Ecology and the Environment

interactive
SCIENCE

PEARSON

Boston, Massachusetts
Chandler, Arizona
Glenview, Illinois
Upper Saddle River, New Jersey

AUTHORS

You're an author!

As you write in this science book, your answers and personal discoveries will be recorded for you to keep, making this book unique to you. That is why you are one of the primary authors of this book.

✎ **In the space below, print your name, school, town, and state. Then write a short autobiography that includes your interests and accomplishments.**

YOUR NAME

SCHOOL

TOWN, STATE

AUTOBIOGRAPHY

Your Photo

Acknowledgments appear on pages 222–223, which constitute an extension of this copyright page.

ISBN-13: 978-0-13-368488-9
ISBN-10:   0-13-368488-1
15 V011 18 17 16

ON THE COVER
Colorful Communication
Did you know that the change in color of a chameleon's skin communicates its mood to other chameleons? Light, temperature, and emotions determine the color changes. The four-horned chameleon, pictured on the cover, is native to Cameroon, Africa. It catches flies with its sticky tongue, which extends twice the length of its body!

Program Authors

DON BUCKLEY, M.Sc.
*Information and Communications Technology Director,
The School at Columbia University, New York, New York*
Mr. Buckley has been at the forefront of K–12 educational
technology for nearly two decades. A founder of New York City
Independent School Technologists (NYCIST) and long-time chair
of New York Association of Independent Schools' annual IT
conference, he has taught students on two continents and
created multimedia and Internet-based instructional systems
for schools worldwide.

ZIPPORAH MILLER, M.A.Ed.
*Associate Executive Director for Professional Programs
and Conferences, National Science Teachers Association,
Arlington, Virginia*
Associate executive director for professional programs and
conferences at NSTA, Ms. Zipporah Miller is a former K–12 science
supervisor and STEM coordinator for the Prince George's County
Public School District in Maryland. She is a science education
consultant who has overseen curriculum development and staff
training for more than 150 district science coordinators.

MICHAEL J. PADILLA, Ph.D.
*Associate Dean and Director, Eugene P. Moore School of
Education, Clemson University, Clemson, South Carolina*
A former middle school teacher and a leader in middle school
science education, Dr. Michael Padilla has served as president of
the National Science Teachers Association and as a writer of the
National Science Education Standards. He is professor of science
education at Clemson University. As lead author of the *Science
Explorer* series, Dr. Padilla has inspired the team in developing a
program that promotes student inquiry and meets the needs of
today's students.

KATHRYN THORNTON, Ph.D.
*Professor and Associate Dean, School of Engineering
and Applied Science, University of Virginia,
Charlottesville, Virginia*
Selected by NASA in May 1984, Dr. Kathryn Thornton is a veteran
of four space flights. She has logged over 975 hours in space,
including more than 21 hours of extravehicular activity. As an
author on the *Scott Foresman Science* series, Dr. Thornton's
enthusiasm for science has inspired teachers around the globe.

MICHAEL E. WYSESSION, Ph.D.
*Associate Professor of Earth and Planetary Science,
Washington University, St. Louis, Missouri*
An author on more than 50 scientific publications, Dr. Wysession
was awarded the prestigious Packard Foundation Fellowship and
Presidential Faculty Fellowship for his research in geophysics. Dr.
Wysession is an expert on Earth's inner structure and has mapped
various regions of Earth using seismic tomography. He is known
internationally for his work in geoscience education and outreach.

Instructional Design Author

GRANT WIGGINS, Ed.D.
*President, Authentic Education,
Hopewell, New Jersey*
Dr. Wiggins is a co-author with
Jay McTighe of *Understanding by Design,
2nd Edition* (ASCD 2005). His approach
to instructional design provides teachers
with a disciplined way of thinking about
curriculum design, assessment, and instruc-
tion that moves teaching from covering
content to ensuring understanding.
   UNDERSTANDING BY DESIGN® and
UbD™ are trademarks of ASCD, and are
used under license.

Planet Diary Author

JACK HANKIN
*Science/Mathematics Teacher,
The Hilldale School, Daly City, California
Founder, Planet Diary Web site*
Mr. Hankin is the creator and writer of
Planet Diary, a science current events
Web site. He is passionate about bringing
science news and environmental awareness
into classrooms and offers numerous Planet
Diary workshops at NSTA and other events
to train middle and high school teachers.

ELL Consultant

JIM CUMMINS, Ph.D.
*Professor and Canada Research Chair,
Curriculum, Teaching and Learning
department at the University of Toronto*
Dr. Cummins focuses on literacy development in multilingual schools and the role of
technology in promoting student learning
across the curriculum. *Interactive Science*
incorporates essential research-based
principles for integrating language with the
teaching of academic content based on his
instructional framework.

Reading Consultant

HARVEY DANIELS, Ph.D.
*Professor of Secondary Education,
University of New Mexico,
Albuquerque, New Mexico*
Dr. Daniels is an international consultant
to schools, districts, and educational
agencies. He has authored or coauthored
13 books on language, literacy, and education. His most recent works are *Compre-
hension and Collaboration: Inquiry Circles
in Action* and *Subjects Matter: Every
Teacher's Guide to Content-Area Reading*.

REVIEWERS

Contributing Writers

Edward Aguado, Ph.D.
Professor, Department of Geography
San Diego State University
San Diego, California

Elizabeth Coolidge-Stolz, M.D.
Medical Writer
North Reading, Massachusetts

Donald L. Cronkite, Ph.D.
Professor of Biology
Hope College
Holland, Michigan

Jan Jenner, Ph.D.
Science Writer
Talladega, Alabama

Linda Cronin Jones, Ph.D.
Associate Professor of Science and Environmental Education
University of Florida
Gainesville, Florida

T. Griffith Jones, Ph.D.
Clinical Associate Professor of Science Education
College of Education
University of Florida
Gainesville, Florida

Andrew C. Kemp, Ph.D.
Teacher
Jefferson County Public Schools
Louisville, Kentucky

Matthew Stoneking, Ph.D.
Associate Professor of Physics
Lawrence University
Appleton, Wisconsin

R. Bruce Ward, Ed.D.
Senior Research Associate
Science Education Department
Harvard-Smithsonian Center for Astrophysics
Cambridge, Massachusetts

Content Reviewers

Paul D. Beale, Ph.D.
Department of Physics
University of Colorado at Boulder
Boulder, Colorado

Jeff R. Bodart, Ph.D.
Professor of Physical Sciences
Chipola College
Marianna, Florida

Joy Branlund, Ph.D.
Department of Earth Science
Southwestern Illinois College
Granite City, Illinois

Marguerite Brickman, Ph.D.
Division of Biological Sciences
University of Georgia
Athens, Georgia

Bonnie J. Brunkhorst, Ph.D.
Science Education and Geological Sciences
California State University
San Bernardino, California

Michael Castellani, Ph.D.
Department of Chemistry
Marshall University
Huntington, West Virginia

Charles C. Curtis, Ph.D.
Research Associate Professor of Physics
University of Arizona
Tucson, Arizona

Diane I. Doser, Ph.D.
Department of Geological Sciences
University of Texas
El Paso, Texas

Rick Duhrkopf, Ph.D.
Department of Biology
Baylor University
Waco, Texas

Alice K. Hankla, Ph.D.
The Galloway School
Atlanta, Georgia

Mark Henriksen, Ph.D.
Physics Department
University of Maryland
Baltimore, Maryland

Chad Hershock, Ph.D.
Center for Research on Learning and Teaching
University of Michigan
Ann Arbor, Michigan

Jeremiah N. Jarrett, Ph.D.
Department of Biology
Central Connecticut State University
New Britain, Connecticut

Scott L. Kight, Ph.D.
Department of Biology
Montclair State University
Montclair, New Jersey

Jennifer O. Liang, Ph.D.
Department of Biology
University of Minnesota–Duluth
Duluth, Minnesota

Candace Lutzow-Felling, Ph.D.
Director of Education
The State Arboretum of Virginia
University of Virginia
Boyce, Virginia

Cortney V. Martin, Ph.D.
Virginia Polytechnic Institute
Blacksburg, Virginia

Joseph F. McCullough, Ph.D.
Physics Program Chair
Cabrillo College
Aptos, California

Heather Mernitz, Ph.D.
Department of Physical Science
Alverno College
Milwaukee, Wisconsin

Sadredin C. Moosavi, Ph.D.
Department of Earth and Environmental Sciences
Tulane University
New Orleans, Louisiana

David L. Reid, Ph.D.
Department of Biology
Blackburn College
Carlinville, Illinois

Scott M. Rochette, Ph.D.
Department of the Earth Sciences
SUNY College at Brockport
Brockport, New York

Karyn L. Rogers, Ph.D.
Department of Geological Sciences
University of Missouri
Columbia, Missouri

Laurence Rosenhein, Ph.D.
Department of Chemistry
Indiana State University
Terre Haute, Indiana

Sara Seager, Ph.D.
Department of Planetary Sciences and Physics
Massachusetts Institute of Technology
Cambridge, Massachusetts

Tom Shoberg, Ph.D.
Missouri University of Science and Technology
Rolla, Missouri

Patricia Simmons, Ph.D.
North Carolina State University
Raleigh, North Carolina

William H. Steinecker, Ph.D.
Research Scholar
Miami University
Oxford, Ohio

Paul R. Stoddard, Ph.D.
Department of Geology and Environmental Geosciences
Northern Illinois University
DeKalb, Illinois

John R. Villarreal, Ph.D.
Department of Chemistry
The University of Texas–Pan American
Edinburg, Texas

John R. Wagner, Ph.D.
Department of Geology
Clemson University
Clemson, South Carolina

Jerry Waldvogel, Ph.D.
Department of Biological Sciences
Clemson University
Clemson, South Carolina

Donna L. Witter, Ph.D.
Department of Geology
Kent State University
Kent, Ohio

Edward J. Zalisko, Ph.D.
Department of Biology
Blackburn College
Carlinville, Illinois

Museum of Science.

Special thanks to the Museum of Science, Boston, Massachusetts, and Ioannis Miaoulis, the Museum's president and director, for serving as content advisors for the technology and design strand in this program.

CONTENTS

 Enter the Lab zone for hands-on inquiry.

Chapter Lab Investigation:
• Directed Inquiry: World in a Bottle
• Open Inquiry: World in a Bottle

Inquiry Warm-Ups: • What's in the Scene?
• Populations • Can You Hide a Butterfly?
• How Communities Change

Quick Labs: • Organisms and Their Habitats
• Organizing an Ecosystem • Growing and
Shrinking • Elbow Room • Adaptations for
Survival • Competition and Predation • Type
of Symbiosis • Primary or Secondary

my science online.com

Go to MyScienceOnline.com to
interact with this chapter's content.
Keyword: Populations and
Communities

UNTAMED SCIENCE
• Clown(fish)ing Around

PLANET DIARY
• Populations and Communities

INTERACTIVE ART
• Changes in Population • Animal Defense
Strategies

ART IN MOTION
• Primary and Secondary Succession

REAL-WORLD INQUIRY
• An Ecological Mystery

CHAPTER 2

Ecosystems and Biomes

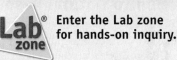

Enter the Lab zone for hands-on inquiry.

Chapter Lab Investigation:
• Directed Inquiry: Ecosystem Food Chains
• Open Inquiry: Ecosystem Food Chains

Inquiry Warm-Ups: • Where Did Your Dinner Come From? • Are You Part of a Cycle? • How Much Rain Is That? • Where Does It Live? • How Can You Move a Seed?

Quick Labs: • Observing Decomposition • Following Water • Carbon and Oxygen Blues • Playing Nitrogen Cycle Roles • Inferring Forest Climates • Dissolved Oxygen • Relating Continental Drift to Dispersal

my science online.com

Go to MyScienceOnline.com to interact with this chapter's content. Keyword: Ecosystems and Biomes

> UNTAMED SCIENCE
• Give Me That Carbon!

> PLANET DIARY
• Ecosystems and Biomes

> INTERACTIVE ART
• Ocean Food Web • Water Cycle • Cycles of Matter • Earth's Biomes • Continental Drift • Seed Dispersal

> VIRTUAL LAB
• Where's All the Food?

CONTENTS

 Enter the Lab zone for hands-on inquiry.

Chapter Lab Investigation:
• Directed Inquiry: Recycling Paper
• Open Inquiry: Recycling Paper

Inquiry Warm-Ups: • How Do You Decide?
• Using Resources • Doubling Time • What
Happened to the Tuna? • How Much Variety
Is There?

Quick Labs: • Environmental Issues
• Comparing Costs and Benefits • Natural
Resources • Human Population Growth
• Comparing Populations • Shelterwood
Cutting • Managing Fisheries • Modeling
Keystone Species • Grocery Gene Pool
• Humans and Biodiversity

my science online

Go to MyScienceOnline.com to
interact with this chapter's content.
Keyword: Resources and Living Things

> **UNTAMED SCIENCE**
• The Great Macaw Debate

> **PLANET DIARY**
• Resources and Living Things

> **INTERACTIVE ART**
• Logging Methods • Exploring
Environmental Impact

> **ART IN MOTION**
• Human Population Growth

> **VIRTUAL LAB**
• Is Variety the Spice of Life?

CHAPTER 4

Land, Air, and Water Resources

 Enter the Lab zone for hands-on inquiry.

Chapter Lab Investigation:
• Directed Inquiry: Waste, Away!
• Open Inquiry: Waste, Away!

Inquiry Warm-Ups: • How Does Mining Affect the Land? • What's in the Trash? • How Does the Scent Spread? • How Does the Water Change? • Is It From the Ocean?

Quick Labs: • Land Use • Modeling Soil Conservation • It's in the Numbers • Half-Life • How Acid Is Your Rain? • Analyzing Ozone • It's in the Air • Where's the Water? • Cleaning Up Oil Spills • Getting Clean • Seaweed Candy • Ocean Trash

my science online.com

**Go to MyScienceOnline.com to interact with this chapter's content.
Keyword:** Land, Air, and Water Resources

> UNTAMED SCIENCE
• Manatee Survival

> PLANET DIARY
• Land, Air, and Water Resources

> INTERACTIVE ART
• Air Pollution • Match the Material

> ART IN MOTION
• Ocean Resource Management

> REAL-WORLD INQUIRY
• Mutation Mystery

CONTENTS

 Enter the Lab zone for hands-on inquiry.

Chapter Lab Investigation:
• Directed Inquiry: Design and Build a Solar Cooker
• Open Inquiry: Design and Build a Solar Cooker

Inquiry Warm-Ups: • What's in a Piece of Coal? • Can You Capture Solar Energy? • Which Bulb Is More Efficient?

Quick Labs: • Observing Oil's Consistency • Fossil Fuels • Producing Electricity • Human Energy Use • Future Energy Use

MY SCIENCE online.com

**Go to MyScienceOnline.com to interact with this chapter's content.
Keyword:** Energy Resources

> **UNTAMED SCIENCE**
• Farming the Wind

> **PLANET DIARY**
• Energy Resources

> **INTERACTIVE ART**
• Hydroelectric Power Plant • Nuclear Power Plant

> **ART IN MOTION**
• Oil: Long to Form, Quick to Use

> **REAL-WORLD INQUIRY**
• Energy Conservation

Untamed Science™

Video Series: Chapter Adventures

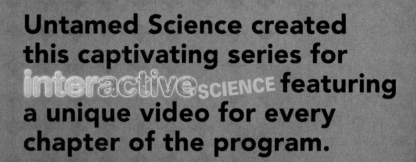

Untamed Science created this captivating series for interactive SCIENCE featuring a unique video for every chapter of the program.

Featuring videos such as

Clown(fish)ing Around
Chapter 1 Follow Jonas of the Untamed Science crew as he dives under water to explore the symbiotic relationship between clownfish and anemones.

Give Me That Carbon!
Chapter 2 The Untamed Science crew examines the journey of a carbon atom as it cycles through an ecosystem.

The Great Macaw Debate
Chapter 3 What happens when a treasured animal's habitat is also valuable land? The Untamed Science crew explores the controversy over the scarlet macaw.

Manatee Survival
Chapter 4 The Untamed Science crew looks at the negative effects people have had on manatees in the past and how they, as well as their environment, can be protected in the future.

Farming the Wind
Chapter 5 This video explores why it is important to have a small carbon footprint and just what can be done to shrink yours.

interactive SCIENCE

This is your book.
You can write in it!

Get Engaged!

At the start of each chapter, you will see two questions: an Engaging Question and the Big Question. Each chapter's Big Question will help you start thinking about the Big Ideas of Science. Look for the Big Q symbol throughout the chapter!

HOW CAN WIND KEEP YOUR LIGHTS ON?

THE BIG ? What are some of Earth's energy sources?

This man is repairing a wind turbine at a wind farm in Texas. Most wind turbines are at least 30 meters off the ground where the winds are fast. Wind speed and blade length help determine the best way to capture the wind and turn it into power. **Develop Hypotheses** Why do you think people are working to increase the amount of power we get from wind?

Wind energy collected by the turbine does not cause air pollution.

> **UNTAMED SCIENCE** Watch the Untamed Science video to learn more about energy resources.

174 Energy Resources

Untamed Science™

Follow the Untamed Science video crew as they travel the globe exploring the Big Ideas of Science.

Interact with your textbook.   **Interact with inquiry.**   **Interact online.**

Build Reading, Inquiry, and Vocabulary Skills

In every lesson you will learn new ↺ Reading and ▲ Inquiry skills. These skills will help you read and think like a scientist. Vocabulary skills will help you communicate effectively and uncover the meaning of words.

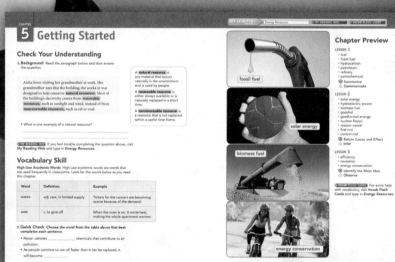

Go Online!

Look for the MyScienceOnline.com technology options. At MyScienceOnline.com you can immerse yourself in amazing virtual environments, get extra practice, and even blog about current events in science.

Explore the Key Concepts.

Each lesson begins with a series of Key Concept questions. The interactivities in each lesson will help you understand these concepts and Unlock the Big Question.

MY PLANET DIARY

At the start of each lesson, My Planet Diary will introduce you to amazing events, significant people, and important discoveries in science or help you to overcome common misconceptions about science concepts.

Desertification If the soil of moisture and nutrients, t advance of desertlike condit fertile is called **desertificat**

One cause of desertificat is a period when less rain th droughts, crops fail. Without blows away. Overgrazing of cutting down trees for firew

Desertification is a serio and graze livestock where d people may face famine and central Africa. Millions of r cities because they can no l

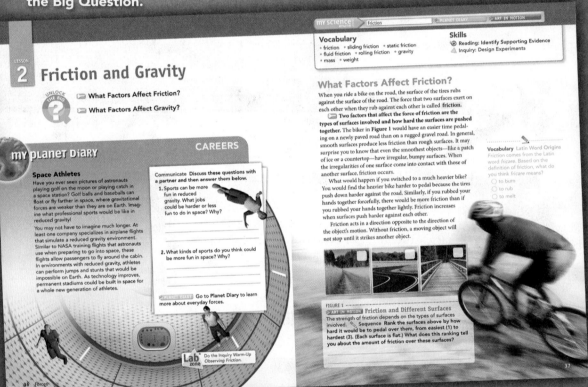

my science ▸ Friction ▸ PLANET DIARY ▸ ART IN MOTION

Vocabulary
• friction • sliding friction • static friction
• fluid friction • rolling friction • gravity
• mass • weight

Skills
○ Reading: Identify Supporting Evidence
△ Inquiry: Design Experiments

LESSON 2 Friction and Gravity

☐ What Factors Affect Friction?
☐ What Factors Affect Gravity?

MY PLANET DIARY CAREERS

Space Athletes

Have you ever seen pictures of astronauts playing golf on the moon or playing catch in a space station? Golf balls and baseballs can float or fly farther in space, where gravitational forces are weaker than they are on Earth. Imagine what professional sports would be like in reduced gravity!

You may not have to imagine much longer. At least one company specializes in airplane flights that simulate a reduced gravity environment. Similar to NASA training flights that astronauts use when preparing to go into space, these flights allow passengers to fly around the cabin. In environments with reduced gravity, athletes can perform jumps and stunts that would be impossible on Earth. As technology improves, permanent stadiums could be built in space for a whole new generation of athletes.

Communicate Discuss these questions with a partner and then answer them below.

1. Sports can be more fun in reduced gravity. What jobs could be harder or less fun to do in space? Why?

2. What kinds of sports do you think could be more fun in space? Why?

▸ PLANET DIARY Go to Planet Diary to learn more about everyday forces.

What Factors Affect Friction?

When you ride a bike on the road, the surface of the tires rubs against the surface of the road. The force that two surfaces exert on each other when they rub against each other is called **friction**.

☐ **Two factors that affect the force of friction are the types of surfaces involved and how hard the surfaces are pushed together.** The biker in **Figure 1** would have an easier time pedaling on a newly paved road than on a rugged gravel road. In general, smooth surfaces produce less friction than rough surfaces. It may surprise you to know that even the smoothest objects—like a patch of ice or a countertop—have irregular, bumpy surfaces. When the irregularities of one surface come into contact with those of another surface, friction occurs.

What would happen if you switched to a much heavier bike? You would find the heavier bike harder to pedal because the tires push down harder against the road. Similarly, if you rubbed your hands together forcefully, there would be more friction than if you rubbed your hands together lightly. Friction increases when surfaces push harder against each other.

Friction acts in a direction opposite to the direction of the object's motion. Without friction, a moving object will not stop until it strikes another object.

Vocabulary Latin Word Origins Friction comes from the Latin word fricare. Based on the definition of friction, what do you think fricare means?
○ to burn
○ to rub
○ to melt

FIGURE 1
▸ ART IN MOTION **Friction and Different Surfaces**
The strength of friction depends on the types of surfaces involved. ✎ Sequence Rank the surfaces above by how hard it would be to pedal over them, from easiest (1) to hardest (3). (Each surface is flat.) What does this ranking tell you about the amount of friction over these surfaces?

Lab zone Do the Inquiry Warm-Up Observing Friction.

37

apply it!

Desertification affects many areas around the world.

❶ **Name** Which continent has the most existing deser

❷ **Interpret Maps** Where i the United States is the grea risk of desertification?

❸ ✎ **Infer** Is desertification is existing desert? Explain. (your answer.

❹ CHALLENGE If an area is things people could do to p

132 Land, Air, and Water

Explain what you know.

Look for the pencil. When you see it, it's time to interact with your book and demonstrate what you have learned.

apply it!

Elaborate further with the Apply It activities. This is your opportunity to take what you've learned and apply those skills to new situations.

Lab Zone

Look for the Lab zone triangle. This means it's time to do a hands-on inquiry lab. In every lesson, you'll have the opportunity to do a hands-on inquiry activity that will help reinforce your understanding of the lesson topic.

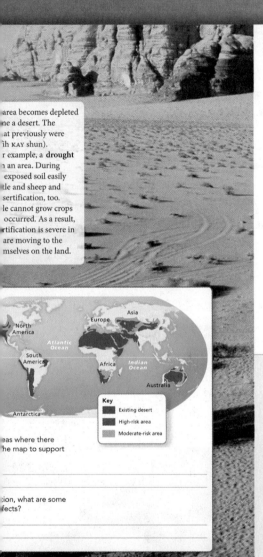

area becomes depleted
me a desert. The
at previously were
(ih KAY shun).
r example, a **drought**
an area. During
exposed soil easily
le and sheep and
sertification, too.
le cannot grow crops
occurred. As a result,
rtification is severe in
are moving to the
mselves on the land.

North America
Europe
Asia
Atlantic Ocean
South America
Africa
Indian Ocean
Australia
Antarctica

Key
- Existing desert
- High-risk area
- Moderate-risk area

eas where there
he map to support

tion, what are some
fects?

Land Reclamation Fortunately, it is possible to replace land damaged by erosion or mining. The process of restoring an area of land to a more productive state is called **land reclamation.** In addition to restoring land for agriculture, land reclamation can restore habitats for wildlife. Many different types of land reclamation projects are currently underway all over the world. But it is generally more difficult and expensive to restore damaged land and soil than it is to protect those resources in the first place. In some cases, the land may not return to its original state.

FIGURE 4
Land Reclamation
These pictures show land before and after it was mined.
✎ **Communicate** Below the pictures, write a story about what happened to the land.

Assess Your Understanding

1a. Review Subsoil has (less/more) plant and animal matter than topsoil.

b. Explain What can happen to soil if plants are removed?

c. Apply Concepts
that could prev
land reclam

Lab zone Do the Quick Lab Modeling S...

got it?

O I get it! Now I know that soil management is important beca...

O I need extra help with

Go to **MY SCIENCE COACH** online for help with this subject.

got it?

Evaluate Your Progress.

After answering the Got It question, think about how you're doing. Did you get it or do you need a little help? Remember, **MY SCIENCE COACH** is there for you if you need extra help.

Explore the Big Question.

At one point in the chapter, you'll have the opportunity to take all that you've learned to further explore the Big Question.

Pollution and Solutions

EXPLORE THE BIG ?

What can people do to use resources wisely?

FIGURE 4 ················

▶ REAL-WORLD INQUIRY All living things depend on land, air, and water. Conserving these resources for the future is important. Part of resource conservation is identifying and limiting sources of pollution.

✏ **Interpret Photos** On the photograph, write the letter from the key into the circle that best identifies the source of pollution.

Land
Describe at least one thing your community could do to reduce pollution on land.

Air
Describe at least one thing your community could do to reduce air pollution.

Water
Describe at least one thing your community could do to reduce water pollution.

Pollution Sources
A. Sediments
B. Municipal solid waste
C. Runoff from development

Lab zone

📖 **Assess Your U[...]**

1a. Define What are sedim[...]

b. Explain How can bacte[...] spill in the ocean?

c. ANSWER What can peop[...] resources wise[...]

d. CHALLENGE Why mig[...] to recycle the waste [...] would reduce water p[...]

got it? ················

○ I get it! Now I know[...] can be reduced by [...]

○ I need extra help w[...]

Go to MY SCIENCE [...] with this subject.

ANSWER THE BIG ?

Answer the Big Question.

Now it's time to show what you know and answer the Big Question.

Review What You've Learned.

Use the Chapter Study Guide to review the Big Question and prepare for the test.

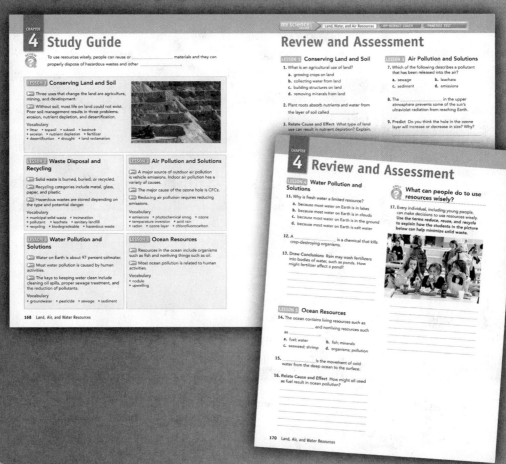

Practice Taking Tests.

Apply the Big Question and take a practice test in standardized test format.

159

INTERACT ... WITH YOUR TEXTBOOK ...

Go to **MyScienceOnline.com** and immerse yourself in amazing virtual environments.

THE BIG QUESTION

Each online chapter starts with a Big Question. Your mission is to unlock the meaning of this Big Question as each science lesson unfolds.

Unit 4 > Chapter 1 > Lesson 1

<< | The Big Question | Unlock the Big Question | Explore the Big Question | >>
The Big Question | Check Your Understanding | Vocabulary Skill

Populations and Communities

Tools

? The Big Question

Unit 2 > Chapter 4 > Lesson 1

Engage & Explore | Expl
Planet Diary

my planet diary

VOCAB FLASH CARDS

Practice chapter vocabulary with interactive flash cards. Each card has an image, definitions in English and Spanish, and space for your own notes.

Unit 4 > Chapter 1 > Lesson 1

<< | The Big Question | Unlock the Big Question | Explore the Big Question | >>
The Big Question | Untamed Science | Check Your Understanding | Vocabulary Skill | Vocabulary Flashcards

Vocabulary Flashcards

Tools

Card List | Create-a-Card | 10 Cards Left | Test Me
Lesson Cards | My Cards

Birth Rate
Carrying Capacity
Commensalism
Community
Competition
Death Rate
Ecology
Ecosystem
Emigration
Habitat
Host
Immigration
Limiting Factor

Science Vocabulary

Term: **Community**

Definition: **All the different populations that live together in a particular area.**

View Spanish

Add Notes

Card 5 of

Unit 6 > Chapter 1 > Le

Engage & Explore
Apply It | Directed Virtua

Color in Light

Exit

Reset Lab

Unit 6 > Chapter 1 > Lesson 1

Engage & Explore | Explain | Elaborate | Evaluate
Apply It | Do the Math | Art in Motion | Interactive Art | Real World Inquiry

The Nebraska Plains

▶ Bald Eagle
Information | Media

Haliaeetus leucocephalus
Bald Eagles are 80-95 cm tall with a wingspan of 180-230 cm. These birds are born with all brown feathers but grow white feathers on their head, neck, and tail.

Layers List | ▲ Show

Next
22 of 22
Back

INTERACTIVE ART

At MyScienceOnline.com, many of the beautiful visuals in your book become interactive so you can extend your learning.

C + 🌐 http://www.myscienceonline.com/

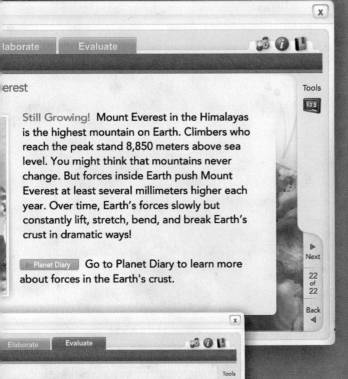

PLANET DIARY

My Planet Diary online is the place to find more information and activities related to the topic in the lesson.

laborate | Evaluate

erest

Tools

Still Growing! Mount Everest in the Himalayas is the highest mountain on Earth. Climbers who reach the peak stand 8,850 meters above sea level. You might think that mountains never change. But forces inside Earth push Mount Everest at least several millimeters higher each year. Over time, Earth's forces slowly but constantly lift, stretch, bend, and break Earth's crust in dramatic ways!

Planet Diary Go to Planet Diary to learn more about forces in the Earth's crust.

Next
22 of 22
Back

Elaborate | Evaluate

Tools

Next
22 of 22
Back

0:35 / 1:30

VIRTUAL LAB

Get more practice with realistic virtual labs. Manipulate the variables on-screen and test your hypothesis.

Find Your Chapter

1 Go to www.myscienceonline.com.

2 Log in with username and password.

3 Click on your program and select your chapter.

Keyword Search

1 Go to www.myscienceonline.com.

2 Log in with username and password.

3 Click on your program and select Search.

4 Enter the keyword (from your book) in the search box.

Other Content Available Online

> **UNTAMED SCIENCE** Follow these young scientists through their amazing online video blogs as they travel the globe in search of answers to the Big Questions of Science.

> **MY SCIENCE COACH** Need extra help? My Science Coach is your personal online study partner. My Science Coach is a chance for you to get more practice on key science concepts. There you can choose from a variety of tools that will help guide you through each science lesson.

> **MY READING WEB** Need extra reading help on a particular science topic? At My Reading Web you will find a choice of reading selections targeted to your specific reading level.

? BIG IDEAS OF SCIENCE

Have you ever worked on a jigsaw puzzle? Usually a puzzle has a theme that leads you to group the pieces by what they have in common. But until you put all the pieces together you can't solve the puzzle. Studying science is similar to solving a puzzle. The big ideas of science are like puzzle themes. To understand big ideas, scientists ask questions. The answers to those questions are like pieces of a puzzle. Each chapter in this book asks a big question to help you think about a big idea of science. By answering the big questions, you will get closer to understanding the big idea.

✎ **Before you read each chapter, write about what you know and what more you'd like to know.**

These prairie dogs live in grasslands and make their homes underground. To stay alive, prairie dogs search for food and water and hide from animals that eat them.

Living things interact with their environment.

What do you already know about how the animals and plants in your neighborhood live together?
✏️ **What more would you like to know?**

_____

_____

_____

_____

Big Questions:

❓ How do living things affect one another?
Chapter 1

❓ How do energy and matter move through ecosystems? Chapter 2

❓ How do people use Earth's resources?
Chapter 3

❓ What can people do to use resources wisely?
Chapter 4

❓ What are some of Earth's energy sources?
Chapter 5

✏️ **After reading the chapters, write what you have learned about the Big Idea.**

_____

_____

_____

_____

_____

Why Do Clownfish Play With Poison?

How do living things affect one another?

Clownfish live among the poisonous and stinging tentacles of sea anemones to avoid being eaten by larger fish. Amazingly, the clownfish do not get stung! This is because a fluid called mucus protects the skin of the fish. ⚠️Develop Hypotheses **How might a sea anemone benefit from having clownfish around?**

_____

_____

_____

_____

_____

_____

_____

▶ UNTAMED SCIENCE Watch the **Untamed Science** video to learn more about interactions between organisms.

Populations and Communities

1 Getting Started

Check Your Understanding

1. **Background** Read the paragraph below and then answer the question.

Raquel planted a garden in a sunny area near her home. First, she loosened the **soil,** so the plant roots could easily grow. If days passed with no **precipitation,** she watered the plants. That was all she had to do—the rest of what the plants needed came from the **atmosphere!**

Soil is made up of rock fragments, water, air, and decaying plant and animal matter.

Rain, hail, sleet, and snow are all types of **precipitation.**

Earth's **atmosphere** contains oxygen, carbon dioxide, nitrogen, and other gases.

• How do soil, precipitation, and the atmosphere help a plant grow?

_____

_____

_____

> **MY READING WEB** If you had trouble completing the question above, visit **My Reading Web** and type in *Populations and Communities.*

Vocabulary Skill

Latin Word Origins Some key terms in this chapter contain word parts with Latin origins. The table below lists two of the Latin words that key terms come from.

Latin Word	Meaning of Latin Word	Example
aptare	to fit	adaptation, *n.* a characteristic that allows an organism to live successfully in its environment
migrare	to move	immigration, *n.* movement into a population

2. **Quick Check** The terms *immigration* and *emigration* both come from the Latin word *migrare*. Circle the meaning of *migrare* in the table above.

organism

immigration

adaptation

predation

Chapter Preview

LESSON 1
- organism • habitat
- biotic factor • abiotic factor
- species • population
- community • ecosystem
- ecology

↻ **Compare and Contrast**

△ **Draw Conclusions**

LESSON 2
- birth rate • death rate
- immigration • emigration
- population density
- limiting factor
- carrying capacity

↻ **Relate Cause and Effect**

△ **Infer**

LESSON 3
- natural selection • adaptation
- niche • competition • predation
- predator • prey • symbiosis
- mutualism • commensalism
- parasitism • parasite • host

↻ **Relate Text and Visuals**

△ **Classify**

LESSON 4
- succession • primary succession
- pioneer species
- secondary succession

↻ **Compare and Contrast**

△ **Observe**

▸ **VOCAB FLASH CARDS** For extra help with vocabulary, visit **Vocab Flash Cards** and type in *Populations and Communities.*

Living Things and the Environment

UNLOCK THE BIG ?

🔑 **What Does an Organism Get From Its Environment?**

🔑 **What Are the Two Parts of an Organism's Habitat?**

🔑 **How Is an Ecosystem Organized?**

MY PLANET DIARY

DISCOVERY

Love Song

The gray, brown, and Goodman's mouse lemurs are some of the world's smallest primates. These three lemurs look similar. Looking so similar makes it difficult for the lemurs to find members of their own kind or species during mating season. However, it seems that the lemurs can identify their own species by song. Scientists recorded the mating calls of the three species of lemurs. They discovered that the lemurs reacted more to the calls from their own species. This allows the lemurs to pick the right mate, even at night.

Communicate Answer these questions. Discuss your answers with a partner.

1. If you were looking for your sneakers among several pairs that looked just like yours, what characteristics would make it easier for you to find them?

   _____

   _____

2. What do you think would happen if a lemur mated with a different kind of lemur?

   _____

   _____

> PLANET DIARY Go to **Planet Diary** to learn more about habitats.

Goodman's mouse lemur

Brown mouse lemur

Gray mouse lemur

Lab zone® Do the Inquiry Warm-Up *What's in the Scene?*

Vocabulary
- organism • habitat • biotic factor • abiotic factor
- species • population • community • ecosystem
- ecology

Skills
↺ Reading: Compare and Contrast
△ Inquiry: Draw Conclusions

What Does an Organism Get From Its Environment?

If you were to visit Alaska, you might see a bald eagle fly by. A bald eagle is one type of **organism,** or living thing. Different types of organisms live in different types of surroundings, or environments. **An organism gets food, water, shelter, and other things it needs to live, grow, and reproduce from its environment.** An environment that provides the things a specific organism needs to live, grow, and reproduce is called its **habitat.**

In a forest habitat, mushrooms grow in the damp soil and wood-peckers build nests in tree trunks. Organisms live in different habitats because they have different requirements for survival and reproduction. Some organisms live on a prairie, with its flat terrain, tall grasses, and low rainfall amounts. A prairie dog, like the one shown in **Figure 1,** obtains the food and shelter it needs from a prairie habitat. It could not survive on this rocky ocean shore. Likewise, the prairie would not meet the needs of a sea star.

FIGURE 1 ·····················
What's Wrong With This Picture?
Most people would never expect to see a prairie dog at the beach.

✎ **List** Give three reasons why this prairie dog would not survive in this habitat.

_____

_____

_____

_____

Lab zone® Do the Quick Lab
Organisms and Their Habitats.

Assess Your Understanding

got it? ···

○ I get it! Now I know that an organism's environment provides _____

_____

○ I need extra help with_____

Go to my science s coach *online for help with this subject.*

What Are the Two Parts of an Organism's Habitat?

To meet its needs, a prairie dog must interact with more than just the other prairie dogs around it. **An organism interacts with both the living and nonliving parts of its habitat.**

Biotic Factors What living things can you see in the prairie dog's habitat shown in **Figure 2**? The parts of a habitat that are living, or once living, and interact with an organism are called **biotic factors** (by AHT ik). The plants that provide seeds and berries are biotic factors. The ferrets and eagles that hunt the prairie dog are also biotic factors. Worms and bacteria are biotic factors that live in the soil underneath the prairie grass. Prairie dog scat, owl pellets, and decomposing plant matter are also biotic factors.

Abiotic Factors Not all of the factors that organisms interact with are living. **Abiotic factors** (ay by AHT ik) are the nonliving parts of an organism's habitat. These factors, as shown in **Figure 2,** include sunlight, soil, temperature, oxygen, and water.

Compare and Contrast In the paragraphs at the right, circle how biotic and abiotic factors are similar and underline how they are different.

FIGURE 2 ·····················
Factors in a Prairie Habitat
A prairie dog interacts with many biotic and abiotic factors in the prairie habitat.

Relate Text and Visuals Add another biotic factor to the picture. For each abiotic factor, draw a line from the text box to an example in the picture.

Sunlight Because sunlight is needed for plants to make their own food, it is an important abiotic factor for most living things.

Soil Soil consists of varying amounts of rock fragments, nutrients, air, water, and the decaying remains of living things. The soil in an area influences the kinds of plants and animals that can live and grow there.

Temperature The temperatures that are typical in an area determine the types of organisms that can live there.

Oxygen Most living things require oxygen to carry out their life processes. Organisms on land obtain oxygen from air. Aquatic organisms obtain oxygen that is dissolved in the water around them.

Water All living things require water to carry out their life processes. Plants and algae need water along with sunlight and carbon dioxide to make their own food. Other living things depend on plants and algae for food.

apply it!

Salt is an abiotic factor found in some environments. To see how the amount of salt affects the hatching of brine shrimp eggs, varying amounts of salt were added to four different 500-mL beakers.

1 **Observe** In which beaker(s) did the eggs, shown as purple circles, hatch? _____

2 **Infer** The manipulated variable was

_____

3 **Infer** The responding variable was _____

_____

4 CHALLENGE Beaker _____ was the control.

5 Draw Conclusions What can you conclude about the amount of salt in the shrimps' natural habitat?

_____

_____

_____

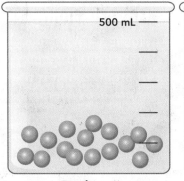

Beaker A
500 mL spring water

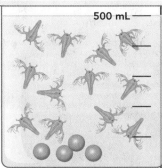

Beaker B
500 mL spring water
+ 2.5 g salt

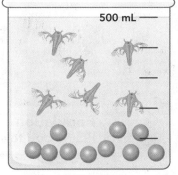

Beaker C
500 mL spring water
+ 7.5 g salt

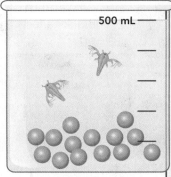

Beaker D
500 mL spring water
+ 15 g salt

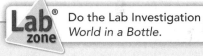

Lab zone® Do the Lab Investigation *World in a Bottle.*

🔑 Assess Your Understanding

1a. Interpret Diagrams List two biotic and two abiotic factors in **Figure 2.**

_____

_____

_____

_____

_____

b. Draw Conclusions Name two abiotic factors in your habitat and explain how your life would be different without them.

_____

_____

_____

_____

_____

got it? ....

O **I get it!** Now I know that the two parts of an organism's habitat are _____

_____

O **I need extra help with** _____

Go to my science s coach *online for help with this subject.*

Ecological Organization

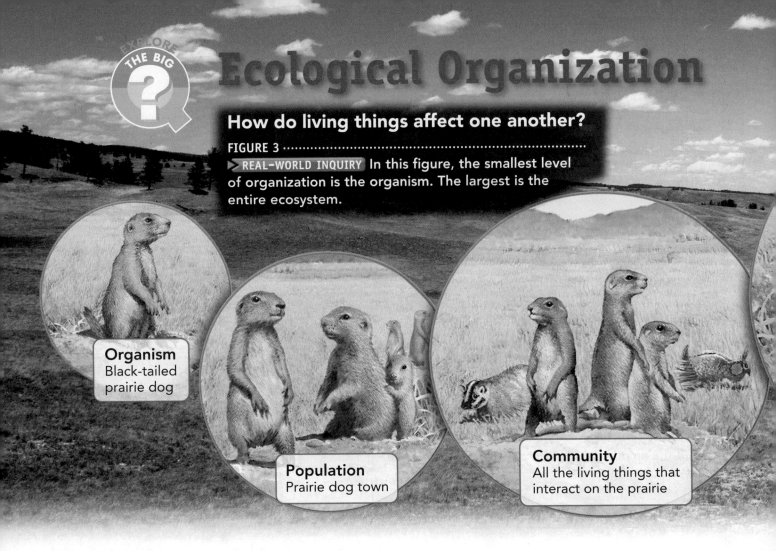

How do living things affect one another?

FIGURE 3 ···

> **REAL-WORLD INQUIRY** In this figure, the smallest level of organization is the organism. The largest is the entire ecosystem.

Organism
Black-tailed
prairie dog

Population
Prairie dog town

Community
All the living things that
interact on the prairie

How Is an Ecosystem Organized?

Most organisms do not live all alone in their habitat. Instead, organisms live together in populations and communities that interact with abiotic factors in their ecosystems.

Organisms Black-tailed prairie dogs that live in prairie dog towns on the Nebraska plains are all members of one species. A **species** (SPEE sheez) is a group of organisms that can mate with each other and produce offspring that can also mate and reproduce.

Populations All the members of one species living in a particular area are referred to as a **population.** The prairie dogs in the Nebraska town are one example of a population.

Communities A particular area contains more than one species of organism. The prairie, for instance, includes prairie dogs, hawks, snakes, and grasses. All the different populations that live together in an area make up a **community.**

Ecosystem
All the living and nonliving things that interact on the prairie

✏️ **Apply Concepts** Draw or write how an ecosystem of your choice is organized. Identify each level. Include biotic and abiotic examples.

Ecosystems The community of organisms that live in a particular area, along with their non-living environment, make up an **ecosystem.** A prairie is just one of the many different ecosystems found on Earth. Other ecosystems are deserts, oceans, ponds, and forests.

Figure 3 shows the levels of organization in a prairie ecosystem. 🔑 **The smallest level of organization is a single organism, which belongs to a population that includes other members of its species. The population belongs to a community of different species. The community and abiotic factors together form an ecosystem.**

Because the populations in an ecosystem interact with one another, any change affects all the different populations that live there. The study of how organisms interact with each other and with their environment is called **ecology.**

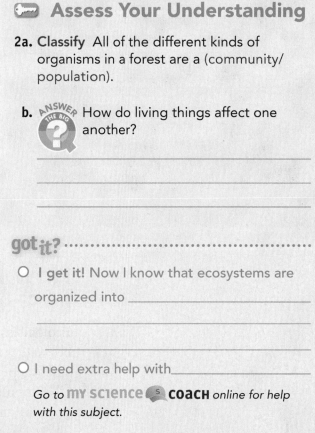

Lab® zone — Do the Quick-Lab *Organizing an Ecosystem.*

🔑 **Assess Your Understanding**

2a. Classify All of the different kinds of organisms in a forest are a (community/population).

b. ANSWER THE BIG ? How do living things affect one another?

_____

_____

_____

got it? •

○ **I get it!** Now I know that ecosystems are organized into _____

_____

_____

○ I need extra help with_____

Go to my science s **coach** *online for help with this subject.*

Populations

🔑 **How Do Populations Change in Size?**

🔑 **What Factors Limit Population Growth?**

my planet diary

Prairie Dog Picker-Upper

Did you know that vacuum cleaners do more than just clean carpets? Across the Great Plains, farmers are using specially designed vacuum cleaners to help them remove black-tailed prairie dogs from the farm land. Prairie dogs can eat crops, cause soil erosion, and endanger cattle and farm machinery. The prairie dog vacuum uses a 4-in. plastic hose to suck prairie dogs out of the ground at 483 km/h! The prairie dogs end up in a padded tank, usually unharmed. They are then relocated or donated to the U.S. Fish and Wildlife Service to be fed to endangered eagles, hawks, and black-footed ferrets.

Prairie dogs

TECHNOLOGY

Communicate Discuss these questions with a group of classmates. Write your answers below.

1. If all of the prairie dogs were removed, how do you think the prairie ecosystem would be affected?

_____

_____

_____

2. Should prairie dogs be used as food for endangered species? Explain.

_____

_____

_____

▶ PLANET DIARY Go to **Planet Diary** to learn more about populations.

Lab zone® Do the Inquiry Warm-Up *Populations.*

How Do Populations Change in Size?

Ecologists are scientists who study biotic and abiotic factors of an ecosystem and the interactions between them. Some ecologists study populations and monitor the sizes of populations over time. 🔑 **Populations can change in size when new members join the population or when members leave the population.**

Vocabulary
- birth rate • death rate • immigration
- emigration • population density
- limiting factor • carrying capacity

Skills
- Reading: Relate Cause and Effect
- Inquiry: Infer

Births and Deaths The most common way in which new individuals join a population is by being born into it. If more individuals are born into a population than die in any period of time, a population can grow. So when the **birth rate,** the number of births per 1,000 individuals for a given time period, is greater than its **death rate,** the number of deaths per 1,000 individuals for a given time period, the population may increase. The main way that individuals leave a population is by dying. If the birth rate is the same as the death rate, then the population may stay the same. In situations where the death rate is higher than the birth rate, then the population may decrease.

do the math!

Depending on the size and age of the female, an American Alligator can lay between 10 and 50 eggs per year.

1 **Graph** Using the data table and colored pencils, create a double bar graph showing alligator births and deaths for four years.

2 Label the x-axis and y-axis.

3 Write a title for the graph.

4 Fill in the graph using the colors shown.

5 **Develop Hypotheses** What factors might explain the number of births and deaths in Year 3?

_____

_____

_____

_____

_____

_____

Data Table		
Year	**Births**	**Deaths**
1	32	8
2	28	13
3	47	21
4	33	16

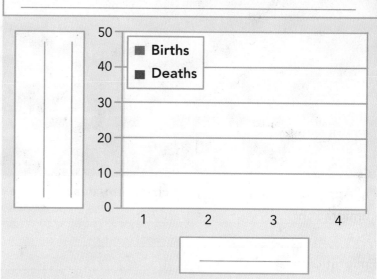

■ Births
■ Deaths

The Population Statement

When the birth rate in a population is greater than the death rate, the population will generally increase. This can be written as a mathematical statement using the "is greater than" sign:

If birth rate > death rate, population size increases.

However, if the death rate in a population is greater than the birth rate, the population size will generally decrease. This can also be written as a mathematical statement:

If death rate > birth rate, population size decreases.

Immigration and Emigration

The size of a population also can change when individuals move into or out of the population. **Immigration** (im ih GRAY shun) means moving into a population. **Emigration** (em ih GRAY shun) means leaving a population. For instance, if food is scarce, some members of an antelope herd may wander off in search of better grassland. If they become permanently separated from the original herd, they will no longer be part of that population.

Vocabulary Latin Word Origins
Both the terms *immigration* ("moving into a population") and *emigration* ("moving out of a population") come from the Latin word *migrare* ("to move"). What do you think the prefixes *im–* and *e–* mean?

_____

_____

_____

FIGURE 1 ··

Immigration

In 1898, white-tailed deer were almost extinct in Iowa due to over-hunting. The deer population was reestablished as animals from Minnesota, Wisconsin, and Missouri immigrated into Iowa.

✎ **Apply Concepts** Using your classroom, describe an example of each of the following.

Immigration: _____

_____

Emigration: _____

_____

population's size can be displayed on a line graph. **Figure 2** shows a graph of the changes in a rabbit population. The vertical axis identifies the number of rabbits in the population, while the horizontal axis shows time. The graph represents the size of the rabbit population over a ten-year period.

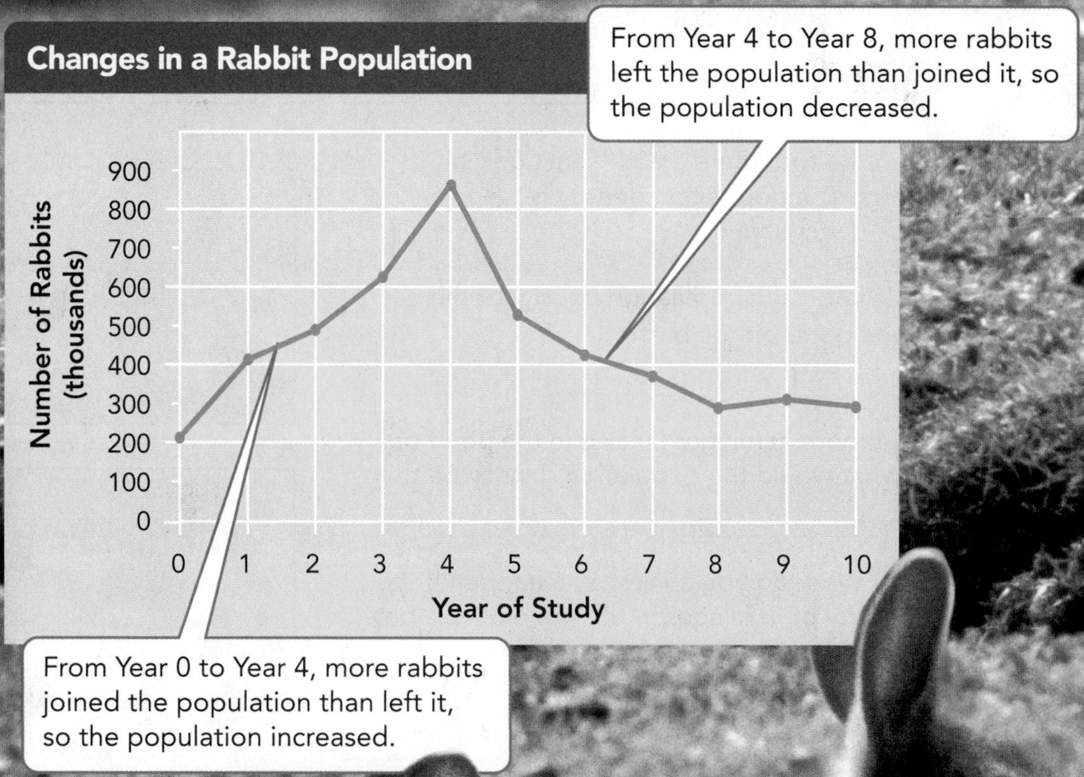

Changes in a Rabbit Population

From Year 4 to Year 8, more rabbits left the population than joined it, so the population decreased.

From Year 0 to Year 4, more rabbits joined the population than left it, so the population increased.

FIGURE 2 ···

▶ INTERACTIVE ART **Changes in a Rabbit Population**

✎ This graph shows how the size of a rabbit population changed over ten years.

1. **Interpret Data** In Year _____, the rabbit population reached its highest point.

2. **Read Graphs** What was the size of the rabbit population in that year? _____

3. **CHALLENGE** How do you think the rabbit population affected the fox population over the same ten-year period? Explain your reasoning.

_____
_____
_____
_____
_____
_____

Population Density Sometimes an ecologist needs to know more than just the total size of a population. In many situations, it is helpful to know the **population density**—the number of individuals in an area of a specific size. Population density can be written as an equation:

$$\text{Population density} = \frac{\text{Number of individuals}}{\text{Unit area}}$$

For example, suppose you counted 20 butterflies in a garden measuring 10 square meters. The population density would be 20 butterflies per 10 square meters, or 2 butterflies per square meter.

apply it!

In the pond on the top, there are 10 flamingos in 8 square meters. The population density is 1.25 flamingos per square meter.

1 **Calculate** What is the population density of the flamingos in the pond on the bottom?

_____

2 **Infer** If 14 more flamingos landed in the pond on the bottom, what would the population density be then?

_____

3 **CHALLENGE** What do you think would happen if the population density of flamingos in the pond on the bottom became too great?

_____
_____
_____
_____

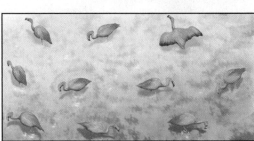

2 meters

← 4 meters →

2 meters

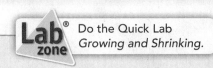 Do the Quick Lab
Growing and Shrinking.

Assess Your Understanding

1a. Review Two ways to join a population are

_____ and _____.

Two ways to leave a population are _____

and _____.

b. Calculate Suppose a population of 8 wolves has produced 20 young in a year. If 7 wolves have died, how many wolves are in the population now? (Assume no wolves have moved into or out of the population for other reasons.)

_____

got it? ....

○ **I get it!** Now I know that population size changes due to _____

_____

○ **I need extra help with** _____

Go to MY SCIENCE ⓢ COACH *online for help with this subject.*

What Factors Limit Population Growth?

When the living conditions in an area are good, a population will generally grow. But eventually some environmental factor will cause the population to stop growing. A **limiting factor** is an environmental factor that causes a population to stop growing or decrease in size. **Some limiting factors for populations are weather conditions, space, food, and water.**

Climate Changes in climate conditions, such as temperature and the amount of rainfall, can limit population growth. A cold spring season can kill the young of many species of organisms, including birds and mammals. Unusual events like floods, hurricanes, and the tornado shown in **Figure 3,** can also have long-lasting effects on population size.

FIGURE 3

Weather as a Limiting Factor

A tornado or flood can destroy nests and burrows.

Identify Name two types of natural disasters that you think can also limit population growth.

____

____

Relate Cause and Effect As you read about the four factors that can limit populations, fill in the graphic organizer below.

Causes

____

____

____

____

Effect

____

____

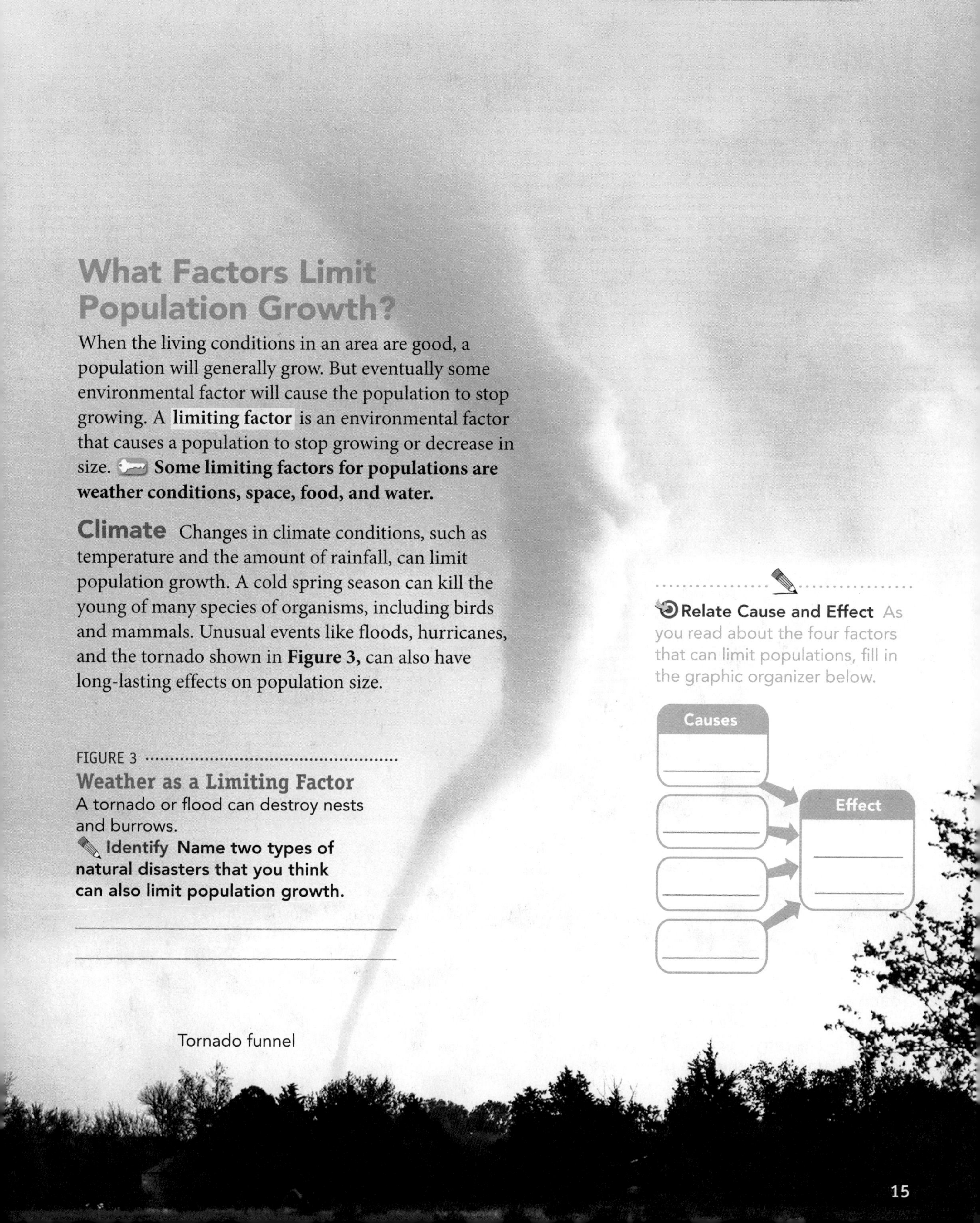

Tornado funnel

Some plants, like the black walnut tree, release chemicals into the environment that prevent other plants from growing too close. This process is called allelopathy (uh luh LOP uh thee).

Space Space is another limiting factor for populations. Gannets are seabirds that are usually seen flying over the ocean. They come to land only to nest on rocky shores. But the nesting shores get very crowded. If a pair does not find room to nest, they will not be able to add any offspring to the gannet population. So nesting space on the shore is a limiting factor for gannets. If there were more nesting space, more gannets would be able to nest. The population could increase.

Figure 4 shows how space is also a limiting factor for plants. The amount of space in which a plant grows determines whether the plant can obtain the sunlight, water, and soil nutrients it needs. For example, many pine seedlings sprout each year in forests. But as the seedlings grow, the roots of those that are too close together run out of space. Branches from other trees may block the sunlight the seedlings need. Some of the seedlings then die, limiting the size of the pine population.

Food and Water Organisms require food and water to survive. When food and water are in limited supply, they can be limiting factors. Suppose a giraffe must eat 10 kilograms of leaves each day to survive. The trees in an area can provide 100 kilograms of leaves a day while remaining healthy. Five giraffes could live easily in this area, because they would need just 50 kilograms of food a day. But 15 giraffes could not all survive—there would not be enough food. No matter how much shelter, water, and other resources there were, the population would not grow much larger than 10 giraffes. The largest population that an area can support is called its **carrying capacity.** The carrying capacity of this giraffe habitat would be 10 giraffes. The size of a population can vary, but usually stays near its carrying capacity because of the limiting factors in its habitat.

FIGURE 4 ·····································
Space as a Limiting Factor
If no more tulip plants can grow in this field, the field has reached its carrying capacity for tulips.

✎ List **Name three things a plant needs to survive.**

_____

apply it!

Giant pandas live in the mountains of south central China. Most (99 percent) of the pandas' diet is made up of the bamboo plant. Bamboo is not nutrient rich. Pandas spend 55 percent of their day eating between 9 and 38 kilograms of bamboo. Getting enough bamboo to eat can be a challenge. Farming and the timber industry have destroyed the pandas' habitat and bamboo forests. In addition, when a bamboo plant flowers, the plant dies and does not regrow for several years. It is difficult for scientists to know exactly how many giant pandas exist in the wild. The best estimate is that there are about 1,600 of them. Due to the small population size, this species is classified as endangered.

✏️ **Communicate** Write a letter to the editor that describes how food and space may be limiting factors for the giant panda species. Add a headline to your letter.

_____

_____

_____

_____

_____

_____

_____

_____

_____

Lab zone® Do the Quick Lab *Elbow Room.*

🔑 Assess Your Understanding

2a. Summarize When the climate changes or there is not enough _____ or _____ or _____, a population can (begin/stop) growing in size.

b. Relate Cause and Effect Choose a limiting factor and describe the factor's effect on population growth.

_____

_____

_____

got it? ···

○ I get it! Now I know that populations can be limited when_____

_____

○ I need extra help with _____

Go to **MY SCIENCE** 🔊 **COACH** online for help with this subject.

Interactions Among Living Things

🔑 **How Do Adaptations Help an Organism Survive?**

🔑 **What Are Competition and Predation?**

🔑 **What Are the Three Types of Symbiosis?**

my planet diary

Predator Power

What predator can close its jaws the fastest? You might think it is a lion or a shark, but you would be wrong. It is the trap-jaw ant that has the fastest strike in the animal kingdom. The trap-jaw ant closes its mouth around its prey in 0.13 milliseconds at speeds of 35 to 64 meters per second! The force created when its jaw snaps shut also helps the ant escape danger by either jumping up to 8.3 centimeters high or 39.6 centimeters sideways.

A trap-jaw ant stalks its prey.

FUN FACT

Communicate **Answer the questions below. Discuss your answers with a partner.**

1. How does the trap-jaw ant's adaptation help it avoid becoming the prey of another organism?

_____

_____

_____

2. What are some adaptations that other predators have to capture prey?

_____

_____

▷ **PLANET DIARY** Go to **Planet Diary** to learn more about predators.

 Do the Inquiry Warm-Up *Can You Hide a Butterfly?*

How Do Adaptations Help an Organism Survive?

As day breaks, a sound comes from a nest tucked in the branch of a saguaro cactus. Two young red-tailed hawks are preparing to fly. Farther down the stem, a tiny elf owl peeks out of its nest in a small hole. A rattlesnake slithers around the base of the saguaro, looking for breakfast. Spying a shrew, the snake strikes it with needle-like fangs. The shrew dies instantly.

Vocabulary

- natural selection • adaptation • niche • competition
- predation • predator • prey • symbiosis • mutualism
- commensalism • parasitism • parasite • host

Skills

- Reading: Relate Text and Visuals
- Inquiry: Classify

Figure 1 shows some organisms that live in, on, and around the saguaro cactus. Each organism has unique characteristics. These characteristics affect the individual's ability to survive and reproduce in its environment.

Natural Selection A characteristic that makes an individual better suited to a specific environment may eventually become common in that species through a process called **natural selection.** Natural selection works like this: Individuals whose unique characteristics are well-suited for an environment tend to survive and produce more offspring. Offspring that inherit these characteristics also live to reproduce. In this way, natural selection results in **adaptations,** the behaviors and physical characteristics that allow organisms to live successfully in their environments. For example, the arctic hare has fur that turns from gray to white in the winter which helps camouflage the hare against the snow.

Individuals with characteristics poorly suited to a particular environment are less likely to survive and reproduce. Over time, poorly suited characteristics may disappear from the species. If a species cannot adapt to changes in its environment, the entire species can disappear from Earth and become extinct.

FIGURE 1 ....
Saguaro Community

✎ **Describe** Circle two examples of how organisms interact in this scene. Describe each one.

_____

_____

_____

_____

Purple martin

Red-tailed hawk

Flycatcher

Woodpecker

Elf owl

Saguaro cactus

Wasps

Gila monster

Rattlesnake

Scorpion

Roadrunner

Niche The organisms in the saguaro community have adaptations that result in specific roles. The role of an organism in its habitat is called its **niche.** A niche includes what type of food the organism eats, how it obtains this food, and what other organisms eat it. A niche also includes when and how the organism reproduces and the physical conditions it requires to survive. Some organisms, like the birds in **Figure 2,** share the same habitat but have very specific niches that allow them to live together. 🔑 **Every organism has a variety of adaptations that are suited to its specific living conditions and help it survive.**

apply it!

Organisms occupy many niches in an environment like the one in this picture.

❶ **Identify** List two abiotic factors in the picture.

_____

❷ **Interpret Diagrams** Describe the niche of the squirrel in the picture.

_____

_____

❸ **Make Generalizations** What adaptations might the squirrel have that make it able to live in this environment?

_____

_____

Lab zone ® Do the Quick Lab
Adaptations for Survival.

🔑 Assess Your Understanding

1a. Define Adaptations are the _____ and _____ characteristics that allow organisms to live successfully in their environments.

b. Explain How are a snake's sharp fangs an adaptation that help it survive in the saguaro community?

_____

_____

got it? ⋯⋯⋯⋯⋯⋯⋯⋯⋯⋯⋯⋯⋯⋯⋯⋯⋯⋯⋯⋯⋯⋯⋯

○ **I get it!** Now I know that adaptations are_____

_____

○ **I need extra help with** _____

Go to **my science 🗩ˢ coach** *online for help with this subject.*

What Are Competition and Predation?

During a typical day in the saguaro community, a range of interactions takes place among organisms. 🔑 **Two major types of interactions among organisms are competition and predation.**

Competition Different species can share the same habitat and food requirements. For example, the flycatcher and the elf owl both live on the saguaro and eat insects. However, these two species do not occupy exactly the same niche. The flycatcher is active during the day, while the owl is active mostly at night. If two species occupy the same niche, one of the species might eventually die off. The reason for this is **competition.** The struggle between organisms to survive as they attempt to use the same limited resources is called competition. For example, weeds in a garden compete with vegetable crops for soil nutrients, water, and sunlight.

In any ecosystem, there are limited amounts of food, water, and shelter. Organisms that share the same habitat often have adaptations that enable them to reduce competition. For example, the three species of warblers in **Figure 2** specialize in feeding only in a certain part of the spruce tree.

Cape May Warbler
This species feeds at the tips of branches near the top of the tree.

Bay-Breasted Warbler
This species feeds in the middle part of the tree.

Yellow-Rumped Warbler
This species feeds in the lower part of the tree and at the bases of the middle branches.

FIGURE 2 ·······

Niche and Competition

✏️ Each of these warbler species occupies a very specific location in its habitat. By feeding on insects in different areas of the tree, the birds avoid competing for food and are able to live together.

1. **Predict** What could happen if these warbler species fed in the same location on the tree?

_____

_____

_____

2. **List** For what resources do the tree and the grass compete?

_____

_____

_____

_____

21

FIGURE 3
Predation
This tiger shark and this albatross are involved in a predator-prey interaction.

✎ **Interpret Photos**
Label the predator and the prey in the photo.

Predation   In **Figure 3,** a tiger shark bursts through the water to seize an albatross in its powerful jaws. An interaction in which one organism kills another for food or nutrients is called **predation.** The organism that does the killing is the **predator.** The organism that is killed is the **prey.** Even though they do not kill their prey, organisms like cows and giraffes are also considered predators because they eat plants.

Predation can have a major effect on a prey population size. Recall that when the death rate exceeds the birth rate in a population, the population size can decrease. So, if there are too many predators in an area, the result is often a decrease in the size of the prey population. But a decrease in the number of prey results in less food for their predators. Without adequate food, the predator population can decline. Generally, populations of predators and their prey rise and fall in related cycles.

FIGURE 4
Predator Adaptations
A jellyfish's tentacles contain a poisonous substance that paralyzes tiny water animals. The sundew is a plant that is covered with sticky bulbs on stalks. When a fly lands on a bulb, it remains snared in the sticky goo while the plant digests it.

✎ **Make Models** Imagine an ideal predator to prey upon a porcupine. Draw or describe your predator below and label its adaptations.

Predator Adaptations Predators, such as those in **Figure 4**, have adaptations that help them catch and kill their prey. A cheetah can run very fast for a short time, enabling it to catch its prey. Some predators, such as owls and bats, have adaptations that enable them to hunt at night when their prey, small mammals and insects, are active.

Prey Adaptations How do organisms avoid being killed by effective predators? The smelly spray of a skunk and the sharp quills of a porcupine help keep predators at a distance. As you can see in **Figure 5,** organisms have many kinds of adaptations that help them avoid becoming prey.

Warning Coloring Like many brightly colored animals, this frog is poisonous. Its bright blue and yellow colors warn predators not to eat it.

False Coloring Predators may be confused by a false eyespot and attack the wrong end of the fish. This allows the fish to swim safely away in the opposite direction.

Mimicry The mimic octopus (top) imitates the coloring, shape, and swimming style of the venomous sole fish (bottom) to discourage predators.

Protective Covering Have you ever seen a pinecone with a face? This is a pangolin, a small African mammal. When threatened, the pangolin protects itself by rolling up into a scaly ball.

Camouflage Is it a leaf? Actually, it's a walking leaf insect. But if you were a predator, you might be fooled into looking else-where for a meal.

FIGURE 5 ···

> INTERACTIVE ART **Defense Strategies**
Organisms display a wide range of adaptations that help them avoid becoming prey. ✎ **Communicate** In a group, rate each prey adaptation from 1 (best) to 5 (worst) in the circles. Explain your best choice.

_____

_____

_____

do the math!

Predator-Prey Interactions

On Isle Royale, an island in Lake Superior, the populations of wolves (the predator) and moose (the prey) rise and fall in cycles. Use the graph to answer the questions.

1 Read Graphs What variable is plotted on the horizontal axis? What two variables are plotted on the vertical axis?

_____

2 Interpret Data How did the moose population change between 2002 and 2007? What happened to the wolf population from 2003 through 2006?

_____
_____
_____

3 Draw Conclusions How might the change in moose population have led to the change in the wolf population?

_____
_____
_____

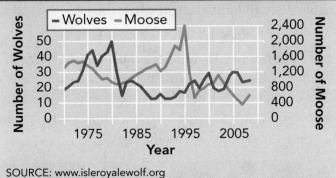

Wolf and Moose Populations on Isle Royale

SOURCE: www.isleroyalewolf.org

4 Explain What adaptations does a wolf have that make it a successful predator?

_____
_____

5 Predict How might disease in the wolf population one year affect the moose population the next year?

_____
_____
_____
_____

Do the Quick Lab
Competition and Predation.

🔑 Assess Your Understanding

2a. Review Two main ways in which organisms interact are_____
and _____.

b. Describe Give an example of competition. Explain your answer.

_____
_____
_____

c. Apply Concepts Owls often prey on mice. What adaptations do you think the mice have that help them avoid becoming prey?

_____
_____
_____
_____

got it? ....

O **I get it!** Now I know that competition and predation_____
_____

O **I need extra help with** _____

Go to MY SCIENCE ⑤ COACH online for help with this subject.

What Are the Three Types of Symbiosis?

In addition to competition and predation, symbiosis is a third type of interaction among organisms. **Symbiosis** (sim bee OH sis) is any relationship in which two species live closely together and at least one of the species benefits. ⟳ **The three main types of symbiotic relationships are mutualism, commensalism, and parasitism.**

Mutualism In some relationships, two species may depend on one another. This is true for some species of acacia trees and stinging ants in South America. The stinging ants nest only in the acacia tree, whose thorns discourage the ants' predators. The tree also provides the ants' only food. The ants, in turn, attack other animals that approach the tree and clear competing plants away from the base of the tree. This relationship is an example of **mutualism** (MYOO choo uh liz um). A relationship in which both species benefit is called mutualism. Other examples of mutualism can be seen in **Figure 6.**

FIGURE 6 ··
Mutualism
✎ An oxpecker rides and snacks aboard an impala. The oxpecker eat ticks living on the impala's ears. This interaction is an example of mutualism because both organisms benefit.

1. Infer How does the oxpecker benefit?

_____

2. Infer How does the impala benefit?

_____

3. [CHALLENGE] Explain how the relationship between the hummingbird and the flower is an example of mutualism.

_____

_____

_____

25

Commensalism

Have you ever seen a bird build a nest in a tree? The bird gets a place to live while the tree is unharmed. This relationship is an example of commensalism. **Commensalism** (kuh MEN suh liz um) is a relationship in which one species benefits and the other species is neither helped nor harmed. In nature, commensalism is not very common because two species are usually either helped or harmed a little by any interaction.

Parasitism

Many family pets get treated with medication to prevent tick and flea bites. Without treatment, pets can suffer from severe health problems as a result of these bites. A relationship that involves one organism living with, on, or inside another organism and harming it is called **parasitism** (PA ruh sit iz um). The organism that benefits is called a **parasite.** The organism it lives on or in is called a **host.** The parasite is usually smaller than the host. In a parasitic relationship, the parasite benefits while the host is harmed. Unlike a predator, a parasite does not usually kill the organism it feeds on. If the host dies, the parasite could lose its source of food or shelter.

Some parasites, like fleas and ticks, have adaptations that enable them to attach to their host and feed on its blood. Other examples of parasitism are shown in **Figure 7.**

✏️ **Relate Text and Visuals** List the names of the parasites and the hosts in **Figure 7**.

Parasites	Hosts

A parasitic cowbird laid its eggs in a yellow warbler's nest. The cowbird chick is outcompeting the warbler chicks for space and food.

Fish lice feed on the blood and other internal fluids of fish.

Dwarf mistletoe is a small parasitic flowering plant that grows into the bark of trees to obtain water and nutrients.

FIGURE 7 ....

Parasitism

There are many examples of parasitic relationships. Besides fleas, ticks, and tapeworms, some plants and birds are parasites. ✏️ **Explain** Why doesn't a parasite usually kill its host?

_____

_____

_____

apply it!

Classify Each photograph on the right represents a different type of symbiosis. Classify each interaction as mutualism, commensalism, or parasitism. Explain your answers.

Interaction 1: A remora fish attaches itself to the underside of a shark without harming the shark, and eats leftover bits of food from the shark's meals.

Interaction 2: A vampire bat drinks the blood of horses.

Interaction 3: A bee pollinates a flower.

1 Interaction 1

_____

_____

2 Interaction 2

_____

_____

3 Interaction 3

_____

_____

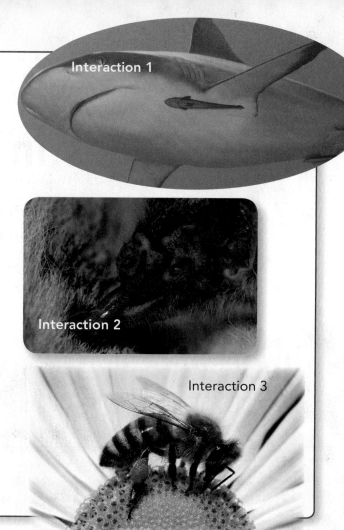

Interaction 1

Interaction 2

Interaction 3

Lab zone® Do the Quick Lab *Type of Symbiosis.*

Assess Your Understanding

3a. Identify The three types of symbiosis are

_____, _____,

and _____.

b. Classify Microscopic mites live at the base of human eyelashes, where they feed on tiny bits of dead skin. What type of symbiosis could this be? Explain your answer.

_____

_____

_____

c. Compare and Contrast Name each type of symbiosis and explain how the two species are affected.

_____

_____

_____

_____

_____

_____

---

got it? ....

○ **I get it!** Now I know that the three types of symbiosis differ in _____

_____

○ I need extra help with _____

Go to my science ⑤ COACH online for help with this subject.

4 Changes in Communities

🔑 How Do Primary and Secondary Succession Differ?

MY PLANET DIARY

Fighting Fire With Fire

Wildfires are often reported in the national news. The images associated with these reports show how damaging these fires can be to property and to some ecosystems. What you may not know is that fire can actually help fight wildfires! Controlled burns, or prescribed burns, are fires that are purposely and carefully set by professional foresters. Prescribed burns are used to remove materials such as dead, dry branches and leaves that can fuel wildfires. A wildfire that occurs in an area that has previously been burned would cause less damage and be easier for firefighters to control.

This forester is carefully igniting a controlled burn.

MISCONCEPTION

Communicate Discuss these questions with a classmate. Write your answers below.

1. Why should only professional foresters set prescribed fires?

_____

_____

_____

2. What do you think could be some other benefits to using prescribed burns in an ecosystem?

_____

_____

_____

> PLANET DIARY Go to **Planet Diary** to learn more about succession.

 Do the Inquiry Warm-Up *How Communities Change.*

How Do Primary and Secondary Succession Differ?

Fires, floods, volcanoes, hurricanes, and other natural disasters can change communities very quickly. But even without disasters, communities change. The series of predictable changes that occur in a community over time is called **succession.**

Vocabulary
- succession • primary succession
- pioneer species • secondary succession

Skills
↻ Reading: Compare and Contrast
△ Inquiry: Observe

Primary Succession

When a new island is formed by the eruption of an undersea volcano or an area of rock is uncovered by a melting sheet of ice, no living things are present. Over time, living things will inhabit these areas. **Primary succession** is the series of changes that occurs in an area where no soil or organisms exist.

Figure 1 shows how an area might change following a volcanic eruption. Just like the pioneers that first settled new frontiers, the first species to populate an area are called **pioneer species.** They are often carried to the area by wind or water. Typical pioneer species are mosses and lichens. Lichens are fungi and algae growing in a symbiotic relationship. As pioneer species grow, they help break up the rocks. When the organisms die, they provide nutrients that enrich the thin layer of soil that is forming on the rocks.

As plant seeds land in the new soil, they begin to grow. The specific plants that grow depend on the climate of the area. For example, in a cool, northern area, early seedlings might include alder and cottonwood trees. Eventually, succession may lead to a community of organisms that does not change unless the ecosystem is disturbed. Reaching this mature community can take centuries.

FIGURE 1 ·····························

> ART IN MOTION **Primary Succession**

Primary succession occurs in an area where no soil and no organisms exist.

✏ **Sequence** In the circles, number the stage of primary succession to show the correct order of events.

Soil Creation
As pioneer species grow and die, soil forms. Some plants grow in this new soil.

Pioneer Species
The first species to grow are pioneer species such as mosses and lichens.

Volcanic Eruption
Shortly after a volcanic eruption, there is no soil, only ash and rock.

Fertile Soil and Maturing Plants
As more plants die, they decompose and make the soil more fertile. New plants grow and existing plants mature in the fertile soil.

29

FIGURE 2 ··

> ART IN MOTION **Secondary Succession**

Secondary succession occurs following a disturbance to an ecosystem, such as clearing a forest for farmland.

✎ **Describe** Write a brief title that describes what happens at each of the four stages of secondary succession.

Increasing time

Title: _____

Grasses and wildflowers have taken over this abandoned field.

Title: _____

After a few years, pine seedlings and other trees replace some of the grasses and wildflowers.

apply it!

↻ **Compare and Contrast** Based on your reading, complete the table below.

Factors in Succession	Primary Succession	Secondary Succession
Possible Cause	Volcanic eruption	
Type of Area		
Existing Ecosystem?		

Secondary Succession In October 2007, huge wildfires raged across Southern California. The changes following the California fires are an example of secondary succession. **Secondary succession** is the series of changes that occurs in an area where the ecosystem has been disturbed, but where soil and organisms still exist. Natural disturbances that have this effect include fires, hurricanes, and tornadoes. Human activities, such as farming, logging, or mining, may also disturb an ecosystem and cause secondary succession to begin.

🔑 **Unlike primary succession, secondary succession occurs in a place where an ecosystem currently exists.** Secondary succession usually occurs more rapidly than primary succession because soil already exists and seeds from some plants remain in the soil. You can follow the process of succession in an abandoned field in **Figure 2.** After a century, a forest develops. This forest community may remain for a long time.

Title: _____
As tree growth continues, the trees begin to crowd out the grasses and wildflowers.

Title: _____
Eventually, a forest of mostly oak, hickory, and some pine dominates the landscape.

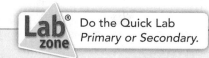 Do the Quick Lab
Primary or Secondary.

Assess Your Understanding

1a. Define Pioneer species are the _____ species to populate an area.

b. 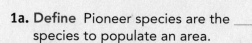 **Observe** Is grass poking through a sidewalk crack primary or secondary succession? Why?

_____

_____

_____

c. [CHALLENGE] Why are the changes during succession predictable?

_____

_____

_____

_____

got it? ....

○ **I get it!** Now I know that primary and secondary succession differ in _____

_____

○ **I need extra help with** _____

_Go to_ **MY SCIENCE ⑤ COACH** _online for help with this subject._

1 Study Guide

Living things interact in many ways, including competition and _____, as well as through symbiotic relationships such as mutualism, commensalism, and _____.

LESSON 1 Living Things and the Environment

🔑 An organism gets the things it needs to live, grow, and reproduce from its environment.

🔑 Biotic and abiotic factors make up a habitat.

🔑 The levels of organization in an ecosystem are organism, population, and community.

Vocabulary
- organism • habitat • biotic factor
- abiotic factor • species • population
- community • ecosystem • ecology

LESSON 2 Populations

🔑 Populations can change in size when new members join the population or when members leave the population.

🔑 Some limiting factors for populations are weather conditions, space, food, and water.

Vocabulary
- birth rate • death rate • immigration
- emigration • population density
- limiting factor • carrying capacity

LESSON 3 Interactions Among Living Things

🔑 Every organism has a variety of adaptations that are suited to its specific living conditions to help it survive.

🔑 Two major types of interactions among organisms are competition and predation.

🔑 The three main types of symbiotic relationships are mutualism, commensalism, and parasitism.

Vocabulary
- natural selection • adaptation • niche • competition
- predation • predator • prey • symbiosis • mutualism
- commensalism • parasitism • parasite • host

LESSON 4 Changes in Communities

🔑 Unlike primary succession, secondary succession occurs in a place where an ecosystem currently exists.

Vocabulary
- succession
- primary succession
- pioneer species
- secondary succession

Review and Assessment

LESSON 1 Living Things and the Environment

1. A prairie dog, a hawk, and a snake are all members of the same
   - a. niche.
   - b. community.
   - c. species.
   - d. population.

2. Grass is an example of a(n) _____ in a habitat.

3. **Sequence** Put these levels in order from the smallest to the largest: population, organism, ecosystem, community.

   _____

   _____

4. **Apply Concepts** Name two biotic and two abiotic factors you might find in a forest ecosystem.

   _____

   _____

5. **Draw Conclusions** In 1815, Mount Tambora, a volcano in Indonesia, erupted. So much volcanic ash and dust filled the atmosphere that 1816 is referred to as the "Year Without a Summer." How might a volcanic eruption affect the abiotic factors in an organism's habitat?

   _____

   _____

   _____

   _____

   _____

6. **Write About It** Write at least one paragraph describing your habitat. Describe how you get the food, water, and shelter you need from your habitat. How does this habitat meet your needs in ways that another would not?

LESSON 2 Populations

7. All of the following are limiting factors for populations except
   - a. space.
   - b. food.
   - c. time.
   - d. weather.

8. _____ occurs when individuals leave a population.

Use the data table to answer the questions below. Ecologists monitoring a deer population collect data during a 30-year study.

Year	0	5	10	15	20	25	30
Population (thousands)	15	30	65	100	40	25	10

9. **Graph** Use the data to make a line graph.

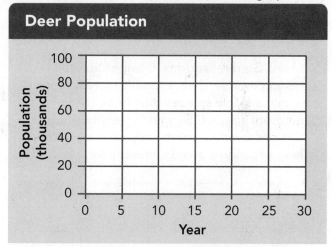

Deer Population

10. **Interpret Data** In which year was the deer population the highest? The lowest?

    _____

11. **Develop Hypotheses** In Year 16 of the study, this region experienced a severe winter. How might this have affected the deer population?

    _____

    _____

    _____

    _____

LESSON 3 Interactions Among Living Things

12. In which type of interaction do both species benefit?

   a. predation   **b.** mutualism

   c. commensalism   **d.** parasitism

13. A parasite lives on or inside its _____ .

14. Relate Cause and Effect Name two prey adaptations. How does each adaptation protect the organism?

_____

_____

_____

_____

_____

15. Make Generalizations Competition for resources in an area is usually more intense within a single species than between two different species. Suggest an explanation for this observation. (*Hint:* Consider how niches help organisms avoid competition.)

_____

_____

_____

_____

_____

16. Write About It Some scientists think that the relationship between clownfish and sea anemones is an example of commensalism. Other scientists think that the relationship is mutualism. If this relationship is actually mutualism, how might both the clownfish and sea anemone benefit?

LESSON 4 Changes in Communities

17. The series of predictable changes that occur in a community over time is called

   a. natural selection   **b.** ecology

   c. commensalism   **d.** succession

18. _____ are the first species to populate an area.

19. Classify Lichens and mosses have just begun to grow on the rocky area shown below. What type of succession is occurring? Explain.

_____

_____

_____

APPLY THE BIG ? How do living things affect one another?

20. Humans interact with their environment on a daily basis. These interactions can have both positive and negative effects. Using at least four vocabulary terms from this chapter, describe a human interaction and the effect it has on the environment.

_____

_____

_____

_____

_____

_____

_____

_____

_____

Standardized Test Prep

Multiple Choice

Circle the letter of the best answer.

1. Symbiotic relationships include mutualism, commensalism, and parasitism. Which of the images below shows mutualism?

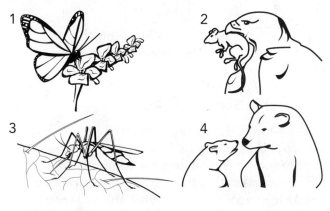

   A   Image 1   B   Image 2
   C   Image 3   D   Image 4

2. In general, which of the following is a true statement about population size?

   A   If birth rate < death rate, population size increases.
   B   If death rate < birth rate, population size decreases.
   C   If birth rate > death rate, population size increases.
   D   If death rate > birth rate, population size increases.

3. Ecosystems have different levels of organization.

   A group of similar organisms makes up a

   _____, which, along with other types

   of organisms, makes up a(n) _____.

   A   species, population
   B   habitat, ecosystem
   C   population, community
   D   population, habitat

4. Three different bird species all live in the same trees in an area, but competition between the birds rarely occurs. Which of the following is a likely explanation for this lack of competition?

   A   The three species occupy different niches.
   B   The three species eat the same food.
   C   The three species have a limited supply of food.
   D   The three species live in the same part of the trees.

5. Which of the following is a typical pioneer species?

   A   grass
   B   lichen
   C   pine trees
   D   soil

Constructed Response

Use the diagram below and your knowledge of science to help you answer Question 6. Write your answer on a separate piece of paper.

6. An organism interacts with both the biotic and abiotic factors in its habitat. List three biotic factors and three abiotic factors shown in the drawing above.

SUCCESSION ECOLOGIST

These lupine plants are growing out of the volcanic ash on Mount St. Helens, 20 years after its last eruption.

Suppose your workplace were on the side of a volcano! Roger del Moral is an ecologist who spends a lot of time on the side of Mount St. Helens, a volcano in Washington State.

When Mount St. Helens erupted in 1980, it destroyed as much as 518 square kilometers of forest. Del Moral and his team study how plant communities form in the aftermath of volcanic eruptions. They visit the volcano regularly to identify plants and estimate the remaining populations of plants to describe how the plant communities are recovering. This work enables researchers to develop more effective ways to help areas recover from human-caused environmental changes.

Del Moral loves his work and says, "My work on Mount St. Helens allows me to follow my passion, train students, and contribute to a better understanding of how the world works."

If you are interested in ecology, try volunteering or interning at a local park or field museum. National parks also have Junior Naturalist programs designed to give you experience in the field.

Compare It Find a park in your neighborhood or town and describe the kinds of plants you find. Make a table in which you list each kind of plant, describe it, describe where it grew, and draw conclusions about the reasons why it might have grown there.

BINOCULAR BOOT CAMP

▼ Populations of common and rare birds can be estimated based on input from students like you!

Scientists need all the help they can get estimating large populations! Binocular Boot Camp, a program for kids in Sonoma Valley, California, trains kids to identify the songs, calls, and flight patterns of birds. Participants form teams and identify and count as many birds as they can in one afternoon. The information they gather gets entered into a huge database of bird observations.

You don't have to go to Binocular Boot Camp to help, though. For four days in February, schools, clubs, and individuals in the United States and Canada take part in the Great Backyard Bird Count (GBBC). All you need to do is count birds for 15 minutes, then fill out a form to help scientists learn how climate change, habitat change, and other factors affect bird populations.

Research It Find out more about the GBBC. Design a poster or use presentation software to create a presentation to convince your school to participate.

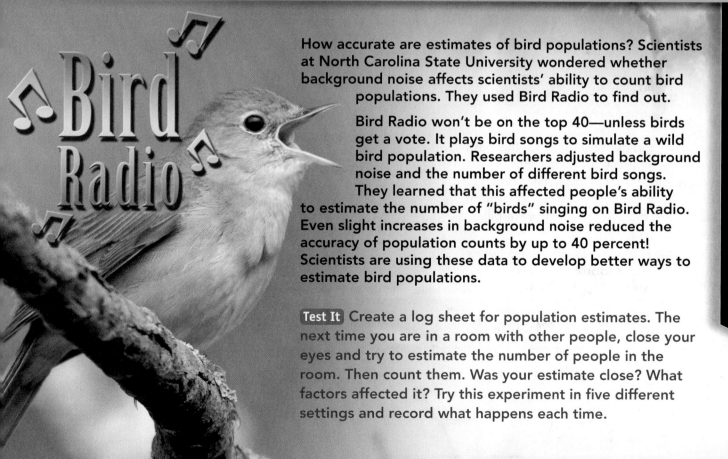

Bird Radio

How accurate are estimates of bird populations? Scientists at North Carolina State University wondered whether background noise affects scientists' ability to count bird populations. They used Bird Radio to find out.

Bird Radio won't be on the top 40—unless birds get a vote. It plays bird songs to simulate a wild bird population. Researchers adjusted background noise and the number of different bird songs. They learned that this affected people's ability to estimate the number of "birds" singing on Bird Radio. Even slight increases in background noise reduced the accuracy of population counts by up to 40 percent! Scientists are using these data to develop better ways to estimate bird populations.

Test It Create a log sheet for population estimates. The next time you are in a room with other people, close your eyes and try to estimate the number of people in the room. Then count them. Was your estimate close? What factors affected it? Try this experiment in five different settings and record what happens each time.

WHERE DOES FOOD COME FROM?

How do energy and matter move through ecosystems?

Flying around hunting for food, this barn owl spots a mouse for dinner. But what did the mouse eat? Perhaps it nibbled on seeds or a caterpillar. Then you might ask, where did the seeds and caterpillar get their food?

⚠ **Develop Hypotheses** Where do living things get their food?

_____

_____

_____

_____

_____

_____

▷ **UNTAMED SCIENCE** Watch the **Untamed Science** video to learn more about ecosystems and biomes.

Ecosystems and Biomes

CHAPTER 2

Check Your Understanding

1. Background Read the paragraph below and then answer the question.

> One morning, Han walks to the park and sits by the pond. He has just studied **ecosystems** in class, and now, looking at the pond, he realizes he sees things in a new way. He notices a turtle sunning itself on a rock, and knows that the sun and rock are **abiotic factors,** while the turtle, and other living things, are **biotic factors.**

The community of organisms that live in a particular area, along with their nonliving environment, make up an **ecosystem.**

Abiotic factors are the nonliving parts of an organism's habitat.

Biotic factors are the living parts of an organism's habitat.

- Name one more biotic factor and one more abiotic factor that Han might see at the pond.

_____

_____

> MY READING WEB If you had trouble answering the question above, visit **My Reading Web** and type in *Ecosystems and Biomes.*

Vocabulary Skill

Prefixes Some words can be divided into parts. A root is the part of the word that carries the basic meaning. A prefix is a word part that is placed in front of the root to change the word's meaning. The prefixes below will help you understand some vocabulary in this chapter.

Prefix	Meaning	Example
bio-	life	biogeography, *n.* the study of where organisms live
inter-	between	intertidal, *adj.* ocean zone between the highest high-tide line and the lowest low-tide line

2. Quick Check Circle the prefix in each boldface word below.

- There was an **intermission** between the acts of the play.
- The **biosphere** is the area where life exists.

consumer

precipitation

desert

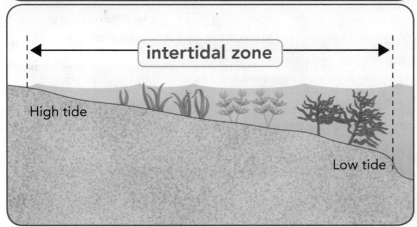

intertidal zone

High tide

Low tide

Chapter Preview

LESSON 1
- producer • consumer
- herbivore • carnivore • omnivore
- scavenger • decomposer
- food chain • food web
- energy pyramid
- ↻ Relate Text and Visuals
- △ Classify

LESSON 2
- evaporation • condensation
- precipitation • nitrogen fixation
- ↻ Sequence
- △ Infer

LESSON 3
- biome • climate • desert
- rain forest • emergent layer
- canopy • understory • grassland
- savanna • deciduous tree
- boreal forest • coniferous tree
- tundra • permafrost
- ↻ Compare and Contrast
- △ Draw Conclusions

LESSON 4
- estuary
- intertidal zone
- neritic zone
- ↻ Outline
- △ Communicate

LESSON 5
- biogeography
- continental drift • dispersal
- exotic species
- ↻ Relate Cause and Effect
- △ Predict

> VOCAB FLASH CARDS For extra help with vocabulary, visit **Vocab Flash Cards** and type in *Ecosystems and Biomes.*

Energy Flow in Ecosystems

UNLOCK THE BIG

🔑 **What Are the Energy Roles in an Ecosystem?**

🔑 **How Does Energy Move Through an Ecosystem?**

MY PLANET DIARY

DISCOVERY

I'll Have the Fish

Scientists have noticed something fishy going on with the wolves in British Columbia, Canada. During autumn, the wolves ignore their typical food of deer and moose and feast on salmon instead. Salmon are very nutritious and lack the big horns and hoofs that can injure or kill wolves. Plus, there are plenty of fish in a small area, making them easier to find and catch.

Many animals, including the wolves, depend upon the salmon's annual mating trip upstream. Losing this important food source to overfishing would hurt the populations of bears, wolves, birds, and many other animals.

Communicate Discuss these questions with a classmate. Write your answers below.

1. What are two reasons the wolves may eat fish in autumn instead of deer or moose?

_____

_____

2. What effect could overfishing salmon have on an ecosystem?

_____

_____

_____

_____

▶ PLANET DIARY Go to **Planet Diary** to learn more about food webs.

 Do the Inquiry Warm-Up *Where Did Your Dinner Come From?*

Vocabulary
- producer • consumer • herbivore • carnivore
- omnivore • scavenger • decomposer • food chain
- food web • energy pyramid

Skills
↺ Reading: Relate Text and Visuals
△ Inquiry: Classify

What Are the Energy Roles in an Ecosystem?

Do you play an instrument in your school band? If so, you know that each instrument has a role in a piece of music. Similar to instruments in a band, each organism has a role in the movement of energy through its ecosystem.

An organism's energy role is determined by how it obtains food and how it interacts with other organisms. ⬤ **Each of the organisms in an ecosystem fills the energy role of producer, consumer, or decomposer.**

Producers Energy enters most ecosystems as sunlight. Some organisms, like the plants and algae shown in **Figure 1,** and some types of bacteria, capture the energy of sunlight and store it as food energy. These organisms use the sun's energy to turn water and carbon dioxide into food molecules in a process called photosynthesis.

An organism that can make its own food is a **producer.** Producers are the source of all the food in an ecosystem. In a few ecosystems, producers obtain energy from a source other than sunlight. One such ecosystem is found in rocks deep beneath the ground. Certain bacteria in this ecosystem produce their own food using the energy in hydrogen sulfide, a gas that is present in their environment.

FIGURE 1 ....
Producers
Producers are organisms that can make their own food.

✎ **Identify** Complete the shopping list below to identify the producers that are part of your diet.
- ○ wheat
- ○ corn
- ○ banana
- ○ _____
- ○ _____
- ○ _____
- ○ _____
- ○ _____
- ○ _____
- ○ _____

Tape grass and water milfoil

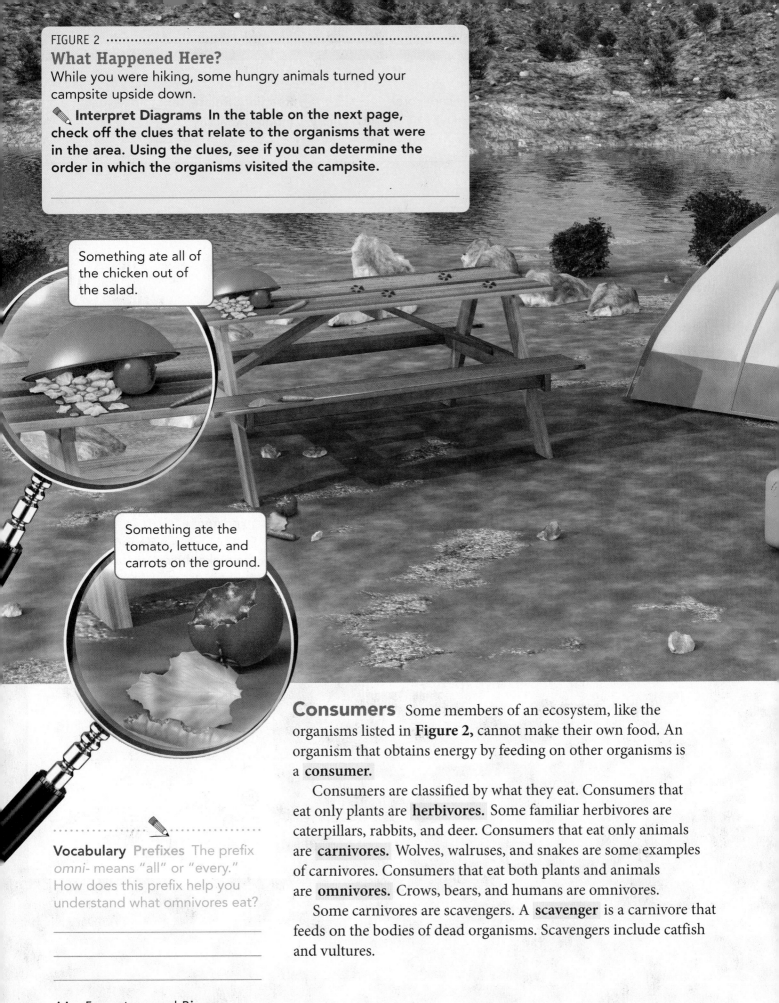

FIGURE 2 ·······························

What Happened Here?

While you were hiking, some hungry animals turned your campsite upside down.

✎ **Interpret Diagrams** In the table on the next page, check off the clues that relate to the organisms that were in the area. Using the clues, see if you can determine the order in which the organisms visited the campsite.

Something ate all of the chicken out of the salad.

Something ate the tomato, lettuce, and carrots on the ground.

Vocabulary Prefixes The prefix *omni-* means "all" or "every." How does this prefix help you understand what omnivores eat?

Consumers Some members of an ecosystem, like the organisms listed in **Figure 2,** cannot make their own food. An organism that obtains energy by feeding on other organisms is a **consumer.**

Consumers are classified by what they eat. Consumers that eat only plants are **herbivores.** Some familiar herbivores are caterpillars, rabbits, and deer. Consumers that eat only animals are **carnivores.** Wolves, walruses, and snakes are some examples of carnivores. Consumers that eat both plants and animals are **omnivores.** Crows, bears, and humans are omnivores.

Some carnivores are scavengers. A **scavenger** is a carnivore that feeds on the bodies of dead organisms. Scavengers include catfish and vultures.

Clues	Bear	Mold	Rabbit	Wolf
Can easily reach the table top				
Grows on food and breaks it down				
Small enough to enter and exit tent				
Gets energy from meat				
Strong enough to open cooler				
Not a picky eater				
Gets energy from plants				

Something ate the apples and beef jerky from inside the tent.

Something ate strawberries, even some of the moldy ones.

Decomposers If an ecosystem had only producers and consumers, the raw materials of life, such as carbon and nitrogen, would stay locked up in wastes and the bodies of dead organisms. However, there are organisms in ecosystems that prevent this from happening. **Decomposers** break down biotic wastes and dead organisms and return the raw materials to the ecosystem.

You can think of decomposers as nature's recyclers. While obtaining energy for their own needs, decomposers return simple molecules to the environment. These molecules can be used again by other organisms. Mushrooms, bacteria, and mold are common decomposers.

Lab® zone Do the Quick Lab *Observing Decomposition.*

🔑 Assess Your Understanding

1a. Describe An organism's energy role is determined by how it obtains _____ and how it _____ with other organisms.

b. Apply Concepts What is the main source of energy for all three energy roles? Why?

_____

_____

_____

_____

_____

_____

_____

got it? ....

○ **I get it!** Now I know that the energy roles in an ecosystem are _____

_____

_____

○ **I need extra help with** _____

_____

Go to MY SCIENCE ⓢ COACH *online for help with this subject.*

45

How Does Energy Move Through an Ecosystem?

As you have read, energy enters most ecosystems as sunlight and is converted into food by producers. This energy is transferred to the organisms that eat the producers, and then to other organisms that feed on the consumers. 🔑 **Energy moves through an ecosystem when one organism eats another.** This movement of energy can be shown as food chains, food webs, and energy pyramids.

Food Chains One way to show how energy moves in an ecosystem is with a food chain. A **food chain** is a series of events in which one organism eats another and obtains energy. You can follow one example of a food chain in **Figure 3.**

Food Webs A food chain shows only one possible path along which energy can move through an ecosystem. Most producers and consumers are part of many food chains. A more realistic way to show the flow of energy through an ecosystem is with a food web. As shown in **Figure 4**, a **food web** consists of many overlapping food chains in an ecosystem.

Organisms may play more than one role in an ecosystem. Look at the crayfish in **Figure 4.** A crayfish is an omnivore that is a first-level consumer when it eats plants. But when a crayfish eats a snail, it is a second-level consumer.

Just as food chains overlap and connect, food webs interconnect as well. A gull might eat a fish at the ocean, but it might also eat a mouse at a landfill. The gull, then, is part of two food webs—an ocean food web and a land food web. All the world's food webs interconnect in what can be thought of as a global food web.

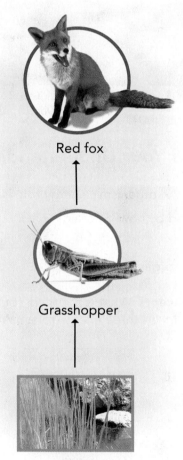

Red fox

Grasshopper

Plants

FIGURE 3 ·······························
Food Chain
In this food chain, you can see how energy moves from plants, to a grasshopper, to the fox. The arrows show how energy moves up the food chain, from one organism to the next.

apply it!

Classify Using what you have learned about food chains, draw or describe a food chain from your local ecosystem. Show at least three organisms in your food chain. Name each organism and label it as a producer, consumer, or decomposer.

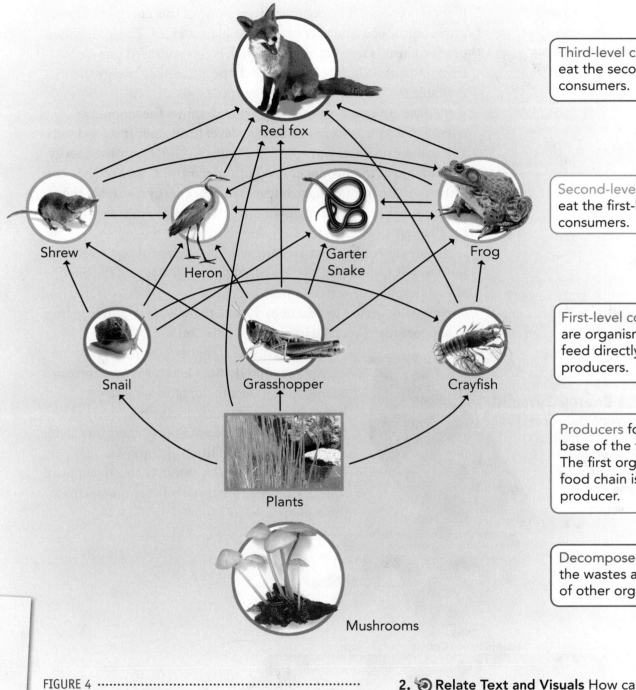

Third-level consumers eat the second-level consumers.

Second-level consumers eat the first-level consumers.

First-level consumers are organisms that feed directly on the producers.

Producers form the base of the food web. The first organism in a food chain is always a producer.

Decomposers consume the wastes and remains of other organisms.

FIGURE 4 ·······························

> INTERACTIVE ART **Food Web**

A food web consists of many interconnected food chains.

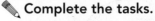 **Complete the tasks.**

1. **Interpret Diagrams** Pick two organisms from the food web. Draw arrows connecting them to the decomposers.

2. ⟳ **Relate Text and Visuals** How can the fox be both a second-level and third-level consumer?

_____

_____

_____

_____

_____

_____

Relate Text and Visuals
Look at the energy pyramid.
Why is a pyramid the best shape
to show how energy moves
through an ecosystem?

_____

_____

_____

_____

_____

_____

Energy Pyramids

When an organism in an ecosystem eats, it obtains energy. The organism uses some of this energy to move, grow, reproduce, and carry out other life activities. These activities produce heat, a form of energy, which is then released into the environment. When heat is released, the amount of energy that is available to the next consumer is reduced.

A diagram called an **energy pyramid** shows the amount of energy that moves from one feeding level to another in a food web. You can see an energy pyramid in **Figure 5**. **The most energy is available at the producer level of the pyramid. As energy moves up the pyramid, each level has less energy available than the level below.** An energy pyramid gets its name from the shape of the diagram—wider at the base and narrower at the top.

In general, only about 10 percent of the energy at one level of a food web is transferred to the next higher level. Most of the energy at each level is converted to heat. Since about 90 percent of the food energy is converted to heat at each step, there is not enough energy to support many feeding levels in an ecosystem.

The organisms at higher feeding levels of an energy pyramid do not necessarily require less energy to live than the organisms at lower levels. Because so much energy is converted to heat at each level, the amount of energy available at the producer level limits the number of consumers that the ecosystem is able to support. As a result, there are usually fewer organisms at the highest level in a food web.

FIGURE 5 ·······················

> VIRTUAL LAB **Energy Pyramid**
This energy pyramid diagram shows the energy available at each level of a food web and how it is calculated. Energy is measured in kilocalories, or kcal.

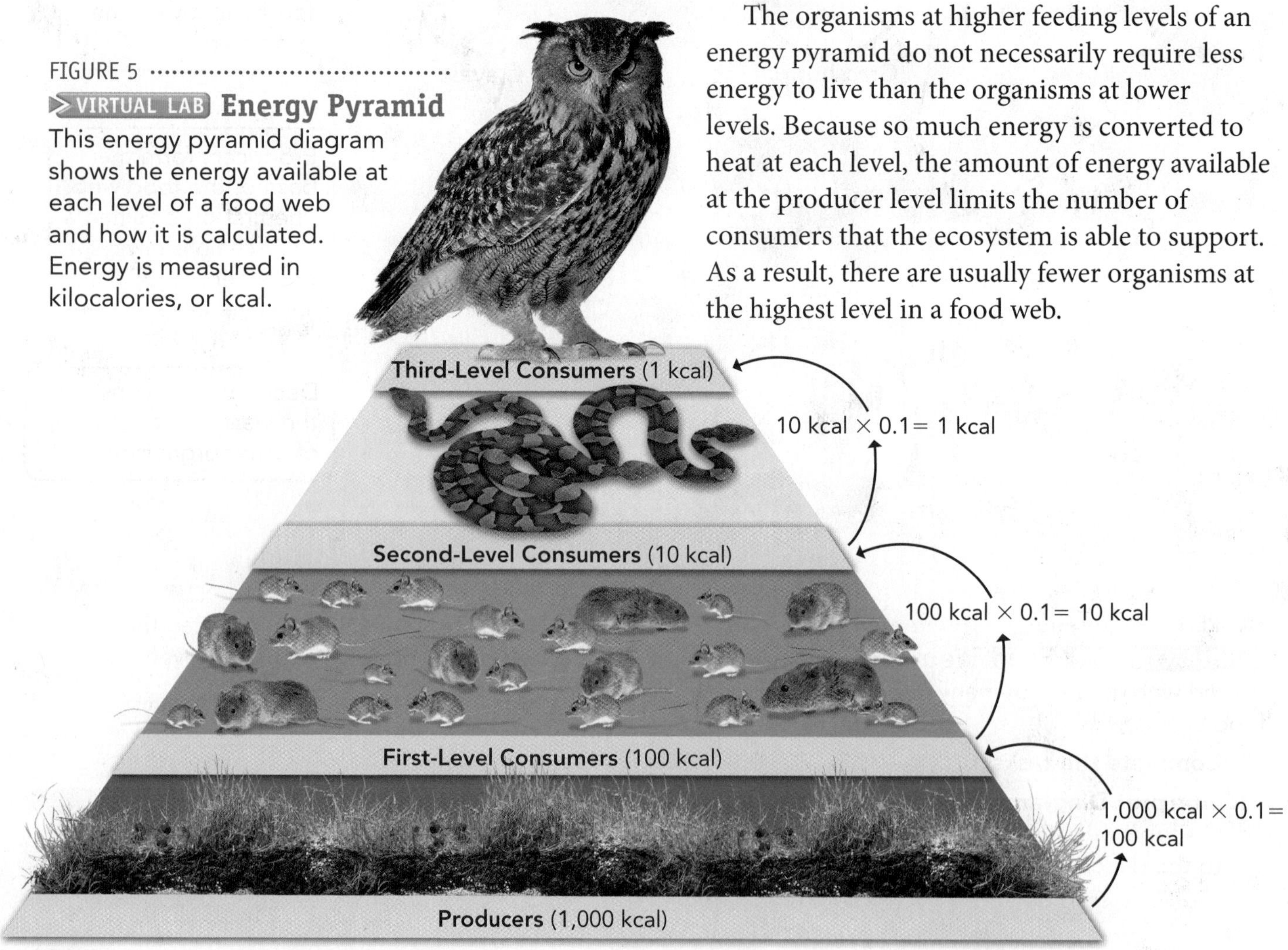

Third-Level Consumers (1 kcal)

10 kcal × 0.1 = 1 kcal

Second-Level Consumers (10 kcal)

100 kcal × 0.1 = 10 kcal

First-Level Consumers (100 kcal)

1,000 kcal × 0.1 = 100 kcal

Producers (1,000 kcal)

do the math!

Energy Pyramids

Suppose that the producers at the base of an energy pyramid contain 330,000 kilocalories.

Calculate Using **Figure 5** as a guide, label how much energy would be available at each level of the pyramid based on the questions below.

1 If mice ate all of the plants, how much energy would be available to them as first-level consumers?

2 If all of the mice were eaten by snakes, how much energy would the snakes receive?

3 If all of the snakes were eaten by the owl, how much energy would the owl receive?

4 [CHALLENGE] About how much energy would the owl use for its life processes or lose as heat? _____

5 [CHALLENGE] How much energy would be stored in the owl's body? _____

Third-Level
Consumers

Second-Level Consumers

First-Level Consumers

330,000 kcal

Producers

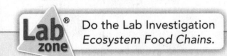

Do the Lab Investigation
Ecosystem Food Chains.

🔑 Assess Your Understanding

2a. Define A food (web/chain) is a series of events in which one organism eats another and obtains energy. A food (web/chain) consists of many overlapping food (webs/chains).

b. Compare and Contrast Why is a food web a more realistic way of portraying an ecosystem than a food chain?

_____

_____

_____

c. Relate Cause and Effect Why are there usually fewer organisms at the top of an energy pyramid?

_____

_____

_____

_____

_____

_____

got it? ●

○ **I get it!** Now I know that energy moves through an ecosystem when_____

_____

○ **I need extra help with** _____

Go to MY SCIENCE COACH *online for help with this subject.*

Cycles of Matter

UNLOCK
THE BIG
?

🔑 **What Processes Are Involved in the Water Cycle?**

🔑 **How Are the Carbon and Oxygen Cycles Related?**

🔑 **How Does Nitrogen Cycle Through Ecosystems?**

my planeT DiaRY

Canaries and Coal

Have you ever stopped to listen to a bird sing? If you were a coal miner in the early 1900s, your life may have depended on it! Sometimes miners stumbled upon pockets of carbon monoxide, a toxic, odorless gas that makes it difficult for the body to get enough oxygen. Without fresh air circulating in the mineshafts, the miners would fall asleep and eventually die. To prevent this disaster from happening, canaries were used to monitor the air quality. A singing canary indicated that all was well. If the canary stopped singing and died, the miners knew that they needed to quickly leave the mine.

DISASTER

Answer the question below.

Do you think it was ethical, or fair, to use canaries this way? Explain.

_____

_____

_____

_____

> PLANET DIARY Go to **Planet Diary** to learn more about cycles of matter.

 Do the Inquiry Warm-Up *Are You Part of a Cycle?*

What Processes Are Involved in the Water Cycle?

Recycling is important for ecosystems because matter is limited. To understand how matter cycles through an ecosystem, you need to know a few terms that describe the structure of matter. Matter is made up of tiny particles called atoms. Two or more atoms that are joined and act as a unit make up a molecule. For example, a water molecule consists of two hydrogen atoms and one oxygen atom.

Water is essential for life. The water cycle is the continuous process by which water moves from Earth's surface to the atmosphere and back. 🔑 **The processes of evaporation, condensation, and precipitation make up the water cycle.**

Vocabulary
- evaporation • condensation
- precipitation • nitrogen fixation

Skills
↻ Reading: Sequence
△ Inquiry: Infer

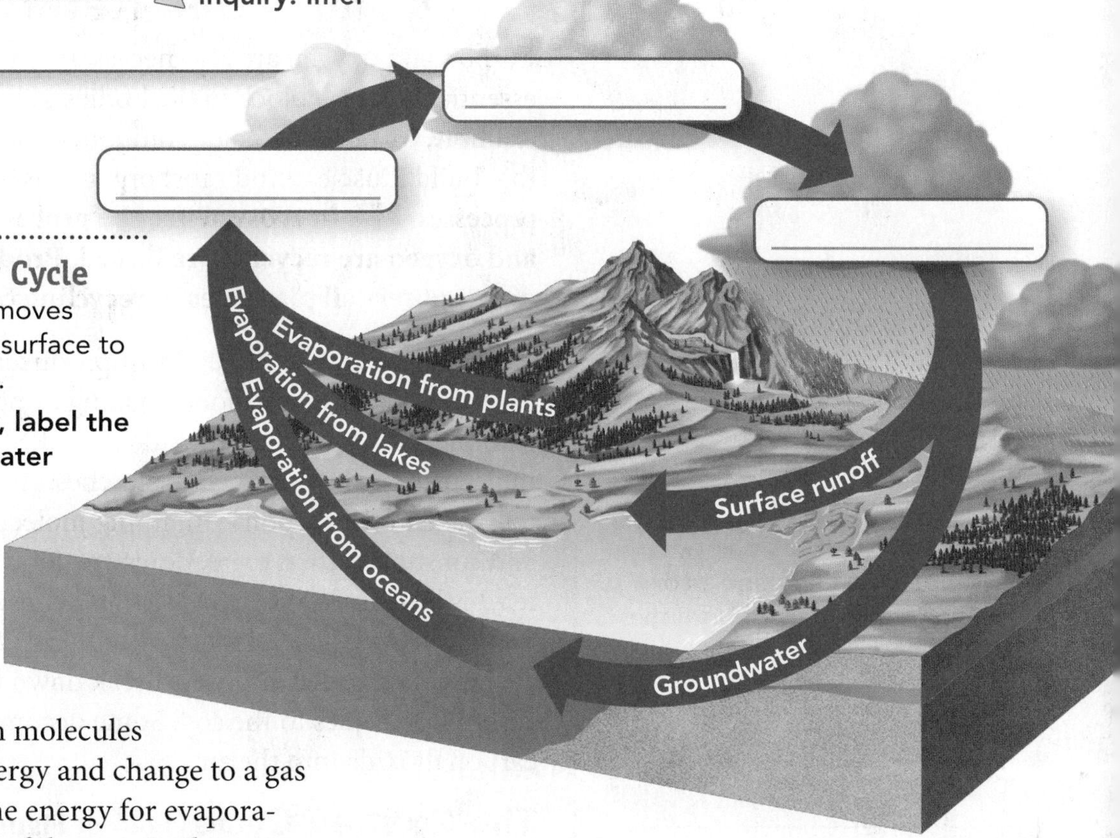

FIGURE 1 ....

> INTERACTIVE ART **Water Cycle**

In the water cycle, water moves continuously from Earth's surface to the atmosphere and back.

✎ **Identify** As you read, label the three processes of the water cycle in the diagram.

Evaporation from plants

Evaporation from lakes

Evaporation from oceans

Surface runoff

Groundwater

Evaporation

How does water from the ground get into the air? The process by which molecules of liquid water absorb energy and change to a gas is called **evaporation.** The energy for evaporation comes from the heat of the sun. In the water cycle, liquid water evaporates from oceans, lakes, and other sources and forms water vapor, a gas, in the atmosphere. Smaller amounts of water also evaporate from living things. Plants release water vapor from their leaves. You release liquid water in your wastes and water vapor when you exhale.

Condensation
As water vapor rises higher in the atmosphere, it cools down. The cooled vapor then turns back into tiny drops of liquid water. The process by which a gas changes to a liquid is called **condensation.** The water droplets collect around dust particles and form clouds.

Precipitation
As more water vapor condenses, the drops of water in the clouds grow larger. Eventually the heavy drops fall to Earth as **precipitation**—rain, snow, sleet, or hail. Precipitation may fall into oceans, lakes, or rivers. The precipitation that falls on land may soak into the soil and become groundwater, or run off the land, flowing back into a river or ocean.

Lab zone® Do the Quick Lab *Following Water.*

🔑 Assess Your Understanding

got**it?** ....

○ **I get it!** Now I know that the processes of the water cycle are _____

_____

_____

○ **I need extra help with** _____

_____

_____

Go to my science ⓢ **coach** *online for help with this subject.*

How Are the Carbon and Oxygen Cycles Related?

Carbon and oxygen are also necessary for life. Carbon is an essential building block in the bodies of living things. For example, carbon is a major component of bones and the proteins that build muscles. And most organisms use oxygen for their life processes. **In ecosystems, the processes by which carbon and oxygen are recycled are linked. Producers, consumers, and decomposers all play roles in recycling carbon and oxygen.**

The Carbon Cycle

Most producers take in carbon dioxide gas from the air during food-making or photosynthesis. They use carbon from the carbon dioxide to make food—carbon-containing molecules such as sugars and starches. As consumers eat producers, they take in the carbon-containing molecules. Both producers and consumers then break down the food to obtain energy. As the food is broken down, producers and consumers release carbon dioxide and water into the environment. When producers and consumers die, decomposers break down their remains and return carbon molecules to the soil. Some decomposers also release carbon dioxide into the air.

The Oxygen Cycle

Look at **Figure 2**. Like carbon, oxygen cycles through ecosystems. Producers release oxygen as a result of photosynthesis. Most organisms take in oxygen from the air or water and use it to carry out their life processes.

Human Impact

Human activities also affect the levels of carbon and oxygen in the atmosphere. When humans burn oil and other plant-based fuels, carbon dioxide is released into the atmosphere. Carbon dioxide levels can also rise when humans clear forests for lumber, fuel, and farmland. Increasing levels of carbon dioxide are a major factor in global warming. As you know, producers take in carbon dioxide during photosynthesis. When trees are removed from the ecosystem, there are fewer producers to absorb carbon dioxide. There is an even greater effect if trees are burned down to clear a forest. When trees are burned down, additional carbon dioxide is released during the burning process.

apply it!

Producers, consumers, and decomposers all play a role in recycling carbon and oxygen.

Infer On the lines below, describe how you think a cow eating grass is part of both the carbon and oxygen cycles.

_____

_____

_____

_____

_____

_____

_____

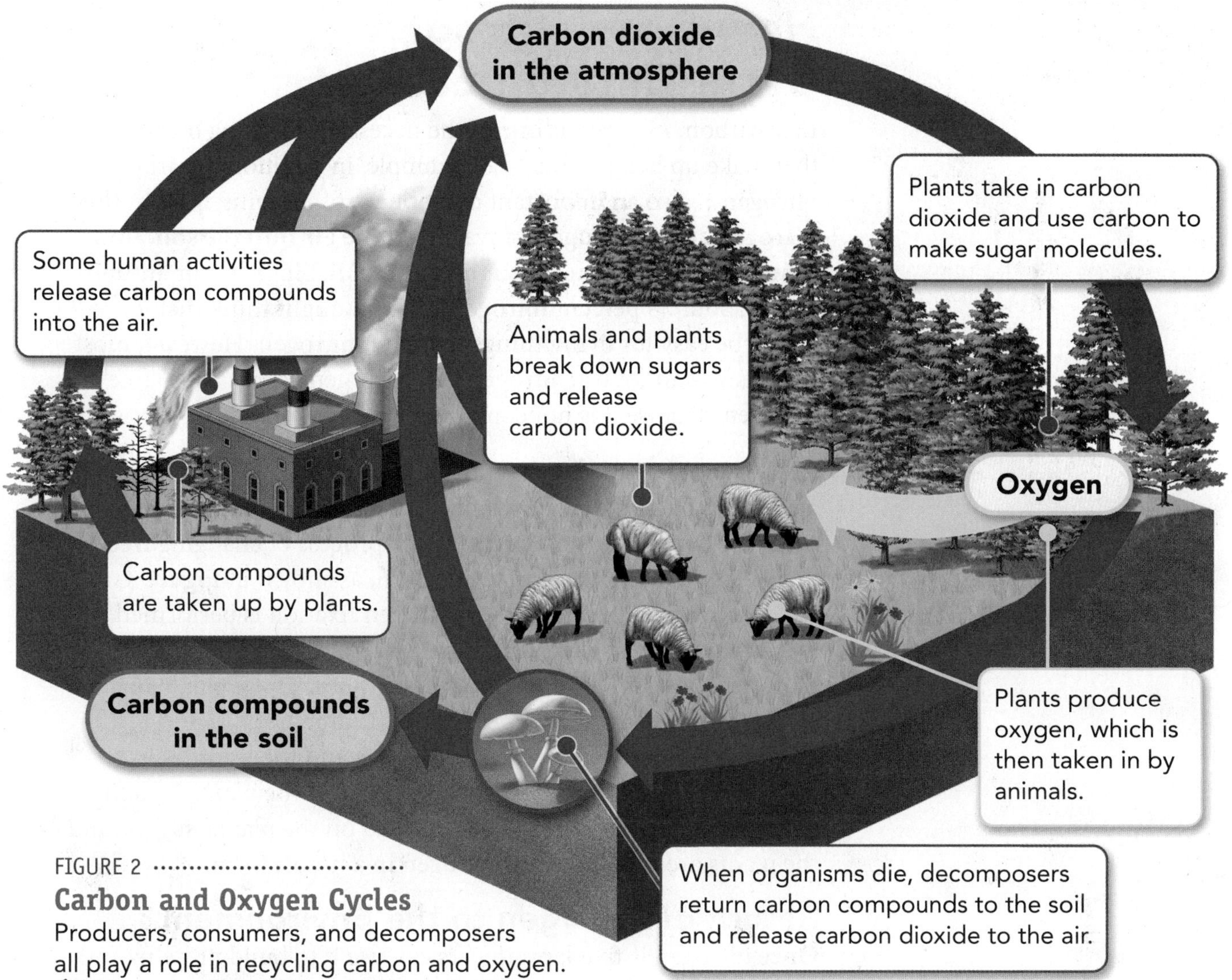

Carbon dioxide in the atmosphere

Some human activities release carbon compounds into the air.

Plants take in carbon dioxide and use carbon to make sugar molecules.

Animals and plants break down sugars and release carbon dioxide.

Oxygen

Carbon compounds are taken up by plants.

Plants produce oxygen, which is then taken in by animals.

Carbon compounds in the soil

When organisms die, decomposers return carbon compounds to the soil and release carbon dioxide to the air.

FIGURE 2 ·······························

Carbon and Oxygen Cycles
Producers, consumers, and decomposers all play a role in recycling carbon and oxygen.
✎ **Describe** When humans burn fuel or cut down trees, they (increase/decrease) levels of carbon dioxide in the atmosphere.

Lab zone® Do the Quick Lab *Carbon and Oxygen Blues.*

🔑 **Assess Your Understanding**

1a. Identify Carbon and oxygen are both

_____ in an ecosystem.

b. Develop Hypotheses How might the death of all the producers in a community affect the carbon and oxygen cycles?

_____

_____

_____

_____

got it?

○ **I get it!** Now I know that the carbon and

oxygen cycles are related by _____

_____

_____

_____

○ **I need extra help with** _____

_____

Go to my science s **coach** *online for help with this subject.*

How Does Nitrogen Cycle Through Ecosystems?

Like carbon, nitrogen is one of the necessary building blocks that make up living things. For example, in addition to carbon, nitrogen is also an important component of proteins. **In the nitrogen cycle, nitrogen moves from the air into the soil, into living things, and back into the air or soil.** Since the air around you is about 78 percent nitrogen gas, you might think that it would be easy for living things to obtain nitrogen. However, most organisms cannot use nitrogen gas. Nitrogen gas is called "free" nitrogen because it is not combined with other kinds of atoms.

Nitrogen Fixation Most organisms can use nitrogen only after it has been "fixed," or combined with other elements to form nitrogen-containing compounds. The process of changing free nitrogen into a usable form of nitrogen, as shown in **Figure 4,** is called **nitrogen fixation.** Most nitrogen fixation is performed by certain kinds of bacteria. These bacteria live in bumps called nodules (NAHJ oolz) on the roots of legumes. These plants include clover, beans, peas, alfalfa, peanuts, and some trees.

The relationship between the bacteria and the legumes is an example of mutualism. Both the bacteria and the plants benefit from this relationship: The bacteria feed on the plants' sugars, and the plants are supplied with nitrogen in a usable form.

Return of Nitrogen to the Environment
Once nitrogen is fixed, producers can use it to build proteins and other complex compounds. Nitrogen can cycle from the soil to producers and then to consumers many times. At some point, however, bacteria break down the nitrogen compounds completely. These bacteria then release free nitrogen back into the air, causing the cycle to continue.

FIGURE 3 ···

Growth in Nitrogen-Poor Soil
Pitcher plants can grow in nitrogen-poor soil because they obtain nitrogen by trapping insects in their tube-shaped leaves. The plants then digest the insects and use their nitrogen compounds.

✎ **Circle the correct word in each sentence.**

1. **Identify** If nitrogen in the soil isn't (fixed/free), then most organisms cannot use it.

2. CHALLENGE The relationship between the pitcher plant and the insects is an example of (competition/predation/symbiosis).

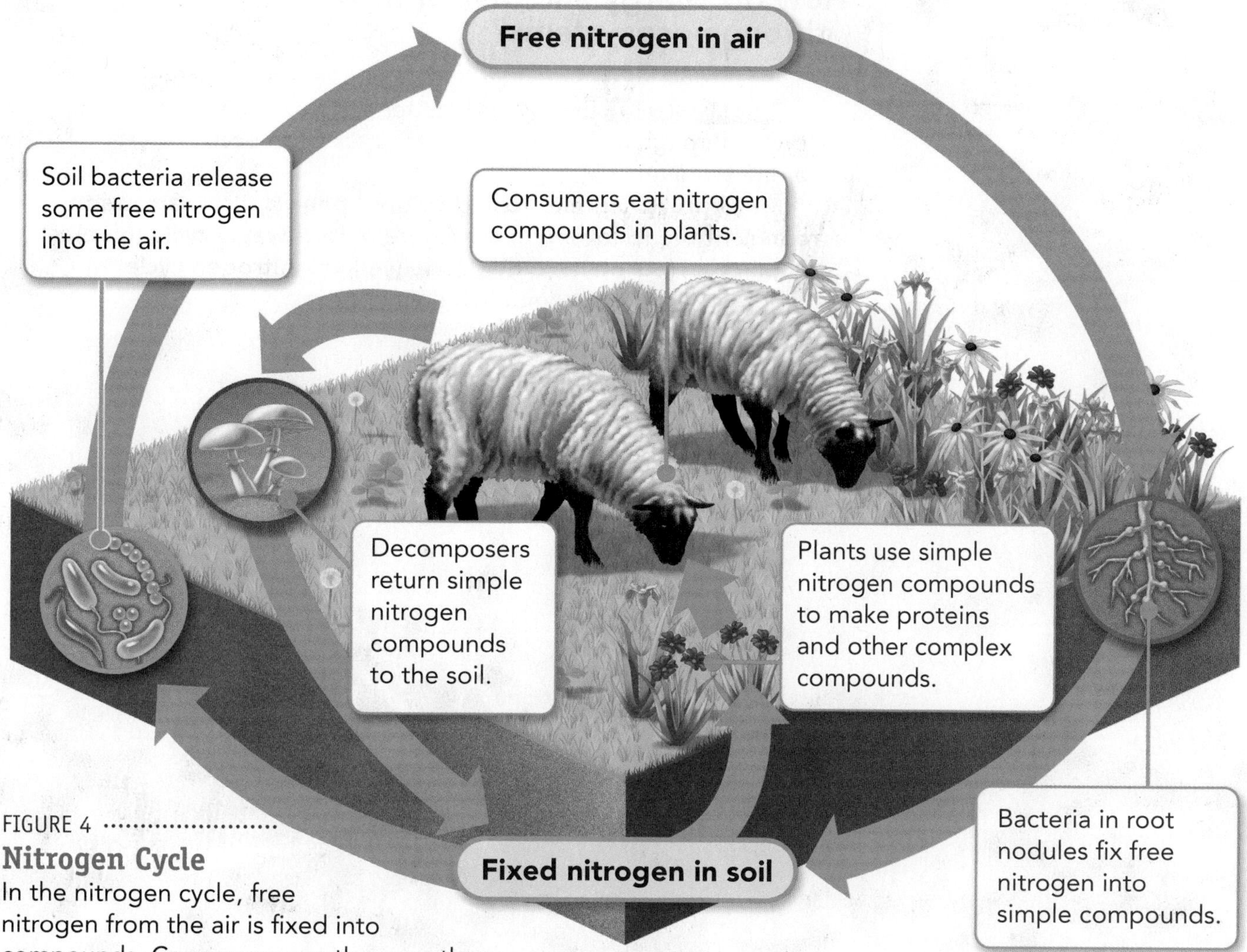

Free nitrogen in air

Soil bacteria release some free nitrogen into the air.

Consumers eat nitrogen compounds in plants.

Decomposers return simple nitrogen compounds to the soil.

Plants use simple nitrogen compounds to make proteins and other complex compounds.

Bacteria in root nodules fix free nitrogen into simple compounds.

Fixed nitrogen in soil

FIGURE 4 ....

Nitrogen Cycle

In the nitrogen cycle, free nitrogen from the air is fixed into compounds. Consumers can then use these nitrogen compounds to carry out their life processes.

✎ **Observe Nitrogen compounds become available to organisms** (in the soil/in the plants/in the air).

⟲ **Sequence** In the frames below, draw a comic strip or describe a situation that shows the order of events in the nitrogen cycle.

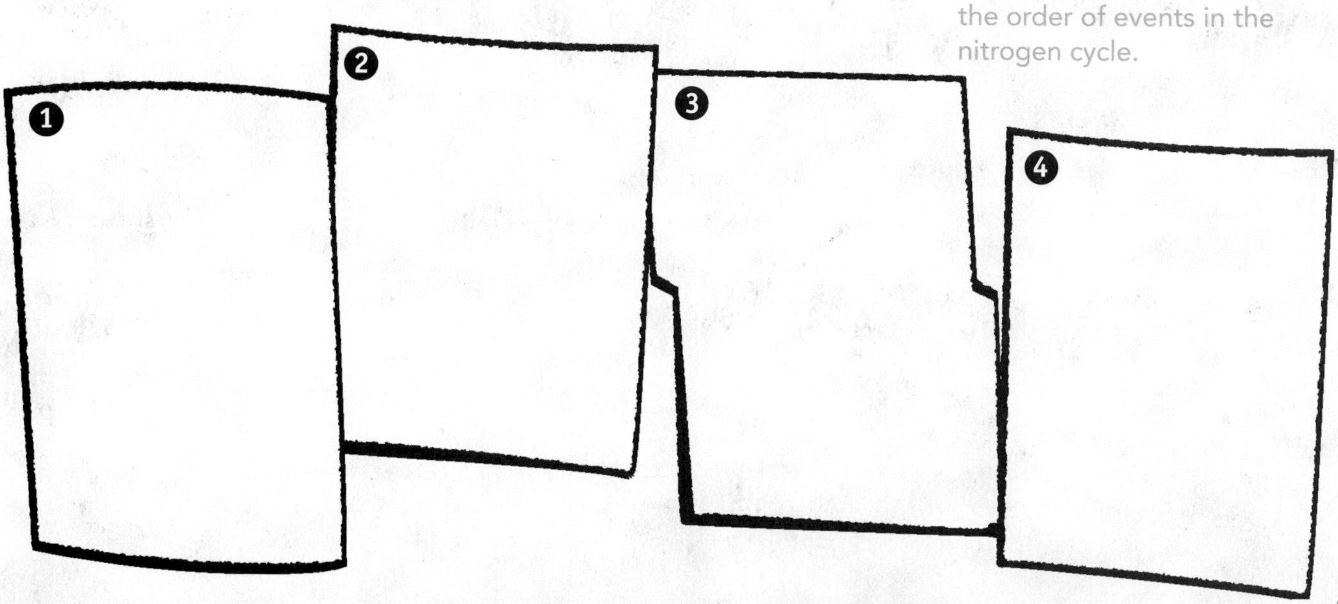

❶

❷

❸

❹

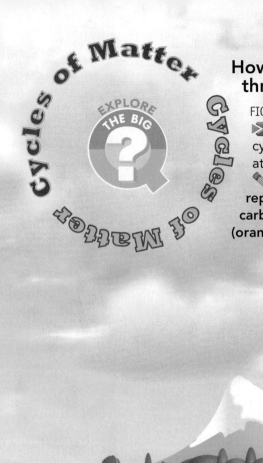

Cycles of Matter

EXPLORE THE BIG ?

How do energy and matter move through ecosystems?

FIGURE 5 ....

> INTERACTIVE ART Energy and matter are constantly being cycled through an ecosystem. These cycles can occur at the same time.

✎ Interpret Diagrams Using colored pencils, draw arrows to represent the following in the figure below: water cycle (blue), carbon cycle (purple), oxygen cycle (yellow), nitrogen cycle (orange), food chain (green). Label each cycle.

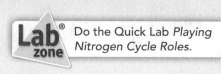
Do the Quick Lab *Playing Nitrogen Cycle Roles.*

🔑 Assess Your Understanding

2a. Describe (Fixed/Free) nitrogen is not combined with other kinds of atoms.

b. Predict What might happen in a community if farmers did not plant legume crops?

_____
_____
_____
_____
_____
_____
_____
_____

c. ANSWER THE BIG ❓ How do energy and matter move through ecosystems?

_____
_____
_____
_____
_____
_____
_____
_____
_____
_____
_____

got it? ....

O I get it! Now I know that the nitrogen cycle _____
_____
_____
_____
_____

O I need extra help with _____
_____

Go to MY SCIENCE ⓢ COACH *online for help with this subject.*

57

Biomes

UNLOCK
THE BIG
?

🔑 **What Are the Six Major Biomes?**

MY PLANET DIARY

That's Super Cool!

Misconception: It is always fatal when body temperatures drop below freezing.

Fact: In the tundra, arctic ground squirrels hibernate up to eight months a year. During this time, a squirrel's body temperature drops below freezing! This is called supercooling and gives the squirrel the lowest body temperature of any mammal. Without waking, a squirrel will shiver for several hours every couple of weeks to increase its body temperature.

MISCONCEPTION

Answer the question below.

What do you think are the advantages of supercooling?

_____

_____

_____

_____

_____

_____

▶ PLANET DIARY Go to **Planet Diary** to learn more about biomes.

Lab® Do the Inquiry Warm-Up
zone *How Much Rain Is That?*

What Are the Six Major Biomes?

Imagine that you are taking part in an around-the-world scientific expedition. On this expedition you will collect data on the typical climate and organisms of each of Earth's biomes. A **biome** is a group of ecosystems with similar climates and organisms.

🔑 **The six major biomes are desert, rain forest, grassland, deciduous forest, boreal forest, and tundra.** It is mostly the **climate**—the average annual temperature and amount of precipitation—in an area that determines its biome. Climate limits the species of plants that can grow in an area. In turn, the species of plants determine the kinds of animals that live there.

Vocabulary

- biome • climate • desert • rain forest
- emergent layer • canopy • understory • grassland
- savanna • deciduous tree • boreal forest
- coniferous tree • tundra • permafrost

Skills

↻ Reading: Compare and Contrast

△ Inquiry: Draw Conclusions

Desert Biomes The first stop on your expedition is a desert. You step off the bus into the searing heat. A **desert** is an area that receives less than 25 centimeters of rain per year. Some of the driest deserts may not receive any precipitation in a year! Deserts often undergo large shifts in temperature during the course of a day. A scorching hot desert like the Namib Desert in Africa cools rapidly each night when the sun goes down. Other deserts, such as the Gobi in central Asia, have a yearly average temperature that is below freezing.

Organisms that live in the desert, like the fennec in **Figure 1,** must be adapted to little or no rain and to extreme temperatures. For example, the stem of a saguaro cactus has folds that are similar to the pleats in an accordion. The stem expands to store water when it is raining. Gila monsters can spend weeks at a time in their cool underground burrows. Many other desert animals are most active at night when the temperatures are cooler.

FIGURE 1 ·······························

Desert

Organisms must be adapted to live in the desert.

✎ **Complete these tasks.**

1. CHALLENGE How do you think the fennec's ears and fur are adaptations to the desert's extreme temperatures?

   _____

   _____

   _____

2. **List** Write five things you'll need to be well adapted to desert conditions. Pack carefully!

Supply List
- ○ wide-brimmed hat
- ○ _____
- ○ _____
- ○ _____
- ○ _____
- ○ _____

Equator

Desert Biomes
☐ Desert

59

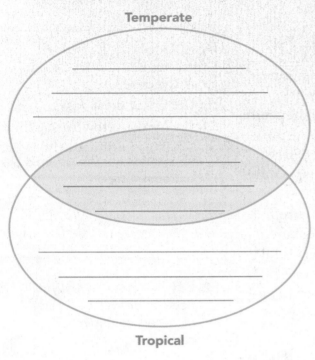
Compare and Contrast As you read about temperate and tropical rain forests, fill in the Venn diagram.

Temperate

Tropical

Rain-Forest Biomes

The second stop on your expedition is a rain forest. **Rain forests** are forests in which large amounts of rain fall year-round. This biome is living up to its name—it's pouring! After a short shower, the sun reappears. However, very little sunlight reaches the ground.

Plants are everywhere in the rain forest. Some plants, like the vines hanging from tree limbs, even grow on other plants! And animals are flying, creeping, and slithering all around you.

Temperate Rain Forests You may think that a rain forest is a warm, humid "jungle" in the tropics. But there is another type of rain forest. The Pacific Northwest of the United States receives more than 300 centimeters of rain a year. Huge trees grow there, including redwoods, cedars, and firs. Many ecologists refer to this ecosystem as a temperate rain forest. The term *temperate* means "having moderate temperatures."

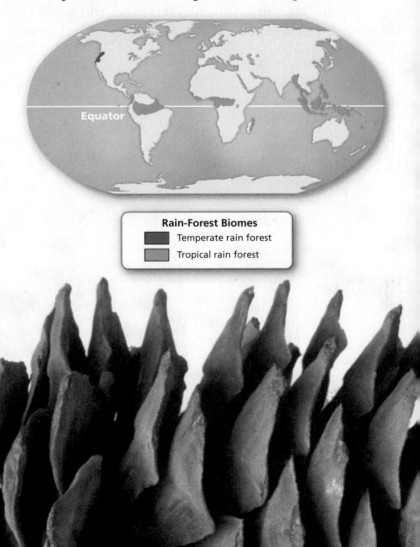

Equator

Rain-Forest Biomes
- Temperate rain forest
- Tropical rain forest

FIGURE 2 ···

Temperate Rain Forests

The sugar pine is the tallest kind of pine tree, reaching heights of 53 to 61 meters. It also produces the largest pine cones. A sugar pine cone can reach a length of 30 to 56 centimeters. The sugar pine cone shown here is actual size!

Identify What conditions do you think allow a tree to grow so tall?

_____

_____

_____

_____

Tropical Rain Forests As you can see on the map, tropical rain forests are found in regions close to the equator. The climate is warm and humid all year long, and there is a lot of rain. Because of these climate conditions, an amazing variety of plants grow in tropical rain forests.

Trees in the rain forest form several distinct layers. The tallest layer of the rain forest which receives the most sunlight and can reach up to 70 meters, is the **emergent layer.** Underneath, trees up to 50 meters tall form a leafy roof called the **canopy.** Below the canopy, a layer of shorter trees and vines, around 15 meters high, form an **understory.** Understory plants grow well in the shade formed by the canopy. The forest floor is nearly dark, so only a few plants live there. Look at the tree layers in **Figure 3.**

The abundant plant life in tropical rain forests provides habitats for many species of animals. Ecologists estimate that millions of species of insects live in tropical rain forests. These insects serve as a source of food for many reptiles, birds, and mammals. Many of these animals, in turn, are food sources for other animals. Although tropical rain forests cover only a small part of the planet, they probably contain more species of plants and animals than all the other biomes combined.

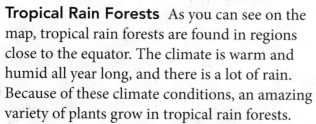

FIGURE 3 ···
Tropical Rain Forests
On the edge of this tropical rain forest, an amazing variety of organisms can be found in the different layers.

✎ **Relate Text and Visuals** Based on your reading, label the four distinct layers of the tropical rain forest in the boxes above.

Rhea, South America A

Cassowary, Australia B

Ostrich, Africa C

FIGURE 4

Grasslands

The rhea, cassowary, and ostrich are grassland birds that live on different continents.

✎ **Interpret Maps** On the world map, identify the continents in which these three birds are located. List three characteristics that these grassland birds all share.

_____

_____

_____

_____

_____

Grassland Biomes

The third stop on the expedition is a grassy plain called a prairie. Temperatures are more comfortable here than they were in the desert. The breeze carries the scent of soil warmed by the sun. This rich soil supports grasses as tall as you. Startled by your approach, sparrows dart into hiding places among the waving grass stems.

Although the prairie receives more rain than a desert, you may notice only a few scattered areas of trees and shrubs. Ecologists classify prairies, which are generally found in the middle latitudes, as grasslands. A **grassland** is an area that is populated mostly by grasses and other nonwoody plants. Most grasslands receive 25 to 75 centimeters of rain each year. Fires and droughts are common in this biome. Grasslands that are located closer to the equator than prairies are known as savannas. A **savanna** receives as much as 120 centimeters of rain each year. Scattered shrubs and small trees grow on savannas, along with grass.

Grasslands are home to many of the largest animals on Earth— herbivores such as elephants, bison, antelopes, zebras, giraffes, kangaroos, and rhinoceroses. Grazing by these large herbivores maintains the grasslands. Their grazing keeps young trees and bushes from sprouting and competing with the grass for water and sunlight. You can see some grassland birds in **Figure 4.**

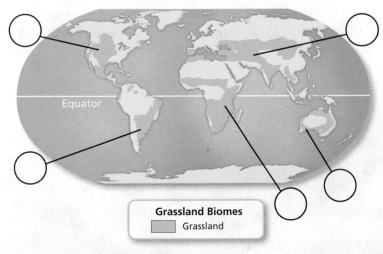

Equator

Grassland Biomes
▢ Grassland

Deciduous Forest Biomes

Your trip to the fourth biome takes you to another forest. It is now late summer. Cool mornings here give way to warm days. Several members of the expedition are busy recording the numerous plant species. Others are looking through binoculars, trying to identify the songbirds.

You are now visiting a deciduous forest biome. Many of the trees in this forest are **deciduous trees** (dee SIJ oo us), trees that shed their leaves and grow new ones each year. Oaks and maples are examples of deciduous trees. Deciduous forests receive enough rain to support the growth of trees and other plants, at least 50 centimeters of rain per year. Temperatures can vary greatly during the year. The growing season usually lasts five to six months.

The variety of plants in a deciduous forest creates many different habitats. Many species of birds live in different parts of the forest, eating the insects and fruits in their specific areas. Mammals such as chipmunks and skunks live in deciduous forests. In a North American deciduous forest you might also see wood thrushes and white-tailed deer.

If you were to return to this biome in the winter, you would not see much wildlife. Many of the bird species migrate, or fly great distances, to warmer areas. Some of the mammals hibernate, or enter a state of greatly reduced body activity similar to sleep. Look at **Figure 5.** During the winter months, animals that hibernate get energy from fat stored in their bodies.

FIGURE 5 ·······················

Deciduous Forest

Most of the trees in a deciduous forest have leaves that change color and drop to the forest floor each autumn. In the leaves, this dormouse hibernates through the winter.

✎ **Infer** Is hibernation an adaptation to life in a deciduous forest? Explain your answer.

_____

_____

_____

_____

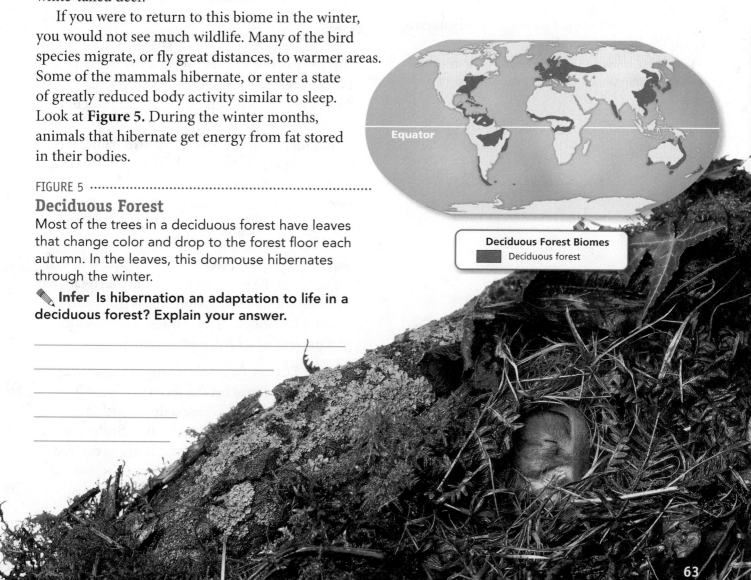

Equator

Deciduous Forest Biomes
◼ Deciduous forest

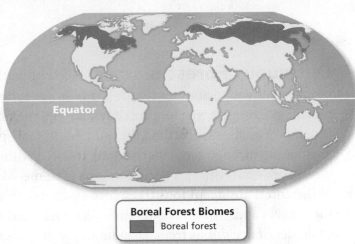

Boreal Forest Biomes
Boreal forest

FIGURE 6 ·······················

Boreal Forest
 This lynx and snowshoe hare are adapted to life in the boreal forest.

1. **Infer** Choose the best answer. The feet of each animal are an adaptation to its

   ○ food.   ○ climate.
   ○ predators.   ○ all of the above

2. **Explain** Defend your answer.

_____

_____

_____

_____

_____

Boreal Forest Biomes Now the expedition heads north to a colder biome, the boreal forest. The term *boreal* means "northern," and **boreal forests** are dense forests found in upper regions of the Northern Hemisphere. The expedition leaders claim they can identify a boreal forest by its smell. When you arrive, you catch a whiff of the spruce and fir trees that blanket the hillsides. Feeling the chilly early fall air, you pull a jacket and hat out of your bag.

Boreal Forest Plants Most of the trees in the boreal forest are **coniferous trees** (koh NIF ur us), trees that produce their seeds in cones and have leaves shaped like needles. The boreal forest is sometimes referred to by its Russian name, the *taiga* (TY guh). Winters in these forests are very cold. The snow can reach heights well over your head! Even so, the summers are rainy and warm enough to melt all the snow.

Tree species in the boreal forest are well adapted to the cold climate. Since water is frozen for much of the year, trees must have adaptations that prevent water loss. Coniferous trees, such as firs and hemlocks, all have thick, waxy needles that prevent water from evaporating.

Boreal Forest Animals Many of the animals of the boreal forest eat the seeds produced by the coniferous trees. These animals include red squirrels, insects, and birds such as finches. Some herbivores, such as moose and beavers, eat tree bark and new shoots. The variety of herbivores in the boreal forest supports many predators, including lynx, otters, and great horned owls. **Figure 6** shows an herbivore and its predator.

Tundra Biomes As you arrive at your last stop, the driving wind gives you an immediate feel for this biome. The **tundra** is extremely cold and dry. Expecting deep snow, many are surprised to learn that the tundra may receive no more precipitation than a desert.

Most of the soil in the tundra is frozen all year. This frozen soil is called **permafrost.** During the short summer, the top layer of soil thaws, but the underlying soil remains frozen. Because rainwater cannot soak into the permafrost, shallow ponds and marshy areas appear in the summer.

Tundra Plants Mosses, grasses, and dwarf forms of a few trees can be found in the tundra. Most of the plant growth takes place during the long days of the short summer season. North of the Arctic Circle, the sun does not set during midsummer.

Tundra Animals In summer, the insects are abundant. Insect-eating birds take advantage of the plentiful food by eating as much as they can. But when winter approaches, these birds migrate south. Mammals of the tundra include caribou, foxes, and wolves. The mammals that remain on the tundra during the winter grow thick fur coats. What can these animals find to eat on the tundra in winter? The caribou scrape snow away to find lichens. Wolves follow the caribou and look for weak members of the herd to prey upon.

FIGURE 7
Tundra
Although the ground is frozen for most of the year, mosses, grasses, and dwarf forms of trees grow here.

✎ **Communicate** Discuss with a partner why there are no tall trees on the tundra. Describe two factors that you think may influence tree growth.

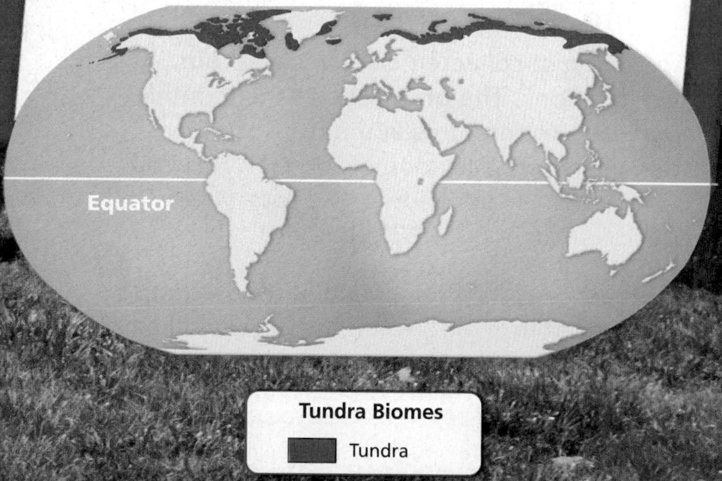

_____

_____

_____

_____

_____

_____

_____

_____

_____

Equator

Tundra Biomes
☐ Tundra

65

Equator

FIGURE 8 ·······························
▶ INTERACTIVE ART **Mountains**
Mountains are not part of any
major biome.

Mountains and Ice Some land areas are
not classified as biomes. Recall that biomes are
defined by abiotic factors such as climate and soil,
and by biotic factors such as plant and animal life.
Because the organisms that live in these areas vary,
mountain ranges and land covered with thick ice
sheets are not considered biomes.

The climate of a mountain changes from its
base to its summit. If you were to hike all the way
up a tall mountain, you would pass through a
series of biomes. At the base, you might find
grasslands. As you climbed, you might pass
through deciduous forest and then boreal forest.
As you neared the top, your surroundings would
resemble the cold, dry tundra.

Other places are covered year-round with thick
ice sheets. Most of Greenland and Antarctica fall
into this category. Organisms that are adapted to
life on ice include leopard seals and polar bears.

do the math!

Biome Climates

An ecologist collected climate data from
two locations. The graph shows the monthly
average temperatures in the two locations. The
total yearly precipitation in Location A is 250
centimeters. In Location B, the total yearly
precipitation is 14 centimeters.

❶ **Read Graphs** Provide a title for the graph.
What variable is plotted on the horizontal axis?
On the vertical axis?

_____

❷ **Interpret Data** Study the graph. How would
you describe the temperature over the course of a
year in Location A? In Location B?

_____

_____

_____

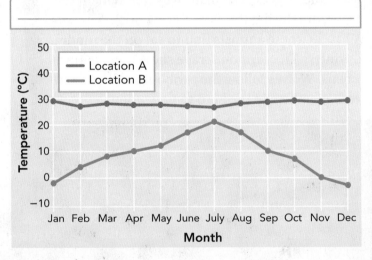

❸ **Draw Conclusions** Given the precipitation
and temperature data for these locations, in which
biome would you expect each to be located?

_____

_____

_____

apply it!

Key of Earth Biomes
- ☐ Desert
- ☐ Temperate rain forest
- ☐ Tropical rain forest
- ☐ Grassland
- ☐ Deciduous rain forest
- ☐ Boreal forest
- ☐ Tundra

❶ Interpret Maps Using the colors shown in the biome maps throughout this lesson, color in the key above. Use the key to color in the areas on the map of North America.

❷ Draw Conclusions Where are most of the boreal forests located? Why are there no boreal forests in the Southern Hemisphere?

_____

_____

_____

_____

_____

❸ Describe Mark the area in which you live with an *X* on the map. What is the climate like where you live? How do you think your climate affects which organisms live there?

_____

_____

_____

_____

_____

_____

_____

Lab zone® Do the Quick Lab *Inferring Forest Climates.*

🔑 Assess Your Understanding

1a. Review _____ and _____ are the two main factors that determine an area's biome.

b. Infer What biome might you be in if you were standing on a bitterly cold, dry plain with only a few, short trees scattered around?

_____

_____

got it? ....

○ **I get it!** Now I know that the six major biomes are _____

_____

○ **I need extra help with** _____

Go to **MY SCIENCE ⑤ COACH** *online for help with this subject.*

67

Aquatic Ecosystems

UNLOCK THE BIG

🔑 **What Are the Two Major Aquatic Ecosystems?**

MY PLANET DIARY

TECHNOLOGY

Underwater *Alvin*

Meet *Alvin*, an HOV (Human-Occupied Vehicle). Equipped with propulsion jets, cameras, and robotic arms, *Alvin* helps scientists gather data and discover ecosystems that exist deep in the ocean. Built in 1964, *Alvin* was one of the world's first deep-ocean submersibles and has made more than 4,500 dives. *Alvin* is credited with finding a lost hydrogen bomb, exploring the first known hydrothermal vents, and surveying the wreck of the *Titanic*.

Calculate Suppose that on each of the 4,500 dives *Alvin* has made, a new pilot and two new scientists were on board. How many scientists have seen the deep ocean through *Alvin's* windows? How many people, in total, traveled in *Alvin*?

_____

_____

▶ PLANET DIARY Go to **Planet Diary** to learn more about aquatic ecosystems.

 Lab zone Do the Inquiry Warm-Up *Where Does It Live?*

What Are the Two Major Aquatic Ecosystems?

Since almost three quarters of Earth's surface is covered with water, many living things make their homes in and near water. 🔑 **There are two types of aquatic, or water-based, ecosystems: freshwater ecosystems and marine (or saltwater) ecosystems.** All aquatic ecosystems are affected by the same abiotic, or nonliving, factors: sunlight, temperature, oxygen, and salt content. Sunlight is an important factor in aquatic ecosystems because it is necessary for photosynthesis in the water just as it is on land. Half of all oxygen produced on Earth comes from floating algae called phytoplankton. Because water absorbs sunlight, there is only enough light for photosynthesis to occur near the surface or in shallow water.

Vocabulary
- estuary
- intertidal zone
- neritic zone

Skills
- ↻ Reading: Outline
- △ Inquiry: Communicate

Freshwater Ecosystems No worldwide expedition would be complete without exploring Earth's waters. Even though most of Earth's surface is covered with water, only 3 percent of the volume is fresh water. Freshwater ecosystems include streams, rivers, ponds, and lakes. On this part of your expedition, you'll find that freshwater biomes provide habitats for a variety of organisms.

Streams and Rivers At the source of a mountain stream, the water flows slowly. Plants take root on the bottom, providing food for insects and homes for frogs. These consumers then provide food for larger consumers. Stream currents increase as streams come together to make larger streams, often called rivers. Animals here are adapted to strong currents. For example, trout have streamlined bodies to swim in the rushing water. As the current speeds up, it can become cloudy with sediment. Few plants or algae grow in this fast-moving water. Consumers such as snails feed on leaves and seeds that fall into the stream. At lower elevations, streams are warmer and often contain less oxygen, affecting the organisms that can live in them.

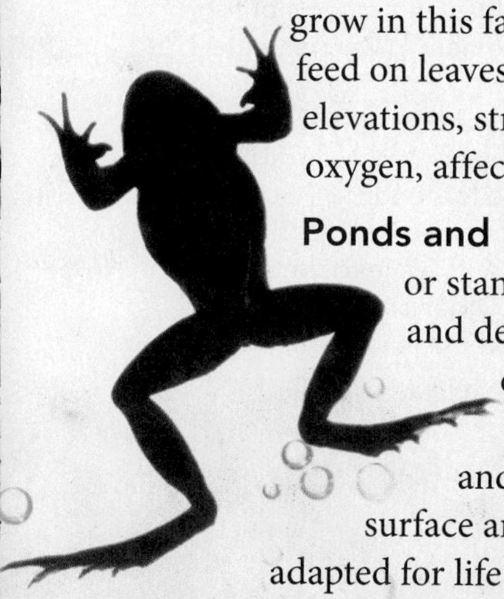

Ponds and Lakes Ponds and lakes are bodies of still, or standing, fresh water. Lakes are generally larger and deeper than ponds. Ponds are often shallow enough that sunlight can reach the bottom, allowing plants to grow there. In large ponds and most lakes, however, algae floating at the surface are the major producers. Many animals are adapted for life in still water. Dragonflies, snails, and frogs live along the shores of ponds. In the open water, sunfish feed on insects and algae close to the surface. Scavengers such as catfish live near the bottoms of ponds. Bacteria and other decomposers also feed on the remains of other organisms.

↻ **Outline** As you read, make an outline on a separate sheet of paper that includes the different types of aquatic ecosystems. Use the red headings for the main ideas and the black headings for the supporting details.

FIGURE 1
Freshwater Ecosystems
Water lilies live in ponds and lakes.

✎ **Answer the questions.**

1. **Identify** What are two abiotic factors that can affect water lilies?

_____
_____
_____
_____

2. [CHALLENGE] What adaptations do fish have that allow them to live in water?

_____
_____
_____
_____

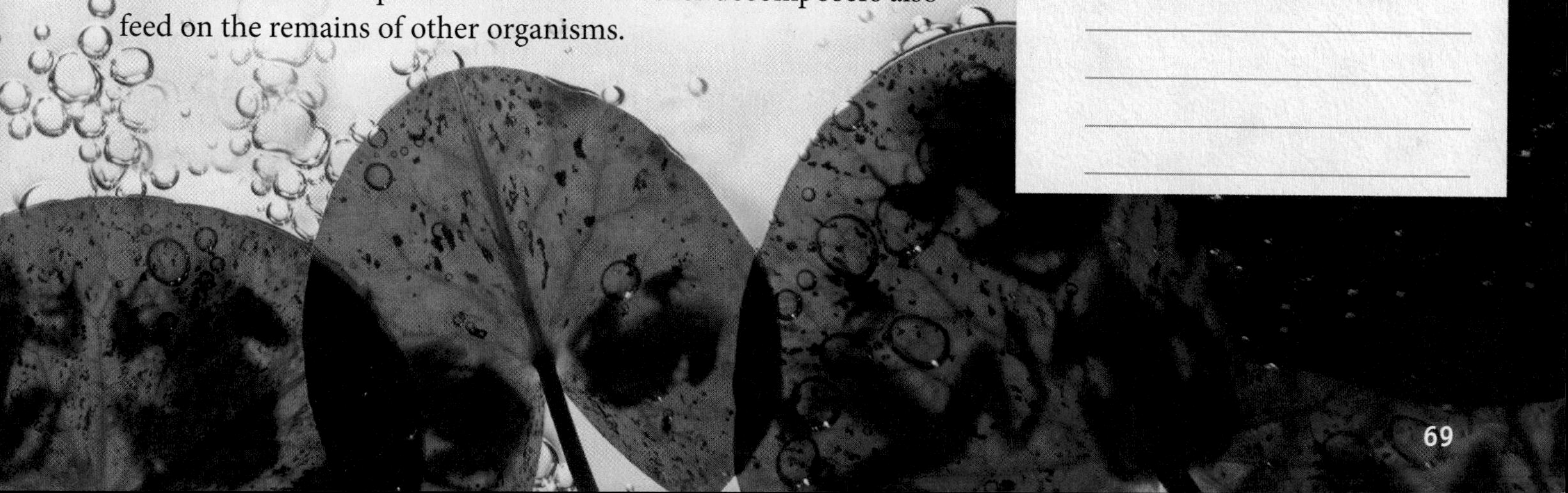

69

High tide

Low tide

Continental shelf

Marine Ecosystems

Marine Ecosystems The expedition now heads to the coast to explore some marine biomes. On your way, you'll pass through an estuary. An **estuary** (ES choo ehr ee), is found where the fresh water of a river meets the salt water of an ocean. Algae and plants provide food and shelter for animals, including crabs and fish. Many animals use the calm waters of estuaries for breeding grounds. Last, you explore the different ocean zones as described in **Figure 2.**

Ocean Zones

Zone	Location	Inhabitants
Intertidal zone	Located on the shore between the highest high-tide line and the lowest low-tide line	Organisms must be able to survive pounding waves and the sudden changes in water levels and temperature that occur with high and low tides. For example, barnacles and sea stars cling to the rocks while clams and crabs burrow in the sand.
Neritic zone	Region of shallow water found below the low-tide line and extending over the continental shelf	Sunlight passes through shallow water, allowing photosynthesis to occur. Many living things, such as algae and schools of fish, live here. Coral reefs can also be found here in warmer waters.
Surface zone, open ocean	Located beyond the neritic zone and extending from the water's surface to about 200 meters deep	Sunlight penetrates this zone, allowing photosynthesis to occur in floating phytoplankton and other algae. Tuna, swordfish, and some whales depend on the algae for food.
Deep zone, open ocean	Located beneath the surface zone to the ocean floor	Little, if any, sunlight passes through. Animals feed on the remains of organisms that sink down. Organisms, like the giant squid and anglerfish, are adapted to life in the dark.

FIGURE 2 ....

Marine Ecosystems

The ocean is home to a number of different ecosystems.

✎ **Classify** Using the clues, determine at which depth each organism belongs. In the circles in the ocean, write the letter for each organism in the correct zone.

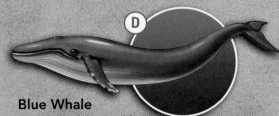

C

Yellowfin Tuna
Found in open waters and has been known to eat squid

D

Blue Whale
Feeds on shrimplike creatures at depths of more than 100 meters during the day

A

Anglerfish
Females have a lighted lure to help them attract prey in the dark.

B

Tripod Fish
This fish has three elongated fins to help it stand.

E

Swordfish
Often seen jumping out of the water to stun smaller fish

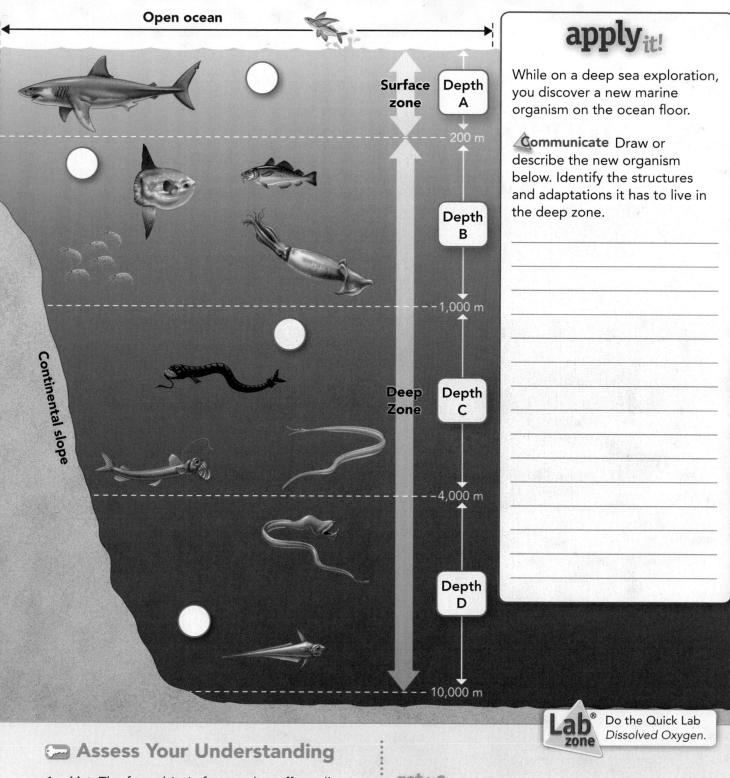

Open ocean

Surface zone

Depth A

— — 200 m

Depth B

— 1,000 m

Continental slope

Deep Zone

Depth C

— — 4,000 m

Depth D

— — 10,000 m

apply it!

While on a deep sea exploration, you discover a new marine organism on the ocean floor.

Communicate Draw or describe the new organism below. Identify the structures and adaptations it has to live in the deep zone.

_____
_____
_____
_____
_____
_____
_____
_____
_____
_____
_____
_____
_____
_____
_____

Lab zone® Do the Quick Lab
Dissolved Oxygen.

🔑 Assess Your Understanding

1a. List The four abiotic factors that affect all aquatic ecosystems are

_____

_____

b. Make Generalizations Why is sunlight important to all aquatic ecosystems?

_____

_____

got it?

○ **I get it!** Now I know that the two major types of aquatic ecosystems are _____

_____

○ **I need extra help with** _____

_____

Go to MY SCIENCE ⬤ COACH *online for help with this subject.*

71

LESSON

5 Biogeography

🔑 **What Factors Affect Species Dispersal?**

my planeT DiaRY

Australia's Animals

When you think of Australia, what animal comes to mind? Most likely, you think of a kangaroo or a koala. Did you know that these animals are marsupials, mammals that carry their young in a pouch? You might be surprised to learn that most marsupials exist only in Australia. Now, can you name any monotremes, or mammals that lay eggs? The only monotremes that exist are platypuses and echidnas, both native to Australia. Lots of unique animals are native to Australia because it is completely surrounded by water.

FUN FACT

Communicate Answer the following questions with a classmate.

1. What are two types of mammals that are common in Australia?

_____

2. Would you ever expect a platypus to move from Australia to the United States? Explain.

_____
_____
_____
_____

> PLANET DIARY Go to **Planet Diary** to learn more about biogeography.

Lab zone® Do the Inquiry Warm-Up
How Can You Move a Seed?

Vocabulary
- biogeography
- continental drift
- dispersal
- exotic species

Skills
- ⟳ Reading: Relate Cause and Effect
- △ Inquiry: Predict

What Factors Affect Species Dispersal?

Do you think all of the people who live in your hometown were born there? Some of them may have come from different cities, states, or countries. Just as humans do, different plants and animals live in different parts of the world. The study of where organisms live and how they got there is called **biogeography.** Biogeographers also study factors that have led to the worldwide distribution of species that exist today.

The movement of the Earth's continents is one factor that has affected how species are distributed. The continents are parts of huge blocks of solid rock, called plates, that make up Earth's surface. These plates have been moving very slowly for millions of years. As the plates move, the continents move with them in a process called **continental drift. Figure 1** shows how the continents have moved over time. Notice that about 225 million years ago, all of the continents were part of one huge landmass, called Pangaea.

Continental drift has had a great impact on species distribution. For example, Australia drifted away from the other landmasses millions of years ago. Organisms from other parts of the world could not reach the isolated island and unique Australian species developed in this isolation.

🔑 **Continental drift, wind, water, and living things are all means of distributing species. Other factors, such as physical barriers, competition, and climate, can limit species dispersal.**

FIGURE 1 ···
▷ **INTERACTIVE ART** **Continental Drift**
The movement of landmasses is one factor affecting the distribution of organisms.

✏️ **Observe** How has Australia's location changed over time?

_____

_____

_____

225 Million Years Ago

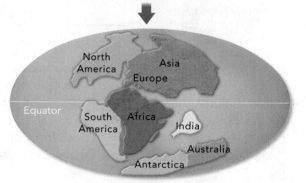

115 Million Years Ago

Earth Today

Means of Dispersal The movement of organisms from one place to another is called **dispersal.** Dispersal can be caused by gravity, wind, water, or living things, such as the blue jay in **Figure 2.**

Wind and Water Many animals move into new areas on their own. But plants and small organisms need help in moving from place to place. Wind can disperse seeds, fungi spores, tiny spiders, and other small, light organisms. Birds use the wind to fly to new locations. Similarly, water transports objects that float, such as coconuts and leaves. Small animals, such as insects or snails, may get a ride to a new home on top of these floating rafts. Water also transports organisms like fish and marine mammals.

Other Living Things Organisms can also be dispersed by other living things. If your dog or cat has ever come home covered with sticky plant burs, you have seen an example of dispersal. Humans have sped up the dispersal of organisms, both intentionally and unintentionally, as they travel around the world. An **exotic species** is an organism that is carried into a new location by people. Exotic species have contributed to the decline or elimination of native species.

FIGURE 2 ••••••••••••••••••••••••

▶ INTERACTIVE ART **Means of Dispersal**
Seeds can be dispersed by the wind or by organisms like this blue jay.

**apply** *it!*

In 1780, a Japanese ship ran aground on one of Alaska's uninhabited Aleutian Islands. Rats from the ship swam to the island. Since then, the rats on this island, now called Rat Island, have preyed upon and destroyed seabird populations and the overall ecosystem. "Rat spills" from ships are one of the leading causes of seabird extinctions on islands worldwide.

1 Communicate With a partner, identify ways in which sailors can control rats on board their ships and prevent them from going ashore.

_____

_____

_____

_____

2 ◢ Predict Do you think the role of humans in the dispersal of species will increase or decrease in the next 50 years? Defend your answer.

_____

_____

_____

_____

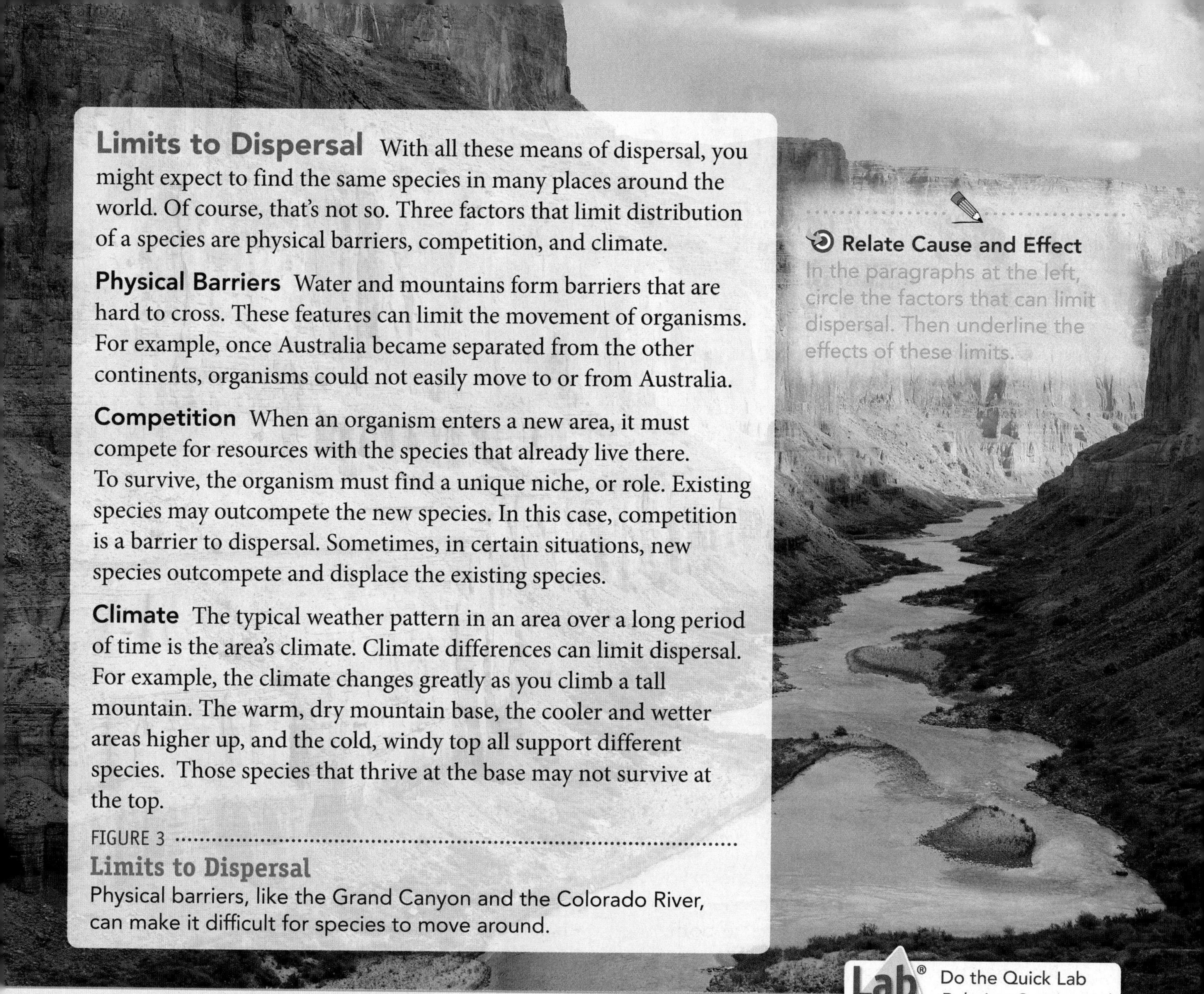

Limits to Dispersal

Limits to Dispersal With all these means of dispersal, you might expect to find the same species in many places around the world. Of course, that's not so. Three factors that limit distribution of a species are physical barriers, competition, and climate.

Physical Barriers Water and mountains form barriers that are hard to cross. These features can limit the movement of organisms. For example, once Australia became separated from the other continents, organisms could not easily move to or from Australia.

Competition When an organism enters a new area, it must compete for resources with the species that already live there. To survive, the organism must find a unique niche, or role. Existing species may outcompete the new species. In this case, competition is a barrier to dispersal. Sometimes, in certain situations, new species outcompete and displace the existing species.

Climate The typical weather pattern in an area over a long period of time is the area's climate. Climate differences can limit dispersal. For example, the climate changes greatly as you climb a tall mountain. The warm, dry mountain base, the cooler and wetter areas higher up, and the cold, windy top all support different species. Those species that thrive at the base may not survive at the top.

FIGURE 3 ···
Limits to Dispersal
Physical barriers, like the Grand Canyon and the Colorado River, can make it difficult for species to move around.

✐ **Relate Cause and Effect**
In the paragraphs at the left, circle the factors that can limit dispersal. Then underline the effects of these limits.

Lab® zone Do the Quick Lab *Relating Continental Drift to Dispersal.*

🔑 Assess Your Understanding

1a. Explain What role do humans play in the dispersal of species?

_____

_____

_____

_____

_____

b. CHALLENGE Suppose that a new species of insect were introduced to your area. Explain how competition might limit its dispersal.

_____

_____

_____

_____

got it? ···

○ **I get it!** Now I know that species dispersal is affected by _____

_____

○ **I need extra help with** _____

Go to **MY SCIENCE** Ⓢ **COACH** online for help with this subject.

2 Study Guide

Producers, _____, and _____ help to cycle energy through ecosystems.

LESSON 1 Energy Flow in Ecosystems

🔑 Each of the organisms in an ecosystem fills the energy role of producer, consumer, or decomposer.

🔑 Energy moves through an ecosystem when one organism eats another.

🔑 The most energy is available at the producer level of the pyramid. As energy moves up the pyramid, each level has less energy available than the level below.

Vocabulary
- producer • consumer • herbivore • carnivore • omnivore
- scavenger • decomposer • food chain • food web • energy pyramid

LESSON 2 Cycles of Matter

🔑 The processes of evaporation, condensation, and precipitation make up the water cycle.

🔑 The processes by which carbon and oxygen are recycled are linked. Producers, consumers, and decomposers play roles in recycling both.

🔑 Nitrogen moves from the air into the soil, into living things, and back into the air or soil.

Vocabulary
- evaporation • condensation
- precipitation • nitrogen fixation

LESSON 3 Biomes

🔑 The six major biomes are desert, rain forest, grassland, deciduous forest, boreal forest, and tundra.

Vocabulary
- biome • climate • desert • rain forest
- emergent layer • canopy • understory
- grassland • savanna • deciduous tree
- boreal forest • coniferous tree • tundra
- permafrost

LESSON 4 Aquatic Ecosystems

🔑 There are two types of aquatic, or water-based, ecosystems: freshwater ecosystems and marine (or saltwater) ecosystems.

Vocabulary
- estuary
- intertidal zone
- neritic zone

LESSON 5 Biogeography

🔑 Continental drift, wind, water, and living things are all means of distributing species. Other factors, such as physical barriers, competition, and climate, can limit species dispersal.

Vocabulary
- biogeography • continental drift
- dispersal • exotic species

Review and Assessment

LESSON 1 Energy Flow in Ecosystems

1. A diagram that shows how much energy is available at each feeding level in an ecosystem is a(n)

   a. food web.   **b.** food chain.

   c. water cycle.   **d.** energy pyramid.

2. A(n) _____ is a consumer that eats only plants.

3. **Interpret Diagrams** Which organisms in the illustration are producers? Consumers?

   _____
   _____
   _____
   _____
   _____
   _____
   _____
   _____

4. **Compare and Contrast** How are food chains and food webs different?

   _____
   _____
   _____
   _____

5. **Write About It** Think about your own food web. Name the producers and consumers that make up your diet.

   _____
   _____
   _____
   _____
   _____
   _____
   _____

LESSON 2 Cycles of Matter

6. When drops of water in a cloud become heavy enough, they fall to Earth as

   a. permafrost.   **b.** evaporation.

   c. precipitation.   **d.** condensation.

7. Evaporation, condensation, and precipitation are the three main processes in the

   _____

8. **Infer** Which process is responsible for the droplets visible on the glass below? Explain.

   _____
   _____
   _____
   _____

9. **Classify** Which group of organisms is the source of oxygen in the oxygen cycle? Explain.

   _____
   _____

10. **Make Generalizations** Describe the roles of producers and consumers in the carbon cycle.

    _____
    _____
    _____
    _____
    _____
    _____

11. **Draw Conclusions** What would happen if all the nitrogen-fixing bacteria disappeared?

    _____
    _____
    _____
    _____

LESSON 3 Biomes

12. Little precipitation and extreme temperatures are main characteristics of which biome?

   a. desert   b. grassland

   c. boreal forest   d. deciduous forest

13. A _____ is a group of ecosystems with similar climates and organisms.

14. **Compare and Contrast** How are the tundra and desert similar? How are they different?

_____

_____

_____

_____

_____

_____

LESSON 4 Aquatic Ecosystems

15. In which ocean zone would you find barnacles, sea stars, and other organisms tightly attached to rocks?

   a. neritic zone   b. intertidal zone

   c. estuary ecosystem d. freshwater ecosystem

16. Coral reefs are found in the shallow, sunny waters of the _____

17. **Compare and Contrast** How are a pond and lake similar? How do they differ?

_____

_____

_____

_____

_____

LESSON 5 Biogeography

18. What is a likely method of dispersal for seeds that are contained within a small berry?

   a. wind   b. water

   c. an animal   d. continental drift

19. The study of where organisms live and how they got there is called

_____

20. **Predict** When might seed dispersal not be beneficial?

_____

_____

_____

_____

_____

APPLY THE BIG ? How do energy and matter cycle through ecosystems?

21. Many acres of the Amazon rain forest have been destroyed to create farmland. Describe how the amount of energy in the food web for this area might be affected. How might the carbon and oxygen cycle also be affected?

_____

_____

_____

_____

_____

_____

_____

_____

_____

_____

Standardized Test Prep

Multiple Choice

Circle the letter of the best answer.

1. At which level of this energy pyramid is the *least* energy available?

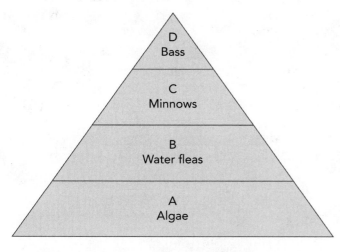

   A Level A   **B** Level B
   C Level C   **D** Level D

2. You are in an area in Maryland where the fresh water of the Chesapeake Bay meets the Atlantic Ocean. Which of the following terms describes where you are?

   A tundra   **B** estuary
   C neritic zone   **D** intertidal zone

3. Which pair of terms could apply to the same organism?

   A carnivore and producer
   B consumer and carnivore
   C scavenger and herbivore
   D producer and omnivore

4. Many Canadian forests contain coniferous trees, such as fir and spruce. The winter is long and cold. Which term describes this biome?

   A tundra   **B** grassland
   C boreal forest   **D** deciduous forest

5. Organisms can be dispersed in all of the following ways *except* by

   A wind.   **B** water.
   C temperature.   **D** other organisms.

Constructed Response

Use the diagram below and your knowledge of science to help you answer Question 6. Write your answer on a separate piece of paper.

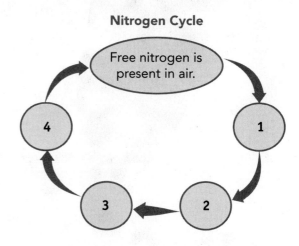

Nitrogen Cycle

6. Describe each numbered part of the cycle shown in the diagram above.

Clothing That FIGHTS BACK

Humans live in every biome on Earth, even some harsh environments that our bodies are not adapted for—deserts, rain forests, and tundra. In less extreme climates, we also face risks from our surroundings. But we have learned to protect ourselves by building shelters and wearing clothing.

UV (ultraviolet) radiation from the sun can damage your skin and cause cancer. A plain T-shirt offers some protection, but not as much as you might think—it may still allow between 7 and 20 percent of the sun's UV radiation through. Now, you can choose clothing made with chemicals that absorb UV radiation. These clothes offer better protection against the sun because they have a higher UPF (ultraviolet protection factor). They are also lightweight, so they're not as sticky in warm weather.

Design It Sun protection is not the only area in which science has helped people develop protective clothing. Scientists have created bug-repellent clothing, waterproof-breathable clothing, and insulated clothing. Research the climate in a biome of your choosing. List characteristics of that climate that might make survival difficult. Design an item of clothing that could help protect humans in that climate. What materials would your garment need in order to work?

Museum of Science.

Trees:
Environmental Factories

Some of the most important members of your community don't volunteer. They consume huge amounts of water and they make a mess. Despite these drawbacks, these long-standing community members do their share. Who are these individuals? They're trees!

Keeping it clean: Trees remove pollutants from the air. Some researchers have calculated the value of the environmental cleaning services that trees provide. One study valued the air-cleaning service that trees in the Chicago area provide at more than $9 million every year.

Keeping it cool: Trees provide shade and lower air temperature by the process of transpiration. Pollutants, like ozone and smog, form more easily when air temperatures are high, so by keeping the air cool, trees also keep it clean.

Acting locally and globally: Trees help fight global environmental problems such as climate change. Trees remove carbon dioxide from the air and store the carbon as they grow. Experts estimate that urban trees in the United States remove more than 700 million tons of carbon from the air every year.

Helping the local economy: Trees are also good for business. One study found that shoppers spend more money in urban areas where trees are planted than they do in similar areas that don't have trees!

Schools, clubs, and civic groups all over the United States volunteer to plant trees in their communities. ▶

Research It Examine a topographical map of the area where you live. Compare it to an aerial photograph from a library or local archive. Identify areas with a lot of trees, and areas that you think could benefit from more trees. Create a proposal to plant trees in one of the areas you identified. What kinds of trees will you plant? What do those trees need in order to grow well?

WHAT
DOES THIS
MACAW CHICK
NEED TO
SURVIVE?

How do people use Earth's resources?

People aren't the only living things that need resources to survive. How we use our planet's resources has an impact on all of Earth's species. Small and helpless, this baby scarlet macaw cannot live on its own. This chick was born featherless and with its eyes closed. Macaw parents feed the chick until it is at least three months old. ◢Infer **What basic things does this chick need to live?**

_____

_____

_____

_____

_____

▷ UNTAMED SCIENCE Watch the **Untamed Science** video to learn more about natural resources.

Resources and Living Things

3 Getting Started

Check Your Understanding

1. Background Read the paragraph below and then answer the question.

Ed is observing his ecology project for the tenth day in a row. He holds the bottle up to see the habitat inside. The snails, fish, and plants inside the bottle all look healthy. He can even see some baby snails. It is a whole ecosystem in a bottle!

> **Ecology** is the study of how organisms interact with each other and their environment.
>
> A **habitat** is an environment that provides the things a specific organism needs to live, grow, and reproduce.
>
> An **ecosystem** is the community of organisms that live in a particular area, along with their nonliving environment.

• How are the terms *ecosystem* and *ecology* related?

_____

_____

▶ MY READING WEB If you had trouble completing the question above, visit **My Reading Web** and type in *Resources and Living Things.*

Vocabulary Skill

Identify Related Word Forms You can increase your vocabulary by learning related forms of a word. For example, if you know the verb *produce* means "to make," you can figure out that the meaning of the noun *product* is "something that is made." The table below shows two vocabulary words in this chapter and their related word forms.

Verb	Noun	Adjective
pollute to contaminate Earth's land, water, or air	**pollution** the contamination of Earth's land, water, or air	**pollutive** contaminating Earth's land, water, or air
conserve to manage resource use wisely	**conservation** the practice of managing resource use wisely	**conservational** managing resource use wisely

2. Quick Check Complete the sentence with the correct form of the word from the table above.

• Air _____ is a problem in many of the world's major cities.

natural resource

nonrenewable resource

exponential growth

keystone species

Chapter Preview

LESSON 1
- natural resource
- pollution • point source
- nonpoint source
- environmental science

○ **Relate Cause and Effect**
△ **Draw Conclusions**

LESSON 2
- renewable resource
- nonrenewable resource
- sustainable use
- ecological footprint
- conservation

○ **Relate Text and Visuals**
△ **Calculate**

LESSON 3
- exponential growth

○ **Identify the Main Idea**
△ **Predict**

LESSON 4
- clear-cutting
- selective cutting
- sustainable yield
- fishery
- aquaculture

○ **Summarize**
△ **Communicate**

LESSON 5
- biodiversity • keystone species
- gene • extinction
- endangered species
- threatened species
- habitat destruction
- habitat fragmentation
- poaching • captive breeding

○ **Compare and Contrast**
△ **Infer**

> VOCAB FLASH CARDS For more help with vocabulary, visit **Vocab Flash Cards** and type in *Resources and Living Things.*

Introduction to Environmental Issues

What Are the Types of Environmental Issues?

How Are Environmental Decisions Made?

my planet diary

How Do You Feel About Nature?

You have probably heard of scientists who study animals, plants, rocks, and everything else in an ecosystem. Social scientists study an often-overlooked but very important part of any ecosystem—the people who use it! These scientists study how people value nature. They study how much people would be willing to pay to preserve nature. They also study how different age groups, genders, races, and social groups use nature. For example, a scuba diver wants coral reefs to remain beautiful and full of all kinds of organisms to enjoy in future dives. A commercial fisherman cares more about a coral reef supporting the kind of fish he wants to catch. You might care about coral reefs because you want to visit one someday.

CAREER

Communicate Discuss the question with a group of classmates. Then write your answer below.

Do you think it is important to consider how people value nature? Explain.

_____

_____

_____

_____

_____

_____

_____

> PLANET DIARY Go to **Planet Diary** to learn more about environmental issues.

Lab zone Do the Inquiry Warm-Up *How Do You Decide?*

Vocabulary

- natural resource • pollution • point source
- nonpoint source • environmental science

Skills

↻ Reading: Relate Cause and Effect

△ Inquiry: Draw Conclusions

What Are the Types of Environmental Issues?

Here is a riddle for you: what place is bigger than the United States and Mexico combined? This place is covered with ice more than two kilometers thick. It is a habitat for many animals and is a source of oil, coal, and iron. Stumped? The answer is Antarctica. Some people think of Antarctica as a useless, icy wasteland, but there are unique wildlife habitats in Antarctica. There are also valuable minerals beneath its thick ice.

What is the best use of Antarctica? Many people want access to its rich deposits of minerals and oil. Others worry that mining will harm its delicate ecosystems. Some people propose building hotels, parks, and ski resorts. Others think that Antarctica should remain undeveloped. Who should decide Antarctica's fate?

In 1998, 26 nations agreed to ban mining and oil exploration in Antarctica for at least 50 years. As resources become more scarce elsewhere in the world, the debate will surely continue.

Antarctica's future is just one environmental issue that people face today. 🔑 **Environmental issues fall into three general categories: population growth, resource use, and pollution.** Because these three types of issues are interconnected, they are very difficult to study and resolve.

FIGURE 1 ·····················

Arguing Over Antarctica
Some people want to leave Antarctica wild. Others want it developed.

✎ **Summarize** Fill in the boxes with points outlining each argument.

Argument One: Keep Antarctica Wild	Argument Two: Develop Antarctica
_____	_____
_____	_____
_____	_____
_____	_____
_____	_____

_____

_____

_____

_____

_____

_____

Population Growth

The human population grew very slowly until about A.D. 1650. Around that time, improvements in medicine, agriculture, and waste disposal led to people's living longer. The human population has been growing faster and faster since then.

When a population grows, the demand for resources also grows. Has your town or city ever experienced a water shortage? If so, you might have noticed that people have been asked to restrict their water use. This sometimes happens in areas with fast-growing populations. The water supplies in such areas were designed to serve fewer people than they now do, so shortages can occur during unusually dry weather.

Resource Use

Earth provides many materials people use throughout their lives. Anything that occurs naturally in the environment and is used by people is called a **natural resource.** Natural resources include trees, water, oil, coal, and other things. However, people do not use resources in the same way. In some areas of the world, people use a wide variety of resources. In other areas, people have little or no access to certain natural resources. For example, people in central Asia live too far away from ocean waters that provide fish and other resources. Conflict arises when a natural resource is scarce or used in a way that people feel is unfair.

FIGURE 2

Everyday Natural Resources

We use natural resources many times a day without even realizing it! A trip to the beach uses land, water, fuel, and many other resources.

✎ **List** On the journal page, list all the ways you have used natural resources so far today. For example, this book is made of paper that started as a tree.

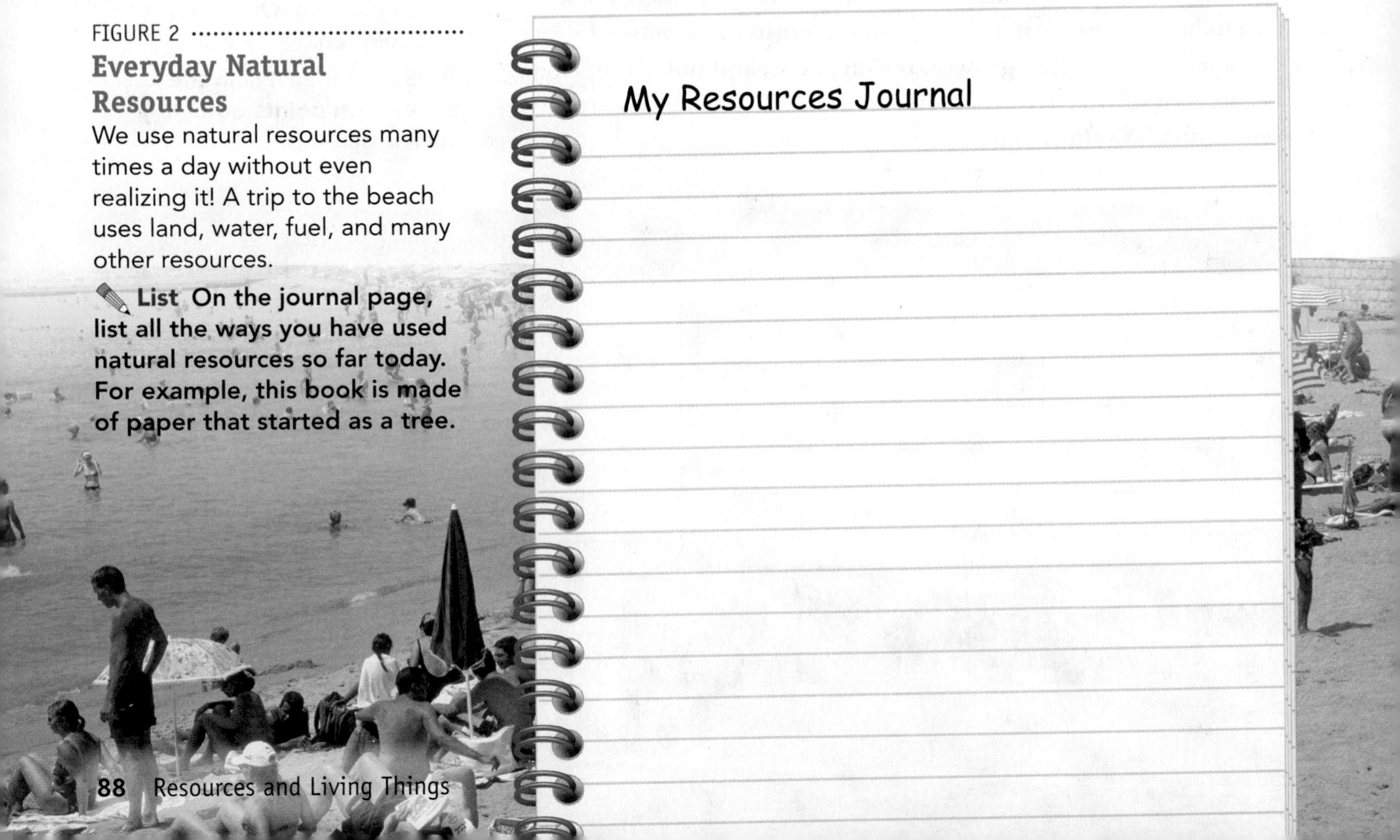

My Resources Journal

Pollution Many environmental factors can contribute to less than ideal conditions on Earth for people or other organisms. The contamination of Earth's land, water, or air is called **pollution.** Pollution can be caused by wastes, chemicals, noise, heat, light, and other sources. Pollution can destroy wildlife and cause human health problems.

Pollution is usually related to population growth and resource use. As you probably know, the burning of gasoline releases pollutants into the air. With more cars on the road, more gasoline is used, so more pollutants are released into the air. As populations grow and more people need to be fed, more fertilizers and other chemicals may be used to produce that food. As these chemicals run off the land, they can pollute bodies of water.

Pollution sources can be grouped into two categories. A **point source** is a specific pollution source that can be identified. A pipe gushing polluted water into a river is an example of a point source. A nonpoint source of pollution is not as easy to identify. A **nonpoint source** is widely spread and cannot be tied to a specific origin. For example, the polluted air that can hang over urban areas comes from vehicles, factories, and other polluters. The pollution cannot be tied to any one car or factory.

⤵ **Relate Cause and Effect**
Use what you have read about pollution so far to fill in the boxes below.

Some Causes of Pollution

_____
_____
_____
_____
_____

Some Effects of Pollution

_____
_____
_____
_____
_____

Lab zone® Do the Quick Lab
Environmental Issues.

🔑 **Assess Your Understanding**

1a. Define What is a natural resource?

_____
_____
_____

b. Make Generalizations How is population growth related to resource use and pollution?

_____
_____
_____
_____

got_{it?}

○ **I get it!** Now I know that the types of environmental issues are_____
_____

○ **I need extra help with** _____

Go to my science ⓢ COACH online for help with this subject.

How Are Environmental Decisions Made?

Dealing with environmental issues means making decisions. Decisions can be made at many levels. Your decision to walk to your friend's house rather than ride in a car is made at a personal level. A town's decision about how to dispose of its trash is made at a local level. A decision about whether the United States should allow oil drilling in a wildlife refuge is made on a national level. Decisions about how to protect Earth's atmosphere are made on a global level. Your personal decisions have a small impact. But when the personal decisions of millions of people are combined, they have a huge impact on the environment.

Balancing Different Needs Lawmakers work with many groups to make environmental decisions. One such group is environmental scientists. **Environmental science** is the study of natural processes in the environment and how humans can affect them. Data provided by environmental scientists are only part of the decision-making process. Environmental decision making requires a balance between the needs of the environment and the needs of people. 🔑 **To help balance the different opinions on an environmental issue, decision makers weigh the costs and benefits of a proposal for change before making a decision.**

apply it!

Suppose you are a member of a city planning board. A company wants to buy a piece of land outside the city and build a factory on it. When you go into work one day, you are met by protesters demanding that the land be turned into a wildlife park.

1 **Solve Problems** How should you decide what to do with the land?

_____

_____

_____

2 [CHALLENGE] What are some ways you could find out people's opinions about the issue?

_____

_____

_____

Types of Costs and Benefits

Costs and benefits are often economic. Will a proposal provide jobs? Will it cost too much money? Costs and benefits are not measured only in terms of money. For example, suppose a state must decide whether to allow logging in a certain area. Removing trees changes the ecosystem, which is an ecological cost. However, the wood and jobs provided by the logging are economic benefits.

It is also important to consider the short-term and long-term costs and benefits of an environmental decision. A plan's short-term costs might be outweighed by its long-term benefits.

Costs of Offshore Drilling	Benefits of Offshore Drilling
• Setting up sites is expensive.	• Creates jobs
• Transporting the oil is risky and expensive.	• A larger oil supply lowers oil prices.
• Oil supply is limited and will not meet energy demands.	• Provides new oil supply to fight shortages
• Oil spills and leaks harm marine organisms and the environment.	• Reduces dependence on foreign oil

FIGURE 3 ....

> INTERACTIVE ART **Weighing Costs and Benefits**
Once you have identified the potential costs and benefits of a decision, you must analyze them.
✏ **Draw Conclusions** Read the chart. Based on these costs and benefits, write a brief letter to your senator explaining your opinion either in favor of or against offshore drilling.

Lab zone — Do the Quick Lab *Comparing Costs and Benefits.*

🔑 Assess Your Understanding

got it? ....

○ I get it! Now I know that environmental decisions are made by _____

_____

○ I need extra help with _____

Go to MY SCIENCE 🅢 COACH online for help with this subject.

Introduction to Natural Resources

🔑 **What Are Natural Resources?**

🔑 **Why Are Natural Resources Important?**

my planet diary

VOICES FROM HISTORY

"It was a spring without voices. On the mornings that had once throbbed with the dawn chorus of robins . . . there was now no sound; only silence lay over the fields and woods and marsh."

—Rachel Carson

In the twentieth century, farmers began to use chemicals to fight insects that killed their crops. People didn't realize that these chemicals were hurting other animals as well. Rachel Carson, born in 1907, was a scientist who wrote about sea life and nature. Carson began to worry about these chemicals. In 1962, she wrote the book *Silent Spring*. She explained what was happening to animals on land, in the air, and in the sea. Today, people are more careful to protect living things.

Write your answers below.

1. What dangers did Rachel Carson warn people about?

_____

_____

_____

2. Do you think the spring Carson wrote about would look different now that some harmful chemicals are banned? Why or why not?

_____

_____

_____

_____

_____

_____

> PLANET DIARY Go to **Planet Diary** to learn more about natural resources.

 Lab zone® Do the Inquiry Warm-Up *Using Resources.*

Vocabulary
- renewable resource • nonrenewable resource
- sustainable use • ecological footprint • conservation

Skills
↻ Reading: Relate Text and Visuals
△ Inquiry: Calculate

What Are Natural Resources?

Did you turn on a light or use an alarm clock today? Flush a toilet or take a shower? Ride in a car or bus? Eat some food? Use any paper—other than this page that you are reading right now? All of these things—and so much more—depend on Earth's resources.

Recall that anything that occurs naturally in the environment and is used by people is called a natural resource. 🔑 **Natural resources include organisms, water, sunlight, minerals, and oil.**

Renewable Resources A **renewable resource** is either always available or is naturally replaced in a relatively short time. Some renewable resources, like wind and sunlight, are almost always available. Other renewable resources, like water and trees, are renewable only if they are replaced as fast as they are used.

Original trees on land

Trees after first harvest

Trees after replanting

↻ **Relate Text and Visuals** The trees in the first diagram are being harvested for wood. The landowner tells you the trees are a renewable resource. Based on the number of trees being harvested and replanted, is the landowner right? Why?

_____

_____

_____

_____

_____

_____

_____

_____

_____

93

Nonrenewable Resources Over millions of years, natural processes changed the remains of organisms into the substances now called oil and coal. Today's world is powered by these fuels. Humans use these resources much faster than they are naturally replaced. Resources that are not replaced in a useful time frame are **nonrenewable resources.** Metals and minerals are also nonrenewable. Remember that some resources, such as trees, may be renewable or nonrenewable, depending on how quickly they are replaced.

FIGURE 1 ·······························

Categorizing Resources
Resources are grouped into two main categories: renewable and nonrenewable. Gold, shown above, is nonrenewable.

✎ **Summarize** Use what you have read to fill in the table comparing renewable and nonrenewable resources.

Renewable Resources	Nonrenewable Resources	Both
Replaced in a short time or always available	Not replaced in a useful time frame	Fits both natural resource categories
Examples:_____ _____ _____ _____ _____	Examples:_____ _____ _____ _____ _____	Examples:_____ _____ _____ _____ _____

 Do the Quick Lab *Natural Resources.*

🔑 **Assess Your Understanding**

1a. Define What is a renewable resource?

_____
_____
_____
_____
_____

b. Compare and Contrast Sunlight and trees are both natural resources. How are they different?

_____
_____
_____
_____

got it? ···

○ I get it! Now I know that natural resources include _____
_____

○ I need extra help with _____

    Go to MY SCIENCE ⓢ COACH online for help with this subject.

Why Are Natural Resources Important?

Humans cannot live without some natural resources, such as sunlight and fresh water. Others, such as metals, are necessary to sustain modern life. 🔑 **Humans depend on Earth's natural resources for survival and for development.**

How People Use Resources

Around the world, people rely on natural resources for the same basic needs. Not all resources are equally available in all parts of the world. In some areas, there is a plentiful supply of clean fresh water. In other areas, water is scarce. In some places, pollution threatens the water supply.

Globally, fuels are used for cooking, heating, and power. Different fuels are common in different parts of the world. Coal is plentiful in some areas of the world and oil is plentiful in others. See **Figure 2.** In some areas, wood is the main fuel, not coal or oil.

FIGURE 2 ·····························

Resources Around the World

People use natural resources in different ways around the world.

✎ **Describe** In the blank box below, draw or describe one way you use natural resources.

In Sierra Leone, entire communities get their drinking water from a main well.

In China, coal is delivered to homes by bicycle to be burned for heat.

In Iceland, most homes get hot water and heat from the energy of the hot, liquidlike rock under Earth's surface.

95

FIGURE 3 ······························
Ecological Footprint
Everything you do contributes to
your ecological footprint, from
how you travel, to the food you
eat, to the home you live in.
Ecological footprints vary among
individuals and among nations,
depending on how people live.

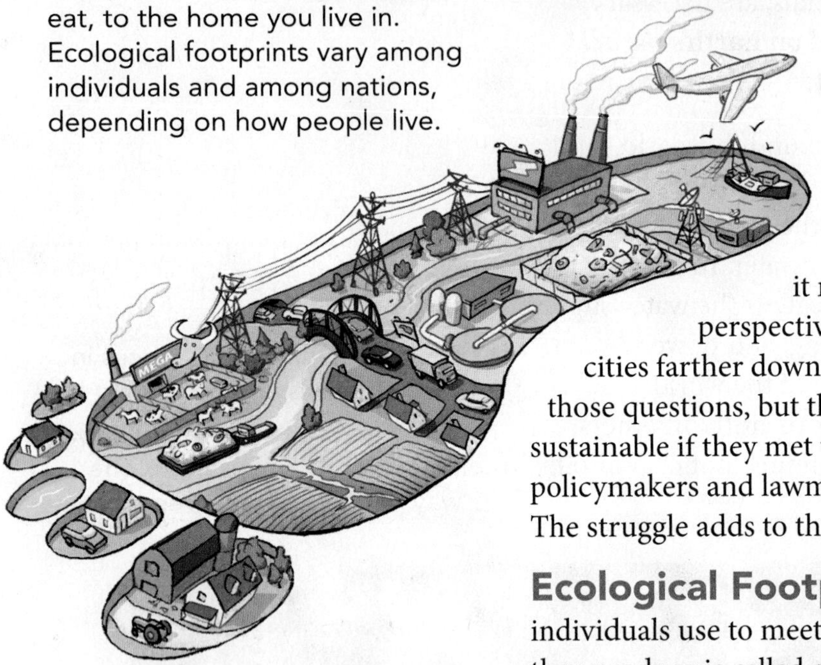

Sustainable Use
How long a resource lasts depends on how people use it. **Sustainable use** of a resource means using it in ways that maintain the resource at a certain quality for a certain period of time. For example, a city may want to manage a river. Does the city want the water to be clean enough to drink or clean enough to swim in? Does the city want the water to be clean for fifty years, two hundred years, or indefinitely? The answers to these questions define what would be considered sustainable use of the river. However, it may not be sustainable from an ecological perspective even if it meets human needs. Other cities farther down the river may have different answers to those questions, but their plans could also be considered sustainable if they met their goals. Because of these differences, policymakers and lawmakers struggle to define sustainable use. The struggle adds to the challenge of regulating resources.

Ecological Footprint
The amount of land and water that individuals use to meet their resource needs and absorb the waste they produce is called an **ecological footprint.** A high level of resource use means a larger footprint. A low level of resource use means a smaller footprint. Refer to **Figure 3.**

apply it!

The chart below gives the average ecological footprints for the people of several countries. It also gives the footprint for each country as a whole. Ecological footprints are measured in global hectares. A global hectare (gha) is a unit of area. It is adjusted to compare how much life different places on Earth can support.

Country	Average Ecological Footprint (gha/person)	Total Ecological Footprint (million gha)
United States	9.6	2,819
United Kingdom	5.6	333
Germany	4.5	375
Mexico	2.6	265
China	1.6	2,152

❶ **Interpret Tables** Which country has the largest ecological footprint? _____

❷ **Calculate** About how many times larger is the average ecological footprint per person in the United States than per person in Mexico?

_____

❸ **CHALLENGE** China has a smaller ecological footprint per person than the United Kingdom, but a much larger total ecological footprint. Why?

_____

_____

_____

_____

_____

_____

Conservation While we cannot avoid using resources, there are better ways to use them. Resource **conservation** is the practice of managing the use of resources wisely so the resources last longer. Conservation cannot make resources last forever, but it can make resources last longer.

Governments and industries greatly affect resource conservation. Even individuals can make a difference. Walking, riding a bike, or riding the bus conserves fuel resources. People can also conserve resources when they turn off lights and unplug equipment that they are not using. Taking shorter showers saves water. When many people make small changes, the results can be huge.

did you know?

If everyone on Earth lived like the average American, it would take the resources of five planets to support us!

Resource Conservation at My School

FIGURE 4

Conserving Resources at School

Students like you can take action to conserve natural resources.

✏ **List** On the notebook paper, write ways your school can conserve resources.

Lab zone Do the Lab Investigation *Recycling Paper.*

🔑 Assess Your Understanding

2a. Review Resources (are/are not) equally available around the world.

b. Summarize What two factors determine whether or not a resource is being used sustainably?

_____

c. Evaluate the Impact on Society As the human population continues to grow, how do you think it will affect the use of natural resources?

_____

_____

_____

got it?

○ **I get it!** Now I know that natural resources are important because_____

_____

○ I need extra help with _____

Go to **MY SCIENCE** 💬 **COACH** *online for help with this subject.*

Human Population Growth

UNLOCK THE BIG Q?

🔑 How Has the Human Population Grown Over Time?

🔑 What Factors Allow the Human Population to Grow?

my planet Diary

DISASTERS

Dangerous Disease

In the mid-1300s, nearly one third of the European population died in what was known as the "Black Death." This was caused by a disease known as the bubonic plague. Around 25 million people died, reducing the regional population from 75 million to 50 million. No treatment was available, and the disease spread. Today, the disease can be treated.

Rodents and rodent fleas carry the plague. It can be passed to humans by a bite from a rodent flea or by handling infected rodents. The most recent outbreak in the United States occurred in 1925. Since then, only 10 to 15 cases have been reported in the United States each year. Around the world, 1,000 to 3,000 cases are reported annually.

Communicate Discuss the question with a group of classmates. Then write your answer below.

Is plague a concern today?

_____
_____
_____
_____
_____
_____
_____
_____

> PLANET DIARY Go to **Planet Diary** to learn more about human population growth.

 Lab zone Do the Inquiry Warm-Up _Doubling Time._

◀ Rodent flea

Vocabulary
• exponential growth

Skills
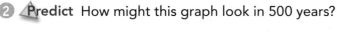 Reading: Identify the Main Idea
△ Inquiry: Predict

How Has the Human Population Grown Over Time?

Five hundred years ago, there were approximately 480 million people on Earth. Today, there are more than 6.7 billion people.

Exponential growth occurs when a population grows at an ever-increasing rate. In exponential growth, the larger a population gets, the faster it grows. 🔑 **Over time, the human population has grown exponentially.** Today, the human population continues to grow, but the growth rate is decreasing. Some experts predict that the human population will stop growing, and possibly decline in the future. Other experts strongly disagree.

do the math!

❶ Interpret Graphs What is the predicted world population for the year 2050?

_____

❷ △ Predict How might this graph look in 500 years?

_____

_____

_____

_____

_____

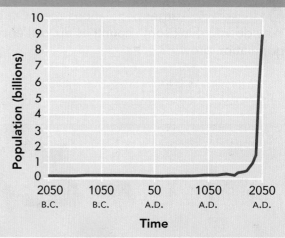

World Population Growth Through History

Population (billions)

10
9
8
7
6
5
4
3
2
1
0

2050 B.C. | 1050 B.C. | 50 A.D. | 1050 A.D. | 2050 A.D.

Time

Lab zone® Do the Quick Lab
Human Population Growth.

🔑 **Assess Your Understanding**

got it? •

○ I get it! Now I know that the human population _____

_____

○ I need extra help with _____

Go to my science COACH online for help with this subject.

What Factors Allow the Human Population to Grow?

A population needs food and other resources to survive. Health and disease can determine life or death. Over time, people have affected these conditions of human survival.  **Advances in medicine and technology have improved human health and allowed for exponential human population growth.**

Birth and Death Rates A population's birthrate is the number of babies born each year per 1,000 people. The death rate of a population is the number of people who die each year per 1,000 people. The global population grows because more people are born each year than die each year. In most areas of the world today, people also live longer than ever before in human history.

apply it!

1 Interpret Tables Circle the countries in the table with decreasing populations.

2 CHALLENGE Larger populations use more resources. Why do you think some countries are still encouraging population growth?

_____

_____

Country	Birthrate (per 1,000 people)	Death Rate (per 1,000 people)
Japan	7.9	9.2
United States	14.0	8.2
Italy	8.4	10.6
Argentina	18.1	7.4
Egypt	22.1	5.1

Medical Care and Technology

Today human survival has increased greatly because of advances in medical care and technology. Antibiotics, vaccines, sanitation, and improved nutrition have lowered death rates and increased birthrates. New technologies have allowed people to build cities, maintain clean water supplies, and produce and distribute more food than ever anticipated. As a result, today's population size is much larger than most experts in the past had predicted.

Population Growth and Natural Resources

As the human population grows, so does the demand for natural resources. If current trends continue, humans will be using resources twice as fast as Earth can replace them within this century. New technologies may allow for a larger human population than ever imagined, but Earth does not have an endless supply of resources. At some point, if it isn't already, the population size will be too large for Earth to support.

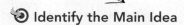

FIGURE 1 ················

> ART IN MOTION **Crowded City**
The photo across these pages is of Hong Kong, China. More than seven million people live in this city of only about 1,100 square kilometers. That's more than 6,000 people per square kilometer!

Healthcare technology	↑	Population	↑
Death rate	↑	Population	
Food production and distribution	↑	Population	
Population	↑	Natural resources	
Birthrate	↑	Population	

✏️ **Identify the Main Idea** Draw arrows in the chart to show the effect of each condition on the human population or natural resources. For example, as healthcare technology improves, the population will increase.

Lab zone® Do the Quick Lab *Comparing Populations.*

🔑 Assess Your Understanding

got it? ················

○ **I get it!** Now I know that the human population has grown exponentially because of_____

_____

_____

○ **I need extra help with** _____

Go to my science 🔊 **COACH** online for help with this subject.

Forests and Fisheries

🔑 **How Can Forests Be Managed as Renewable Resources?**

🔑 **How Can Fisheries Be Managed for a Sustainable Yield?**

my planet Diary

What happened to all the trees?

We get all kinds of things from forests, from food to oxygen to medicine to beautiful places for exploring. The world's forests are disappearing at an alarming rate. We lose a piece of forest the size of a soccer field every two seconds. In a year, that's about an area as big as the state of Illinois! Many people are trying to save the forests. Some countries have passed laws to stop farmers, miners, loggers, and ranchers from cutting down the forests. And some organizations are replanting trees.

SCIENCE STATS

Communicate Discuss the questions with a group of classmates. Then write your answers below.

1. Why should people care about losing trees?

_____

_____

_____

_____

2. How could your class raise awareness about the importance of trees in your community?

_____

_____

_____

_____

▶ PLANET DIARY Go to **Planet Diary** to learn more about forests and fisheries.

Lab zone® Do the Inquiry Warm-Up *What Happened to the Tuna?*

Vocabulary
- clear-cutting • selective cutting • sustainable yield
- fishery • aquaculture

Skills
↻ Reading: Summarize

△ Inquiry: Communicate

How Can Forests Be Managed as Renewable Resources?

Forests contain many valuable resources. Many products are made from the fruits, seeds, and other parts of forest plants. Some of these products, such as maple syrup, rubber, and nuts, come from living trees. Other products, such as lumber and wood pulp for making paper, require cutting trees down. Coniferous trees, including pine and spruce, are used for construction and for making paper. Hardwoods, such as oak, cherry, and maple, are used for furniture because of their strength and beauty. Some products made from trees are shown in **Figure 1.**

Trees and other plants produce oxygen that organisms need to survive. They also absorb carbon dioxide and many pollutants from the air. Trees help prevent flooding and control soil erosion. Their roots absorb rainwater and hold the soil together.

There are about 300 million hectares of forests in the United States. That's nearly a third of the nation's area! Many forests are located on public land. Others are owned by individuals or by private timber and paper companies. Forest industries in the United States provide jobs for more than 1.5 million people.

🔑 **Because new trees can be planted to replace trees that are cut down, forests can be renewable resources.** The United States Forest Service and environmental organizations work with forestry companies to conserve forest resources. They try to develop logging methods that maintain forests as renewable resources.

FIGURE 1 ·······································
Forest Products
Many common products have at least one thing in them that came from trees. The soles on the shoes below came from the sap of the rubber tree.

✏️ **Identify** Besides the shoes, circle the three items that were made from tree products. Pick one of the items and explain why you think it contains tree products.

_____

_____

_____

Logging Methods   There are two major methods of logging: clear-cutting and selective cutting. **Clear-cutting** is the process of cutting down all the trees in an area at once. Cutting down only some trees in a forest and leaving a mix of tree sizes and species behind is called **selective cutting.** See **Figure 2.**

Each logging method has advantages and disadvantages. Clear-cutting is usually quicker and cheaper than selective cutting. It may also be safer for the loggers. In selective cutting, the loggers must move the heavy equipment and logs around the remaining trees in the forest. But selective cutting is usually less damaging to the forest environment than clear-cutting. When an area of forest is clear-cut, the ecosystem changes. After clear-cutting, the soil is exposed to wind and rain. Without the protection of the trees, the soil is more easily blown or washed away. Soil washed into streams may harm the fish and other organisms that live there. However, clear-cutting can provide habitats for species such as rabbits and some birds.

FIGURE 2 ·······································
> **INTERACTIVE ART** **Tree Harvest**
Clear-cutting and selective cutting are two methods of tree harvesting.

✎ **Relate Text and Visuals**
Based on what you have read, label the original forest, the clear-cut forest, and the selectively cut forest.

Replanted Growth

Diverse Growth

Sustainable Forestry

Forests can be managed to provide a sustainable yield. A **sustainable yield** is an amount of a renewable resource such as trees that can be harvested regularly without reducing the future supply. Sustainable forestry works sort of like a book swap: as long as you donate a book each time you borrow one, the total supply of books does not change. Planting a tree to replace one that was cut down is like donating a book to replace a borrowed one.

In sustainable forestry, after trees are harvested, young trees are planted. Trees must be planted frequently enough to keep a constant supply. Different species grow at different rates. Forests containing faster-growing trees, such as pines, can be harvested and replanted every 20 to 30 years. On the other hand, some forests containing hardwood trees, such as hickory, oak, and cherry, may be harvested only every 40 to 100 years. One sustainable approach is to log small patches of forest. This way, different sections of forest can be harvested every year.

Certified Wood

The Forest Stewardship Council is an international organization dedicated to sustainable forest management. This organization oversees certification of forests that are well managed and that provide good working conditions for their employees. Once a forest is certified, its wood may carry a "well-managed" label. This label allows businesses and individuals to select wood from forests that are managed for sustainable yields.

apply it!

You are an advertising writer for a company that makes products from sustainable wood.

1 Communicate Write a slogan to help sell the products.

_____

_____

_____

2 Design a company logo.

Lab zone ® Do the Quick Lab *Shelterwood Cutting.*

🔑 Assess Your Understanding

1a. Define What is a sustainable yield of a natural resource like trees?

_____

_____

_____

_____

b. CHALLENGE Should the government buy only certified wood for construction projects? Why?

_____

_____

_____

_____

got it? ●

○ **I get it!** Now I know that forests can be managed as renewable resources by _____

_____

○ **I need extra help with** _____

Go to MY SCIENCE COACH online for help with this subject.

How Can Fisheries Be Managed for a Sustainable Yield?

Fish are an important global food resource. An area with a large population of valuable ocean organisms is called a **fishery.**

Until recently, fisheries seemed to have unlimited resources. The waters held such huge schools of fish, and fish reproduce in incredible numbers. A single codfish can lay as many as nine million eggs in one year! But people have discovered that this resource has limits. After many years of big catches, the number of sardines off the California coast suddenly declined. The same thing happened to the huge schools of cod off the New England coast. What caused these changes?

The fish were caught faster than they could breed, so the population decreased. This situation is known as overfishing. Scientists estimate that 70 percent of the world's major fisheries have been overfished. But if fish populations recover, a sustainable yield can again be harvested. **Managing fisheries for a sustainable yield includes strategies such as setting fishing limits, changing fishing methods, developing aquaculture techniques, and finding new resources.**

Fishing Limits Laws can ban the fishing of certain species. Laws can also limit the number or size of fish that can be caught. These laws ensure that all of the largest adult fish aren't caught and that young fish survive long enough to reproduce. If a fishery has been severely overfished, however, the government may ban fishing completely until the populations recover.

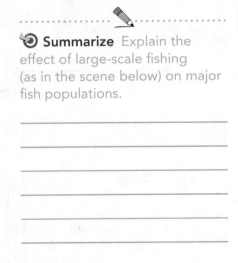

Summarize Explain the effect of large-scale fishing (as in the scene below) on major fish populations.

_____

_____

_____

_____

_____

_____

_____

Fishing Methods Today many fishing crews use nets with a larger mesh size that allow small, young fish to escape. Many other fishing practices are also regulated by laws. Some harmful fishing methods have been outlawed. These methods include poisoning fish with cyanide and stunning them by exploding dynamite under water. These techniques harm all the fish in an area rather than targeting certain fish.

Aquaculture The practice of raising fish and other water-dwelling organisms for food is called **aquaculture.** The fish may be raised in artificial ponds or bays. Salmon, catfish, and shrimp are farmed in this way in the United States.

However, aquaculture is not a perfect solution. The artificial ponds and bays often replace natural habitats such as salt marshes. Maintaining the farms costs money, and the farms can cause pollution and spread diseases into wild fish populations.

New Resources Today about 9,000 different fish species are harvested for food. More than half the animal protein eaten by people throughout the world comes from fish. One way to help feed a growing human population is to fish for new species. Scientists and chefs are working together to introduce people to deep-water species such as monkfish and tile fish, as well as easy-to-farm freshwater fish such as tilapia.

FIGURE 3 ....

Aquaculture
Fish like tilapia, shown below, can be farmed.

✎ **Analyze Costs and Benefits** Fill in the boxes to explain the costs and benefits of aquaculture.

Benefits of Aquaculture
_____
_____
_____
_____

Costs of Aquaculture
_____
_____
_____
_____

Lab zone® Do the Quick Lab
Managing Fisheries.

🔑 **Assess Your Understanding**

got it? ....

○ **I get it!** Now I know managing fisheries for a sustainable yield includes _____

_____

○ **I need extra help with** _____

Go to MY SCIENCE ⬤ COACH online for help with this subject.

107

Biodiversity

🔑 **What Is Biodiversity's Value?**

🔑 **What Factors Affect Biodiversity?**

🔑 **How Do Humans Affect Biodiversity?**

MY PLANET DiARY

BLOG

Posted by: Max

Location: Hagerstown, Maryland

I went to summer camp to learn about wildlife and how to protect it. One of the activities that I liked the most was making "bat boxes." These are wooden homes for brown bats, which often need places to nest. Making these houses is important, because without brown bats, there would be too many mosquitoes. I hope the bats like their new homes as much as I loved making them.

Communicate Discuss the question with a group of classmates. Then write your answers below.

How do you think helping the bats in an area helps other species nearby?

_____

_____

_____

_____

_____

_____

_____

▷ PLANET DIARY Go to **Planet Diary** to learn more about biodiversity.

Lab
zone
Do the Inquiry Warm-Up
How Much Variety Is There?

What Is Biodiversity's Value?

No one knows exactly how many species live on Earth. As you can see in **Figure 1,** scientists have identified more than 1.6 million species so far. The number of different species in an area is called the area's **biodiversity.** It is difficult to estimate the total biodiversity on Earth because many areas have not been thoroughly studied.

Vocabulary
- biodiversity • keystone species • gene • extinction
- endangered species • threatened species
- habitat destruction • habitat fragmentation
- poaching • captive breeding

Skills
↻ Reading: Compare and Contrast
△ Inquiry: Infer

There are many reasons why preserving biodiversity is important. One reason to preserve biodiversity is that wild organisms and ecosystems are a source of beauty and recreation. 🔑 **In addition, biodiversity has both economic value and ecological value within an ecosystem.**

Economic Value Many plants, animals, and other organisms are economically valuable for humans. These organisms provide people with food and supply raw materials for clothing, medicine, and other products. No one knows how many other useful species have not yet been identified. Ecosystems are economically valuable, too. Many companies now run wildlife tours to rain forests, savannas, mountains, and other places. This ecosystem tourism, or ecotourism, is an important source of jobs and money for such nations as Brazil, Costa Rica, and Kenya.

Ecological Value All the species in an ecosystem are connected to one another. Species may depend on each other for food and shelter. A change that affects one species can affect all the others.

Some species play a particularly important role in their ecosystems. A **keystone species** is a species that influences the survival of many other species in an ecosystem. Sea otters, as shown in **Figure 2,** are one example of a keystone species.

FIGURE 1 ·······························
Species Diversity
There are many more species of insects than plant or other animal species on Earth!

✎ **Calculate** What percentage of species shown on the pie graph do insects represent? Round your answer to the nearest tenth.

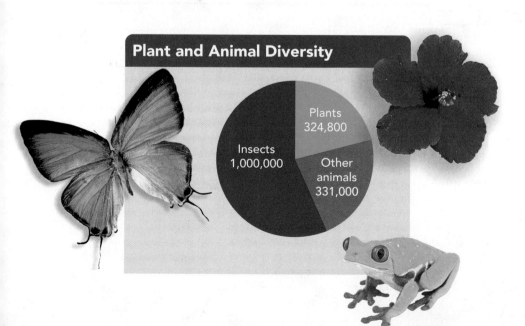

Plant and Animal Diversity

Plants 324,800

Insects 1,000,000

Other animals 331,000

FIGURE 2 ....

Keystone Otters

Sea otters are a keystone species in the kelp forest ecosystem.

✏ **Describe** Read the comic. In the empty panel, draw or explain what happened to the kelp forest when the otters returned. Write a caption for your panel.

The sea otter is a keystone species in a kelp forest ecosystem.

In the 1800s, many otters were killed for their fur.

Without otters preying on them, the population of kelp-eating sea urchins exploded, destroying kelp forests.

Under new laws that banned the hunting of sea otters, the sea otter population grew again.

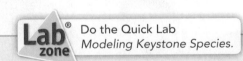

Lab zone ® Do the Quick Lab
Modeling Keystone Species.

🔑 Assess Your Understanding

got it? ....

○ I get it! Now I know that biodiversity has _____

_____

○ I need extra help with _____

Go to MY SCIENCE ⓢ COACH online for help with this subject.

What Factors Affect Biodiversity?

Biodiversity varies from place to place on Earth. **Factors that affect biodiversity in an ecosystem include climate, area, niche diversity, genetic diversity, and extinction.**

Climate The tropical rain forests of Latin America, southeast Asia, and central Africa are the most diverse ecosystems in the world. The reason for the great biodiversity in the tropics is not fully understood. Many scientists hypothesize that it has to do with climate. For example, tropical rain forests have fairly constant temperatures and large amounts of rainfall throughout the year. Many plants grow year-round. This continuous growing season means that food is always available for other organisms.

Area See **Figure 3.** Within an ecosystem, a large area will usually contain more species than a small area. For example, you would usually find more species in a 100-square-meter area than in a 10-square-meter area.

FIGURE 3 ··

Park Size

A park manager has received three park plans. The dark green area represents the park.

✎ **Complete each task.**

1. **Identify** Circle the plan the manager should choose to support the most biodiversity.

2. **Calculate** Suppose that 15 square meters of the park could support seven species of large mammals. About how many species could the park you circled support?

10 m

10 m

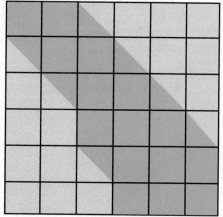

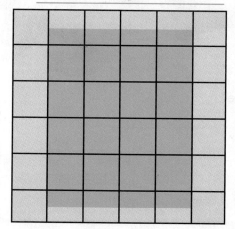

Niche Diversity

Coral reefs are the second most diverse ecosystems in the world. Found only in shallow, warm waters, coral reefs are often called the rain forests of the sea. A coral reef supports many different niches. Recall that a niche is the role of an organism in its habitat, or how it makes its living. A coral reef enables a greater number of species to live in it than a more uniform habitat, such as a flat sandbar, does.

Genetic Diversity

Diversity is very important within a species. The greatest genetic diversity exists among species of unicellular organisms. Organisms in a healthy population have diverse traits such as color and size. **Genes** are located within cells and carry the hereditary information that determines an organism's traits. Organisms inherit genes from their parents.

The organisms in one species share many genes. But each organism also has some genes that differ from those of other individuals. Both the shared genes and the genes that differ among individuals make up the total gene pool of that species. Species that lack a diverse gene pool are less able to adapt to and survive changes in the environment.

apply it!

New potato plants are created from pieces of the parent plant. So a potato crop has the same genetic makeup as the parent plant. In 1845, Ireland was struck by a potato famine. A rot-causing fungus destroyed potato crops, which were an important part of the Irish diet. Many people died of starvation, and many more left the country to find food.

❶ **Apply Concepts** How did a potato crop without a variety of different genes lead to the Irish potato famine of 1845?

_____

_____

_____

_____

❷ [CHALLENGE] What could farmers do to prevent another potato famine?

_____

_____

_____

_____

Extinction of Species The disappearance of all members of a species from Earth is called **extinction.** Extinction is a natural process that occurs when organisms do not adapt to changes in their environment. In the last few centuries, the number of species becoming extinct has increased dramatically. Once a population drops below a certain level, the species may not recover. People have directly caused the extinction of many species through habitat destruction, hunting, or other actions.

Species in danger of becoming extinct in the near future are called **endangered species.** Species that could become endangered in the near future are called **threatened species.** Endangered and threatened species are found on every continent and in every ocean.

Green sea turtle ▲

Blackburn's ▲
sphinx moth

FIGURE 4 ·······················
Endangered Species
Large animals, like the green sea turtle, are the most publicized endangered species. Did you know insects and plants can also be endangered? ✎ **Infer** Why do you think some endangered species get more attention than others?

_____
_____
_____
_____
_____

Hawaiian alula ▲

Do the Quick Lab
Grocery Gene Pool.

🔑 **Assess Your Understanding**

1a. Review A (smaller/larger) area will contain more species than a (smaller/larger) area.

b. Explain How is biodiversity related to niches?

_____
_____
_____

c. ↻ **Compare and Contrast** What is the difference between an endangered species and a threatened species?

_____
_____
_____

got it? ···

○ **I get it!** Now I know that the factors that affect biodiversity include _____
_____

○ **I need extra help with** _____

Go to MY SCIENCE ⓢ COACH online for help with this subject.

How Do Humans Affect Biodiversity?

Humans interact with their surroundings every day. The many choices people make impact the environment and affect species. 🔑 **Biodiversity can be negatively or positively affected by the actions of humans.**

Damaging Biodiversity A natural event, such as a hurricane, can damage an ecosystem, wiping out populations or even entire species. Human activities can also threaten biodiversity and cause extinction. These activities include habitat destruction, poaching, pollution, and the introduction of exotic species.

Habitat Destruction The major cause of extinction is **habitat destruction,** the loss of a natural habitat. Clearing forests or filling in wetlands changes those ecosystems. Breaking larger habitats into smaller, isolated pieces, or fragments, is called **habitat fragmentation.** See **Figure 5.** Some species may not survive such changes to their habitats.

Poaching The illegal killing or removal of wildlife from their habitats is called **poaching.** Some endangered species are valuable to poachers. Animals can be sold as pets or used to make jewelry, coats, belts, or shoes. Plants can be sold as houseplants or used to make medicines.

Pollution Some species are endangered because of pollution. Pollution may reach animals through the water they drink, the air they breathe, or the food they eat. Pollutants may kill or weaken organisms or cause birth defects.

Exotic Species Introducing exotic species into an ecosystem can threaten biodiversity. Exotic species can outcompete and damage native species. The gypsy moth was introduced into the United States in 1869 to increase silk production. Gypsy moth larvae have eaten the leaves off of millions of acres of trees in the northeastern United States.

FIGURE 5 ···

Habitat Fragmentation

Breaking habitats into pieces can have negative effects on the species that live there.

✏️ **Interpret Diagrams** In the first diagram below, a road divides a habitat in two. On the second diagram, redraw the road so it divides the habitat's resources equally.

Protecting Biodiversity

Protecting Biodiversity Some people who preserve biodiversity focus on protecting individual endangered species. Others try to protect entire ecosystems. Three methods of protecting biodiversity are captive breeding, laws and treaties, and habitat preservation.

Captive Breeding Captive breeding is the mating of animals in zoos or on wildlife preserves. Scientists care for the young, and then release them into the wild. Much of the sandhill crane habitat in the United States has been destroyed. To help the population, some cranes have been taken into captivity. The young are raised and trained by volunteers to learn the correct behaviors, such as knowing how and where to migrate. They are then released into the wild.

Compare and Contrast
The photos on top show young sandhill cranes being raised by their parents. The photos on the bottom show humans copying this process to increase the crane population. What is a possible disadvantage of the human approach?

_____

_____

_____

_____

_____

Same Land, Different Use

How do people use Earth's resources?

EXPLORE THE BIG ?

FIGURE 6 ·····································

> VIRTUAL LAB   The cattle ranch in this photo is in Wyoming. You may think the photo on the opposite page is of a completely different place, but it was also taken in Wyoming, in Yellowstone National Park. As you can see, the same land resources can be used in two very different ways to meet very different needs.

✎ **Make Judgments** Write one benefit and one cost of each of the land uses in the boxes. Then answer the question.

Ranch

Benefit _____

_____

Cost _____

_____

Laws and Treaties In the United States, the Endangered Species Act prohibits trade of products made from threatened or endangered species. This law also requires the development of plans to save endangered species. The Convention on International Trade in Endangered Species is an international treaty that lists more than 800 threatened and endangered species that cannot be traded for profit or other reasons anywhere in the world.

Habitat Preservation The most effective way to preserve biodiversity is to protect whole ecosystems. Protecting whole ecosystems saves endangered species, the species they depend upon, and those that depend upon them. Many countries have set aside wildlife habitats as parks and refuges. Today, there are about 7,000 nature parks, preserves, and refuges in the world.

National Park

Benefit _____

_____

Cost _____

_____

Do you think we should preserve our resources, use them, or have a balance of both? Explain your answer.

_____
_____
_____
_____
_____
_____
_____

Lab® Do the Quick Lab
zone Humans and Biodiversity.

Assess Your Understanding

2a. Define What is poaching?

_____
_____
_____
_____

b. ANSWER THE BIG ? How do people use Earth's resources?

_____
_____
_____
_____

got it? ....

○ **I get it!** Now I know that humans affect biodiversity_____

_____

○ **I need extra help with** _____

Go to MY SCIENCE ⓢ COACH online for help with this subject.

3 Study Guide

People use both _____ and nonrenewable resources. Reducing
resource use through _____ can help make resources last longer.

LESSON 1 Introduction to Environmental Issues

🔑 Environmental issues fall into three main categories: resource use, population growth, and pollution.

🔑 To balance opinions, decision makers weigh the costs and benefits of a proposal.

Vocabulary
• natural resource   • pollution
• point source   • nonpoint source
• environmental science

LESSON 2 Introduction to Natural Resources

🔑 Natural resources include organisms, water, sunlight, minerals, and oil.

🔑 Humans depend on Earth's natural resources for survival and for development.

Vocabulary
• renewable resource   • nonrenewable resource
• sustainable use   • ecological footprint
• conservation

LESSON 3 Human Population Growth

🔑 Over time, the human population has grown exponentially.

🔑 Advances in medicine and technology have improved human health and allowed for exponential human population growth.

Vocabulary
• exponential growth

LESSON 4 Forests and Fisheries

🔑 Forests can be renewable resources if new trees are planted to replace trees that are cut.

🔑 Managing fisheries for a sustainable yield includes setting fishing limits, changing fishing methods, developing aquaculture techniques, and finding new resources.

Vocabulary
• clear-cutting   • selective cutting   • sustainable yield
• fishery   • aquaculture

LESSON 5 Biodiversity

🔑 Biodiversity has both economic value and ecological value within an ecosystem.

🔑 Factors that affect biodiversity include climate, area, niche diversity, genetic diversity, and extinction.

🔑 Biodiversity can be negatively or positively affected by the actions of humans.

Vocabulary
• biodiversity   • keystone species   • gene   • extinction
• endangered species   • threatened species   • habitat destruction
• habitat fragmentation   • poaching   • captive breeding

Review and Assessment

LESSON 1 Introduction to Environmental Issues

1. Coal and sunlight are examples of

   a. environmental sciences.

   b. pollution.

   c. natural resources.

   d. extinction.

2. _____ can take many forms, including chemical wastes, noise, heat, and light.

3. Relate Cause and Effect Fill in the blank circles with the other main categories of environmental issues. How are they related?

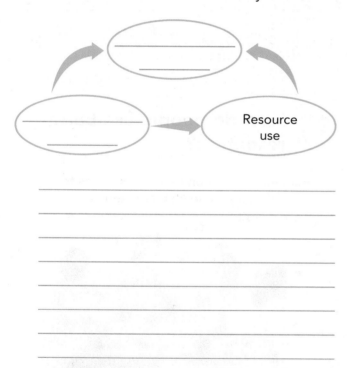

Resource use

_____

_____

_____

_____

_____

_____

_____

4. **Write About It** Suppose your town is considering building a new coal-burning power plant. The benefits of the new facility include providing power and jobs for the town's growing population. What are some of the costs of this project? What do you think your town should do?

LESSON 2 Introduction to Natural Resources

5. Which of the following actions can increase an individual's ecological footprint?

   a. riding a bicycle more often

   b. reducing the use of plastic bags

   c. reusing materials before disposal

   d. turning on the air conditioner

6. Like oil, metals are an example of

_____

7. Apply Concepts When is water a renewable resource? When is it nonrenewable?

_____

_____

_____

_____

LESSON 3 Human Population Growth

8. Under which of the following conditions would the global population decrease?

   a. birthrate > death rate

   b. birthrate = death rate

   c. death rate > birthrate

   d. death rate = birthrate

9. _____, or growth at an ever-increasing rate, describes the pattern of human population growth.

10. Infer How would continued population growth affect Earth's natural resources?

_____

_____

_____

_____

119

LESSON 4 Forests and Fisheries

11. The practice of raising fish for food is called

   a. poaching.

   b. overfishing.

   c. captive breeding.

   d. aquaculture.

12. A _____ is the amount of a resource that can be harvested regularly without reducing the future supply.

13. Compare and Contrast How does selective cutting compare with clear-cutting?

_____

_____

_____

_____

_____

_____

14. Make Judgments Do you think the government should encourage more aquaculture, the use of new fish species, or both? Explain your answer.

_____

_____

_____

_____

_____

_____

_____

_____

_____

LESSON 5 Biodiversity

15. The most effective way to preserve biodiversity is through

   a. captive breeding.

   b. habitat destruction.

   c. habitat preservation.

   d. habitat fragmentation.

16. _____ occurs when all members of a species disappear from Earth.

17. Predict How could the extinction of a species today affect your life in 20 years?

_____

_____

_____

_____

APPLY THE BIG Q How do people use Earth's resources?

18. Humans depend on Earth's resources to survive. Name at least four resources that were used to produce the scene below.

_____

_____

_____

_____

Standardized Test Prep

Multiple Choice

Circle the letter of the best answer.

1. Study the table below. Then choose the list that correctly ranks each country's ecological footprint per person, from smallest to largest.

Country	Average Ecological Footprint (gha/person)
United States	9.6
Germany	4.5
Mexico	2.6
China	1.6

  A China, Germany, Mexico, United States
  B United States, Mexico, Germany, China
  C China, Mexico, Germany, United States
  D Mexico, China, United States, Germany

2. Which words best describe the growth patterns of the human population?
  A decreasing growth
  B exponential growth
  C extended growth
  D incremental growth

3. In some areas, foresters plant one tree for every tree they cut. This activity is an example of
  A a sustainable approach to a renewable resource.
  B an unsustainable approach to a renewable resource.
  C a sustainable approach to a nonrenewable resource.
  D an unsustainable approach to a nonrenewable resource.

4. How do conservation practices affect natural resources?
  A They cause existing natural resources to last longer.
  B They increase Earth's natural resources.
  C They increase people's ecological footprint.
  D They cause natural resources to be depleted.

5. Which of the following terms describes a species that is in danger of becoming extinct in the near future?
  A captive species
  B keystone species
  C threatened species
  D endangered species

Constructed Reponse

Use the chart below to help you answer Question 6. Write your answer on a separate sheet of paper.

Some Costs	Some Benefits
• Changes ecosystem • Makes forest less attractive	• Provides jobs • Provides wood

6. A city is considering whether or not to allow logging in a large forest nearby. Based on the costs and benefits of this decision, what do you think the city should do? Give at least three reasons to support your answer.

SUSTAINABLE SEAFOOD

Fish and seafood are a tasty part of many foods all over the United States. Blackened Cajun shrimp, New England clam chowder, and smoked west-coast salmon are a few popular examples. But for how long? Overharvesting and habitat loss threaten many types of marine organisms. How do you know which types of seafood are sustainable? To identify sustainable seafood, ask yourself the following questions.

How healthy is the wild population? Some animals have been overharvested. Others are threatened by habitat loss.

What is the organism's life cycle? Some fish grow slowly. Some do not reproduce in large numbers. If these fish are overharvested, the population can take a long time to recover.

How are the fish harvested? Some fishing methods, such as bottom trawling, are much more damaging to the environment than others are.

What is the impact of farming? Sustainable fish farming can help save some wild populations. However, fish farms can also release waste and pollutants that harm the environment.

Research It Identify three types of fish or seafood that you can buy locally. Find out where each came from. Use a spreadsheet to record the answers to the questions above for each type of fish or seafood.

▲ Knowing the source of the seafood you eat can help you make decisions that support sustainable fishing practices.

THE CONSERVATION PRESIDENT

In 1901, if you wanted to go camping or hiking, you might run into a mine or a logging site. Although a lot of natural space existed in the United States when Theodore Roosevelt became president, the country had only five national parks. Years of uncontrolled mining, logging, and hunting threatened many of the country's natural areas. Roosevelt, at left in the photograph, was a passionate conservationist. He signed laws that protected over 93 million hectares of land in the United States. Today, the area of the United States that is protected as wilderness is greater than the area of France, Belgium, and the Netherlands combined!

Map It Create a map of national parks in your state or region. Your map should include interesting details about each park.

Environmental Lawyer

As a child, Melissa Scanlan loved boating on the Fox River with her family. As she grew older, she learned that the river was polluted with industrial and agricultural chemicals. Scanlan went to law school and became an environmental lawyer. As a lawyer, she formed Midwest Environmental Advocates—a law firm that helps midwestern communities work with industries and the government to find solutions to local environmental problems. Scanlan says that seeing her work affect the world around her "is like dropping a pebble into water and seeing the rings echo out."

Debate It Research an environmental issue in your region. Choose a possible solution and stage a class debate. Make sure you support your opinion with facts and evidence from your research.

Environmental lawyer Melissa Scanlan finds inspiration from her childhood home in Wisconsin.

HOW IS THIS HOUSE SAVING OUR PLANET?

What can people do to use resources wisely?

Have you ever thought of ways to reuse something you would normally throw away? This home is made from the shipping containers you see transporting goods on ships and trucks. These containers would have been thrown away but an architect thought of a new way to use them.

> UNTAMED SCIENCE Watch the **Untamed Science** video to learn more about reusing resources.

⚠ **Infer** How can reusing shipping containers and other objects help our planet?

_____

_____

_____

_____

_____

Land, Air, and Water Resources

4 Getting Started

Check Your Understanding

1. Background Read the paragraph below and then answer the question.

On a lazy summer day, Mia pours water on the hot sidewalk and imagines where the water will go as it travels through the **water cycle.** After the water **evaporates,** it may float through the **atmosphere** and fall as rain in faraway lands or the ocean.

- What makes the water cycle a *cycle*?

_____

_____

The **water cycle** is the continuous process by which water moves from Earth's surface to the atmosphere and back.

Evaporation is the process by which molecules of liquid water absorb energy and change to a gas.

The **atmosphere** is the envelope of gases that surrounds the planet.

> MY READING WEB If you had trouble answering the question above, visit **My Reading Web** and type in *Land, Air, and Water Resources.*

Vocabulary Skill

Prefixes Some words can be divided into parts. A root is the part of the word that carries the basic meaning. A prefix is a word part placed in front of the root to change the word's meaning. The prefixes below will help you understand some of the vocabulary in this chapter.

Prefix	Meaning	Example
bio-	life	biodegradable, *adj.* describes a material that can be broken down and recycled by bacteria and other decomposers
aqua-	water	aquaculture, *n.* the farming of saltwater and freshwater organisms

2. Quick Check In the definitions of the example words in the table, circle the part that includes the prefix meaning.

topsoil

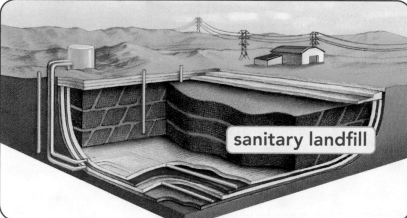

sanitary landfill

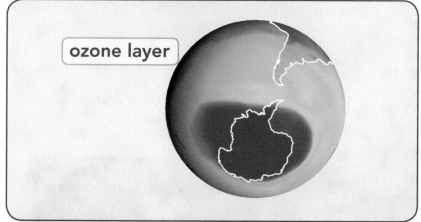

ozone layer

pesticide

Chapter Preview

> **VOCAB FLASH CARDS** For extra help with vocabulary, visit **Vocab Flash Cards** and type in *Land, Air, and Water Resources.*

Conserving Land and Soil

UNLOCK THE BIG

🔑 **How Do People Use Land?**

🔑 **Why Is Soil Management Important?**

MY PLANET DIARY

VOICES FROM HISTORY

Land Inspiration

Conservation is a state of harmony between men and land.
—Aldo Leopold

Aldo Leopold spent his life in beautiful landscapes. He was so inspired by what he saw that he sought to better understand it. Leopold realized that land and all it contains—living and nonliving—are connected. He believed people should use land in a way that protects it for all living things as well as for future generations. Leopold called his idea the "land ethic." He wrote several books on conservation using this philosophy, including his most famous book, *A Sand County Almanac.*

Communicate **Discuss this question with a group of classmates. Write your answer below.**

How do you think land should be used?

_____

_____

_____

_____

_____

 **PLANET DIARY** Go to **Planet Diary** to learn more about conserving land and soil.

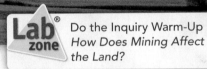 **Lab** ®
zone Do the Inquiry Warm-Up *How Does Mining Affect the Land?*

How Do People Use Land?

Less than a quarter of Earth's surface is dry, ice-free land. All people on Earth must share this limited amount of land to produce their food, build shelter, and obtain resources. As the American author Mark Twain once said about land, "They don't make it anymore."

People use land in many ways. 🔑 **Three uses that change the land are agriculture, mining, and development.** See **Figure 1.**

Vocabulary
- litter • topsoil • subsoil • bedrock • erosion
- nutrient depletion • fertilizer • desertification
- drought • land reclamation

Skills
↻ **Reading:** Relate Cause and Effect
△ **Inquiry:** Infer

Agriculture Land provides most of the food that people eat. Crops such as wheat require lots of fertile land, but less than a third of Earth's land can be farmed. The rest is too dry, too salty, or too mountainous. New farmland is created by clearing forests, draining wetlands, and irrigating deserts. Land can also be used to grow food for animals, to provide grazing for livestock, or to grow crops such as cotton.

Mining Mining is the removal of nonrenewable resources from the land. Resources just below the surface are strip mined. Strip mining removes a strip of land to obtain minerals. The strip is then replaced. Strip mining exposes soil, which can then be blown or washed away. The area may remain barren for years. Resources can also be removed from deeper underground by digging tunnels to bring the minerals to the surface.

Development People settled in areas that had good soil near fresh water. As populations grew, the settlements became towns and cities. People developed the land by constructing buildings, bridges, and roads. In the United States, an area half the size of New Jersey is developed each year.

FIGURE 1 ···

Land Use
The ways that people use land vary greatly. For example, about 93 percent of land in Nebraska is used for agriculture, while only 10 percent of land in Massachusetts is used for agriculture.

✎ **Describe** How is land used in your area?

_____

_____

Agriculture

Strip Mining

Development

Lab zone Do the Quick Lab *Land Use.*

🔑 Assess Your Understanding
got it? ···

○ **I get it!** Now I know the ways people use and change land include _____

_____

○ **I need extra help with** _____

Go to MY SCIENCE ⊙ COACH online for help with this subject.

Why Is Soil Management Important?

To understand why soil management is important, you need to know about the structure and function of fertile soil. It can take hundreds of years to form just a few centimeters of new soil. Soil contains the minerals and nutrients that plants need to grow. Soil also absorbs, stores, and filters water. Bacteria, fungi, and other organisms in soil break down the wastes and remains of living things. See **Figure 2.**

FIGURE 2 ················

Structure of Fertile Soil
Fertile soil is made up of several layers, including litter, topsoil, and subsoil.

✎ **Identify** Underline the organisms that make up or play a role in each soil layer.

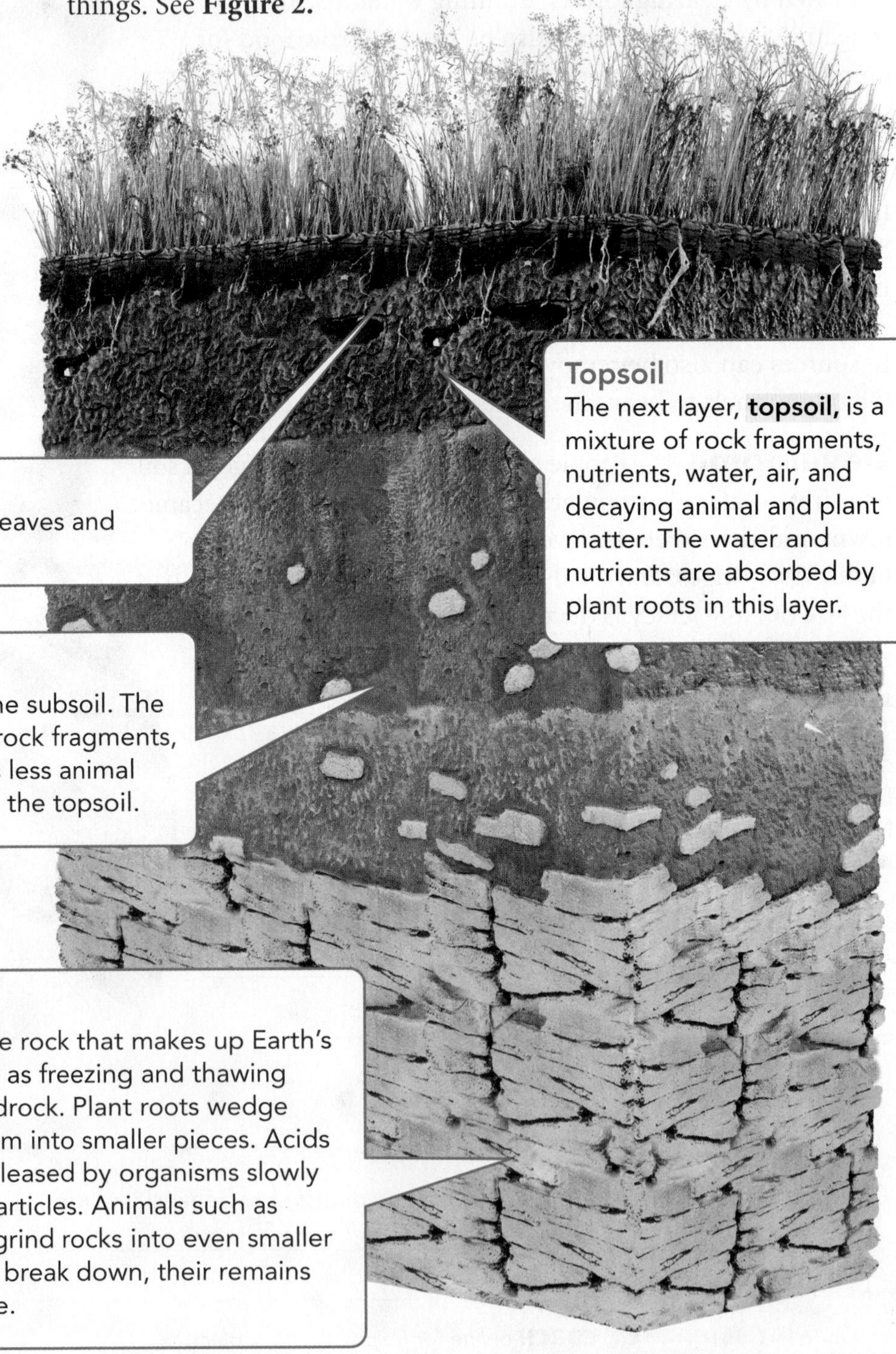

Litter
The top layer of dead leaves and grass is called **litter.**

Subsoil
Below the topsoil is the subsoil. The **subsoil** also contains rock fragments, water, and air, but has less animal and plant matter than the topsoil.

Topsoil
The next layer, **topsoil,** is a mixture of rock fragments, nutrients, water, air, and decaying animal and plant matter. The water and nutrients are absorbed by plant roots in this layer.

Bedrock
All soil begins as **bedrock,** the rock that makes up Earth's crust. Natural processes such as freezing and thawing gradually break apart the bedrock. Plant roots wedge between rocks and break them into smaller pieces. Acids in rainwater and chemicals released by organisms slowly break the rock into smaller particles. Animals such as earthworms and moles help grind rocks into even smaller particles. As dead organisms break down, their remains also contribute to the mixture.

Soil Use Problems Because rich topsoil takes so long to form, it is important to protect Earth's soil. 🔑 **Without soil, most life on land could not exist. Poor soil management can result in three problems: erosion, nutrient depletion, and desertification.** Fortunately, damaged soil can sometimes be restored.

Erosion Normally, plant roots hold soil in place. But when plants are removed during logging, mining, or farming, the soil is exposed and soil particles can easily move. The process by which water, wind, or ice moves particles of rocks or soil is called **erosion.** Terracing, one farming method that helps reduce erosion, is shown in **Figure 3.**

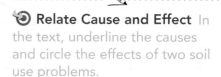

🖉 **Relate Cause and Effect** In the text, underline the causes and circle the effects of two soil use problems.

Nutrient Depletion Plants make their own food through photosynthesis. Plants also need nutrients such as the nitrogen, potassium, and phosphorus found in soil to grow. Decomposers supply these nutrients to the soil as they break down the wastes and remains of organisms. But if a farmer plants the same crops in a field every year, the crops may use more nutrients than the decomposers can supply. The soil becomes less fertile, a situation called **nutrient depletion.**

When soil becomes depleted, farmers usually apply **fertilizers,** which include nutrients that help crops grow better. Farmers may choose other methods of soil management, too. They may periodically leave fields unplanted. The unused parts of crops, such as cornstalks, can be left in fields to decompose, adding nutrients to the soil. Farmers also can alternate crops that use many nutrients with crops that use fewer nutrients.

FIGURE 3 ⋯⋯⋯⋯⋯⋯⋯⋯⋯⋯
Terracing
🖉 A terrace is a leveled section of a hill used to grow crops and prevent erosion. The flat surfaces allow crops to absorb water before the water flows downhill.

1. **Interpret Photos** Draw the path of water down the first hill and the terraced hill.

2. ⚠ **Infer** Why do you think terracing helps prevent erosion?

_____

_____

_____

Desertification If the soil in a once-fertile area becomes depleted of moisture and nutrients, the area can become a desert. The advance of desertlike conditions into areas that previously were fertile is called **desertification** (dih zurt uh fih KAY shun).

One cause of desertification is climate. For example, a **drought** is a period when less rain than normal falls in an area. During droughts, crops fail. Without plant cover, the exposed soil easily blows away. Overgrazing of grasslands by cattle and sheep and cutting down trees for firewood can cause desertification, too.

Desertification is a serious problem. People cannot grow crops and graze livestock where desertification has occurred. As a result, people may face famine and starvation. Desertification is severe in central Africa. Millions of rural people there are moving to the cities because they can no longer support themselves on the land.

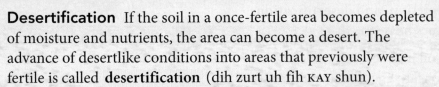

Desertification affects many areas around the world.

1 Name Which continent has the most existing desert?

_____

2 Interpret Maps Where in the United States is the greatest risk of desertification?

_____

3 Infer Is desertification a threat only in areas where there is existing desert? Explain. Circle an area on the map to support your answer.

_____

_____

4 CHALLENGE If an area is facing desertification, what are some things people could do to possibly limit its effects?

_____

_____

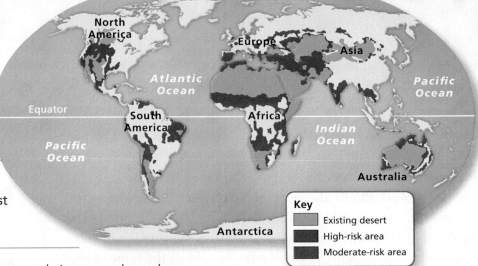

Key
- Existing desert
- High-risk area
- Moderate-risk area

Land Reclamation Fortunately, it is possible to replace land damaged by erosion or mining. The process of restoring an area of land to a more productive state is called **land reclamation.** In addition to restoring land for agriculture, land reclamation can restore habitats for wildlife. Many different types of land reclamation projects are currently underway all over the world. But it is generally more difficult and expensive to restore damaged land and soil than it is to protect those resources in the first place. In some cases, the land may not return to its original state.

FIGURE 4 ······························
Land Reclamation
These pictures show land before and after it was mined.

✏ **Communicate** Below the pictures, write a story about what happened to the land.

_____

_____

_____

Lab zone Do the Quick Lab
Modeling Soil Conservation.

🔑 Assess Your Understanding

1a. Review Subsoil has (less/more) plant and animal matter than topsoil.

b. Explain What can happen to soil if plants are removed?

_____

_____

c. Apply Concepts What are some problems that could prevent people from supporting land reclamation?

_____

_____

_____

_____

got it? ···

○ **I get it!** Now I know that soil management is important because _____

_____

○ **I need extra help with** _____

Go to **MY SCIENCE** ⑤ **COACH** *online for help with this subject.*

Waste Disposal and Recycling

🔑 What Are Three Solid Waste Disposal Methods?

🔑 What Are the Major Categories of Recycling?

🔑 How Are Hazardous Wastes Safely Disposed Of?

my planet Diary

Trash Talk

Here are some interesting facts about trash:

- Every hour, people throw away 2.5 million plastic bottles.

- Recycling one aluminum can saves enough energy to run a TV for three hours.

- Americans create two kilograms of trash per day. That trash could fill 63,000 garbage trucks each day!

- In 2005 the U.S. government recorded the first-ever drop in the amount of trash produced from the previous year. Trash declined by 1.5 million metric tons from 2004 to 2005, partly due to an increase in recycling.

SCIENCE STATS

Communicate Discuss these questions with a group of classmates. Write your answers below.

1. Do you think the amount of trash we produce will increase or decrease in the future? Explain.

_____

_____

_____

2. What can you do to reduce the amount of trash you create?

_____

_____

_____

▶ PLANET DIARY Go to Planet Diary to learn more about waste disposal and recycling.

Lab® zone Do the Inquiry Warm-Up *What's in the Trash?*

Vocabulary
- municipal solid waste
- incineration
- pollutant
- leachate
- sanitary landfill
- recycling
- biodegradable
- hazardous waste

Skills
- Reading: Compare and Contrast
- Inquiry: Graph

What Are Three Solid Waste Disposal Methods?

People generate many types of waste, including empty packaging, paper, and food scraps. The wastes produced in homes, businesses, schools, and in the community are called **municipal solid waste.** Other sources of solid waste include construction debris, agricultural wastes, and industrial wastes. **Three methods of handling solid waste are burning, burying, and recycling.** Each method has its advantages and disadvantages.

Incineration The burning of solid waste is called **incineration** (in sin ur AY shun). The burning facilities, or incinerators, do not take up much space. They do not directly pollute groundwater. The heat produced by burning solid waste can be used to produce electricity. Incinerators supply electricity to many homes.

Unfortunately, incinerators do have drawbacks. Even the best incinerators create some air pollution. Although incinerators reduce the volume of waste by as much as 90 percent, some waste still remains and needs to be disposed of somewhere. Incinerators are also expensive to build.

apply it!

What happens to all the trash?

❶ **Graph** Use the data in the table and the key to fill in the bar graph. The graph represents the methods of municipal waste disposal in the United States in 2007. Give the graph a title.

Disposal Method	Waste (Percent)
Incineration	13%
Landfills	54%
Recycling	33%

❷ **CHALLENGE** Why do you think incineration is the least popular method of solid waste disposal?

_____

_____

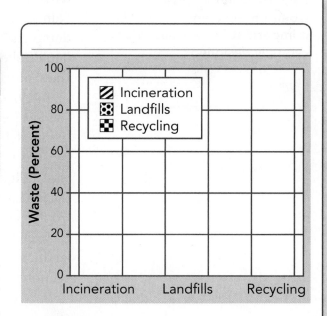

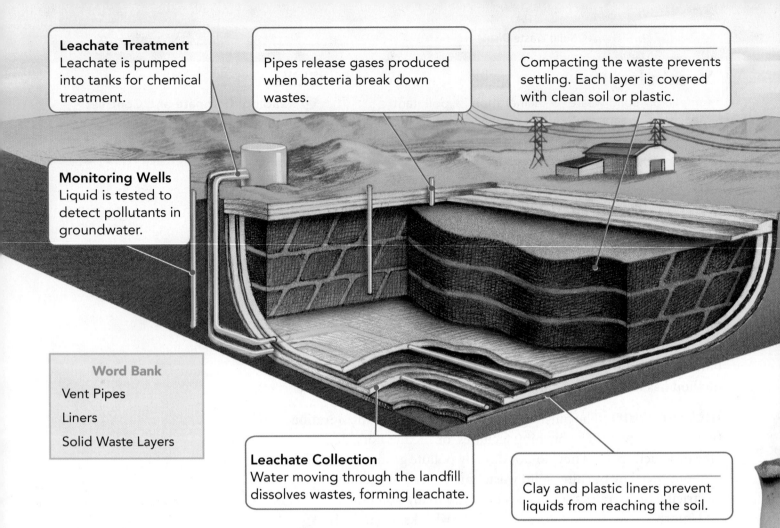

Leachate Treatment
Leachate is pumped into tanks for chemical treatment.

Pipes release gases produced when bacteria break down wastes.

Compacting the waste prevents settling. Each layer is covered with clean soil or plastic.

Monitoring Wells
Liquid is tested to detect pollutants in groundwater.

Word Bank
Vent Pipes
Liners
Solid Waste Layers

Leachate Collection
Water moving through the landfill dissolves wastes, forming leachate.

Clay and plastic liners prevent liquids from reaching the soil.

FIGURE 1 ·······························
Sanitary Landfill Design
Sanitary landfills are designed to protect the surrounding area.

✏ **Interpret Diagrams** Use the terms listed in the word bank to fill in the missing labels on the diagram. Why is it important for landfills to be carefully designed?

_____
_____
_____
_____
_____

Landfills Until fairly recently, people disposed of waste in open holes in the ground called dumps. Some of this waste polluted the environment. Any substance that causes pollution is a **pollutant.** Dumps were dangerous and unsightly. Rainwater falling on a dump dissolved chemicals from the wastes, forming a polluted liquid called **leachate.** Leachate could run off into streams and lakes, or trickle down into the groundwater.

In 1976, the government banned open dumps. Now much solid waste is buried in landfills that are built to hold the wastes more safely. A **sanitary landfill** holds municipal solid waste, construction debris, and some types of agricultural and industrial waste. **Figure 1** shows the parts of a well-designed sanitary landfill. Once a landfill is full, it is covered with a clay cap to keep rainwater from entering the waste.

Even well-designed landfills can pollute groundwater. Capped landfills can be reused as parks and sites for sports arenas. They cannot be used for housing or agriculture.

Recycling You may have heard of the "three R's"—reduce, reuse, and recycle. *Reduce* refers to creating less waste from the beginning, such as using cloth shopping bags rather than disposable ones. *Reuse* refers to finding another use for an object rather than discarding it, such as refilling reusable bottles with drinking water instead of buying new bottled water.

The process of reclaiming raw materials and reusing them to create new products is called **recycling.** You can recycle at home and encourage others to recycle. You can buy products made from recycled materials. Your purchase makes it more profitable for companies to use recycled materials in products.

Another way to reduce solid waste is to start a compost pile. The moist, dark conditions in a compost pile allow natural decomposers to break down grass clippings, leaves, and some food wastes. Compost is an excellent natural fertilizer for plants.

🔄 **Compare and Contrast**
In the table below, write one pro and one con for each of the three solid waste disposal methods.

	Incineration	Sanitary Landfills	Recycling
Pro			
Con			

Lab zone Do the Lab Investigation *Waste, Away!*

🔑 **Assess Your Understanding**

1a. Define What is incineration?

_____

b. Design a Solution What could be some possible uses for the space over a landfill once it is capped? _____

_____

c. Make Judgments Which solid waste disposal method do you think is best? Why?

_____
_____
_____
_____

got it? ....

○ **I get it!** Now I know solid waste can be disposed of through _____

_____

○ **I need extra help with** _____

Go to **MY SCIENCE** Ⓢ **COACH** online for help with this subject.

What Are the Major Categories of Recycling?

Recycling reduces the volume of solid waste by reusing materials. Recycling uses energy, but it also saves the energy that would be needed to obtain, transport, and process raw materials. Recycling is also cheaper than making new materials. Additionally, recycling conserves nonrenewable resources and limits the environmental damage caused by mining for raw materials.

Materials that can be broken down and recycled by bacteria and other decomposers are **biodegradable** (by oh dih GRAY duh bul). Many products people use today are not biodegradable, such as plastic containers, metal cans, rubber tires, and glass jars. Instead, people have developed different ways to recycle the raw materials in these products.

A wide range of materials can be recycled. 🔑 **Most recycling focuses on four major categories of products: metal, glass, paper, and plastic.**

Vocabulary Prefixes The prefix *bio-* means "life." A material is biodegradable if it can be broken down and recycled by living things such as

_____

_____

Material	Recycling Process	Products Made From Recycling
Metal	Metals are melted in furnaces and rolled into sheets.	Cars, cans, bicycles, jewelry, office supplies, house siding
Glass	Glass pieces are melted in furnaces and cast into new glass.	Bottles, floor tiles, countertops, jewelry, jars
Paper	Paper is shredded and mixed with water to form pulp. The pulp is washed, dried, and rolled into new sheets.	Toilet paper, notebook paper, paper cups, paper plates, napkins, envelopes
Plastic	Plastic containers are chopped, washed, and melted. The molten plastic is turned into pellets that can be heated and molded.	Picnic tables, park benches, speed bumps, recycling bins, playground equipment, deck lumber, fleece (see girl's jacket at left)

Is recycling worthwhile? Besides conserving resources, recycling saves energy. Making aluminum products from recycled aluminum rather than from raw materials uses about 90 percent less energy overall. For certain materials, recycling is usually worthwhile. However, recycling is not a complete answer to the solid waste problem. For some cities, recycling is not cost-effective. Scientists have not found good ways to recycle some materials, such as plastic-coated paper and plastic foam. Some recycled products, such as low-quality recycled newspaper, have few uses. All recycling processes require energy and create pollution. The value of recycling must be judged on a case-by-case basis.

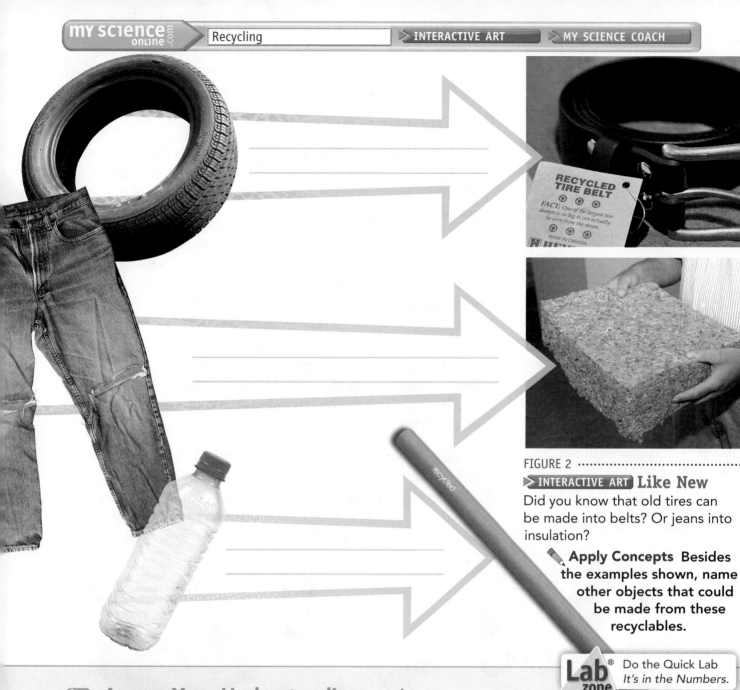

RECYCLED TIRE BELT

FACT: One of the largest tire dumps is so big it can actually be seen from the moon.
MADE IN CANADA

FIGURE 2 ....

› INTERACTIVE ART **Like New**
Did you know that old tires can be made into belts? Or jeans into insulation?

✎ **Apply Concepts** Besides the examples shown, name other objects that could be made from these recyclables.

Lab zone® Do the Quick Lab *It's in the Numbers.*

🔑 **Assess Your Understanding**

2a. Explain How does recycling save energy?

_____

_____

_____

_____

b. Solve Problems How could your community solve its solid waste problem?

_____

_____

_____

_____

got it?

○ **I get it!** Now I know recyclable materials are categorized as _____

_____

_____

_____

○ **I need extra help with** _____

_____

Go to my science ⓢ coach *online for help with this subject.*

How Are Hazardous Wastes Safely Disposed Of?

Many people picture hazardous wastes as bubbling chemicals or oozing slime. Any material that can be harmful to human health or the environment if it is not properly disposed of is a **hazardous waste.**

Types of Hazardous Wastes Toxic wastes can damage the health of humans and other organisms. Explosive wastes can react very quickly when exposed to air or water, or explode when dropped. Flammable wastes easily catch fire. Corrosive wastes can dissolve many materials. Everyday hazardous wastes include electronic devices, batteries, and paint.

Other wastes that require special disposal are radioactive wastes. Radioactive wastes give off radiation that can cause cancer and other diseases. Some radioactive waste can remain dangerous for millions of years.

Health Effects A person can be exposed to hazardous wastes by breathing, eating, drinking, or touching them. Even short-term exposure to hazardous wastes can cause problems such as skin irritation or breathing difficulties. Long-term exposure can cause diseases such as cancer, damage to body organs, or death.

FIGURE 3 ·····································

Sort It Out!
Wastes can be thrown away, recycled, or disposed of as hazardous waste.

✏ **Summarize Draw a line from each object to its appropriate disposal container.**

Disposal Methods

It is difficult to safely dispose of hazardous wastes. Hazardous wastes are most often disposed of in carefully designed landfills. The landfills are lined and covered with clay and plastic. These materials prevent chemicals from leaking into the soil and groundwater. **Hazardous wastes that are not disposed of in carefully designed landfills may be incinerated or broken down by organisms. Liquid wastes may be stored in deep rock layers.**

Scientists are still searching for methods that will provide safe and permanent disposal of radioactive wastes. Some wastes are currently stored in vaults dug hundreds of meters underground or in concrete and steel containers above ground.

Disposal Sites

It is a challenge to decide where to build hazardous waste disposal facilities. In general, people would prefer to have a single large facility located in an area where few people live. However, it may be safer, cheaper, and easier to transport wastes to small local facilities instead.

Reducing Hazardous Waste

The best way to manage hazardous wastes is to produce less of them in the first place. Industries are eager to develop safe alternatives to harmful chemicals. At home, you can find substitutes for some hazardous household chemicals. For example, you could use citronella candles instead of insect spray to repel insects.

FIGURE 4 ·

Hazardous Wastes

Hazardous waste can be harmful if improperly handled.

✎ **Review** What is the best way to manage hazardous wastes?

- ◯ Store waste in small facilities.
- ◯ Produce less waste to start.
- ◯ Incinerate waste.

Lab zone® Do the Quick Lab *Half-Life.*

🔑 Assess Your Understanding

3a. Name What are some negative health effects of exposure to hazardous wastes?

_____

_____

_____

b. Make Judgments Do you think hazardous wastes should be disposed of at one large central facility? Explain.

_____

_____

_____

got it? ·

⊙ **I get it!** Now I know that hazardous wastes are disposed of by_____

_____

⊙ I need extra help with _____

Go to MY SCIENCE ⓢ COACH online for help with this subject.

Air Pollution and Solutions

🔑 **What Causes Outdoor and Indoor Air Pollution?**

🔑 **What Causes Damage to the Ozone Layer?**

🔑 **How Can Air Pollution Be Reduced?**

my planet diary

Drawing for a Difference

Some people may think that kids can't help the environment. Kids in the San Joaquin Valley of California know better! Each year, students enter their drawings into a contest for a Clean Air Kids Calendar sponsored by the San Joaquin Valley Air Pollution Control District. Lisa Huang and Saira Delgada are two middle school students whose work was chosen to be a part of the 2008 calendar. Their drawings show people why healthy air is important. Every time people looked at the calendar, the drawings reminded them of the simple ways they can help the planet.

Communicate Discuss the question with a group of classmates. Then, write your answer below.

How could you raise awareness about air pollution in your community?

_____

_____

_____

_____

▷ **PLANET DIARY** Go to **Planet Diary** to learn more about air pollution and solutions.

Lab zone® Do the Inquiry Warm-Up *How Does the Scent Spread?*

Vocabulary

- emissions • photochemical smog • ozone
- temperature inversion • acid rain • radon
- ozone layer • chlorofluorocarbon

Skills

↩ Reading: Relate Text and Visuals

△ Inquiry: Communicate

What Causes Outdoor and Indoor Air Pollution?

You can't usually see it, taste it, or smell it, but you are surrounded by air. Air is a mixture of nitrogen, oxygen, carbon dioxide, water vapor, and other gases. Almost all living things depend on these gases to survive. Recall that these gases cycle between living things and the atmosphere. These cycles guarantee that the air supply will not run out, but they don't guarantee that the air will be clean.

Outdoor Air Pollution What causes air pollution? Until the mid-1900s in the United States, factories and power plants that burned coal produced most of the pollutants, or **emissions,** that were released into the air. 🔑 **Today, a large source of emissions resulting in air pollution outdoors comes from motor vehicles such as cars and trucks.** There are also some natural causes of air pollution. Methane released from animals such as cows also sends pollutants into the atmosphere.

Air pollution sources can be grouped as point or nonpoint sources. A point source is a specific source of pollution that is easy to identify, such as a smokestack. A nonpoint source is a source that is widely spread and cannot be tied to a specific origin, such as vehicle emissions. So the pollution cannot be traced to any specific vehicle.

FIGURE 1 ···

Volcanoes and Air Pollution

Not all air pollution is caused by people. Gases released by volcanic eruptions can also harm the atmosphere.

✎ **Infer** In the text, underline one natural source of air pollution. Name at least one other natural source of air pollution.

_____

_____

_____

FIGURE 2 ·······················

Temperature Inversion
Normally, pollutants rise into the atmosphere and blow away. During a temperature inversion, warm air traps the pollution close to the ground.

✎ **Interpret Photos** On the photo above, label the warm air, cool air, and polluted air.

Smog Have you ever heard a weather forecaster talk about a "smog alert"? A smog alert is a warning about a type of air pollution called photochemical smog. **Photochemical smog** is a thick, brownish haze formed when certain gases in the air react with sunlight. When the smog level is high, it settles as a haze over a city. Smog can cause breathing problems and eye and throat irritation. Exercising outdoors can make these problems worse.

The major sources of smog are the gases emitted by cars and trucks. Burning gasoline in a car engine releases gases into the air. These gases include hydrocarbons (compounds containing hydrogen and carbon) and nitrogen oxides. The gases react in the sunlight and produce a form of oxygen called **ozone.** Ozone, which is toxic, is the major chemical found in smog. Ozone can cause lung infections and damage the body's defenses against infection.

Normally, air close to the ground is heated by Earth's surface. As the air warms, it rises into the cooler air above it. Any pollutants in the air are carried higher into the atmosphere and are blown away from the place where they were produced.

Certain weather conditions can cause a condition known as a temperature inversion. During a **temperature inversion,** as shown in **Figure 2,** a layer of warm air prevents the rising air from escaping. The polluted air is trapped and held close to Earth's surface. The smog becomes more concentrated and dangerous.

Acid Rain Precipitation that is more acidic than normal because of air pollution is called **acid rain.** Acid rain can also take the form of snow, sleet, or fog. Acid rain is caused by the emissions from power plants and factories that burn coal and oil. These fuels produce nitrogen oxides and sulfur oxides when they are burned. The gases that are released react with water vapor in the air, forming nitric acid and sulfuric acid. The acids dissolve in precipitation and return to Earth's surface.

As you can imagine, acid falling from the sky has some negative effects. When acid rain falls into a pond or lake, it changes the conditions there. Many fish, particularly their eggs, cannot survive in more acidic water. When acid rain falls on plants, it can damage their leaves and stems. Acid rain that falls on the ground can also damage plants by affecting the nutrient levels in the soil. Whole forests have been destroyed by acid rain. Fortunately, some of the effects of acid rain are reversible. Badly damaged lakes have been restored by adding lime or other substances that neutralize the acid.

Acid rain doesn't just affect living things. The acid reacts with stone and metal in buildings and statues. Statues and stonework damaged by acid rain may look as if they are melting, as seen in **Figure 3.** Automobiles rust more quickly in areas with acid rain. These effects are not reversible and the damage can be costly.

FIGURE 3 ·······································

Acid Rain
Acid rain harms plants, animals, buildings, and statues.

✎ **Review** In the text, underline the cause of acid rain.

apply it!

You are a scientist called to testify before Congress about acid rain. The government is proposing putting limits on emissions that lead to acid rain.

❶ **Communicate** Some of the members of Congress do not think acid rain causes real damage. What do you tell them?

_____

_____

❷ **Explain** Is rain the only form of precipitation you would identify as being potentially acidic? Explain.

_____

❸ CHALLENGE What could you tell a company that was unwilling to reduce its emissions because the initial cost was high?

_____

_____

_____

FIGURE 4 ····························

Indoor Air Pollution

Indoor air pollution has many sources. ✎ **Identify** Circle the sources of indoor air pollution in this room.

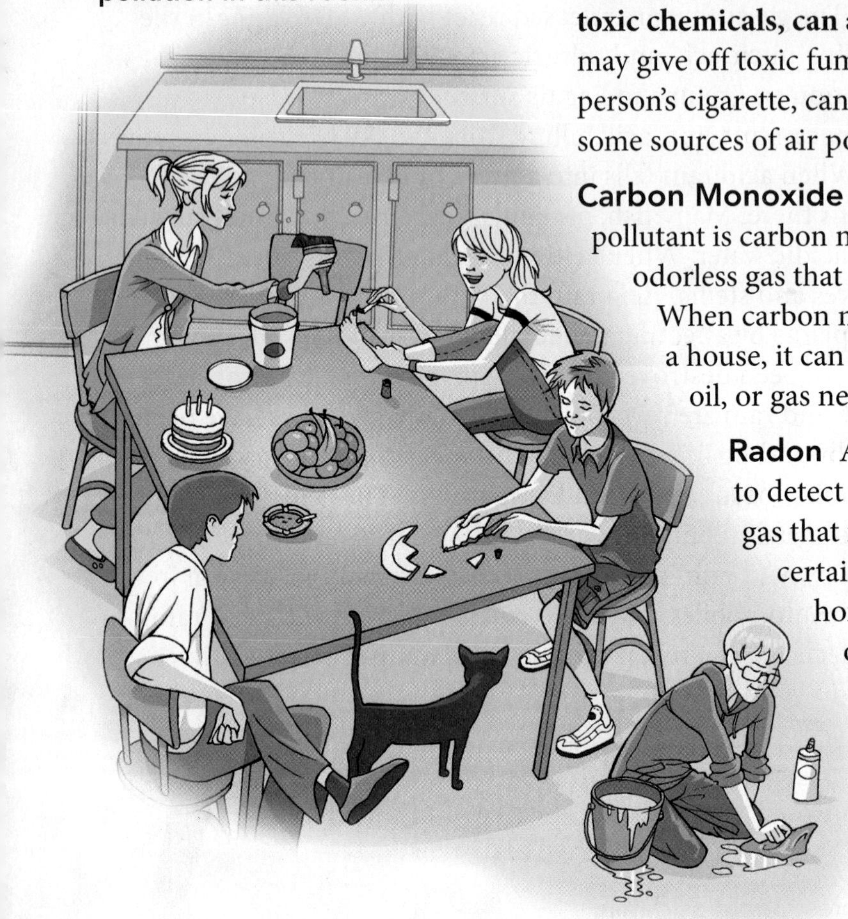

Indoor Air Pollution You might think that you can avoid air pollution by staying inside. The air inside buildings can be polluted, too. 🔑 **Some substances that cause indoor air pollution, such as dust and pet hair, bother only those people who are sensitive to them. Other indoor air pollutants, such as toxic chemicals, can affect anyone.** Glues and cleaning supplies may give off toxic fumes. Cigarette smoke, even from another person's cigarette, can damage the lungs and heart. **Figure 4** shows some sources of air pollution that can be found in homes.

Carbon Monoxide One particularly dangerous indoor air pollutant is carbon monoxide. Carbon monoxide is a colorless and odorless gas that forms when fuels are not completely burned. When carbon monoxide builds up in an enclosed space, like a house, it can be deadly. Any home heated by wood, coal, oil, or gas needs a carbon monoxide detector.

Radon Another indoor air pollutant that is difficult to detect is radon. **Radon** is a colorless, odorless gas that is radioactive. It is formed naturally by certain rocks underground. Radon can enter homes through cracks in basement walls or floors. Breathing radon gas over many years may cause lung cancer and other health problems. Homeowners can install ventilation systems to prevent radon from building up in their homes.

Lab zone® Do the Quick Lab
How Acid Is Your Rain?

🔑 **Assess Your Understanding**

1a. Name (Photochemical smog/Methane) is a thick, brownish haze formed when gases in the air are exposed to sunlight.

b. Make Judgments Do you think the government should regulate sources of air pollution such as factory and car emissions? Explain.

_____

_____

_____

_____

got it? ··

○ **I get it!** Now I know outdoor air pollution is

caused by _____

_____

and indoor air pollution is caused by _____

_____

○ **I need extra help with**_____

_____

Go to MY SCIENCE 🄢 COACH *online for help with this subject.*

What Causes Damage to the Ozone Layer?

If you have ever had a sunburn, you have experienced the painful effects of the sun's ultraviolet radiation. But did you know that sunburns would be even worse without the protection of the ozone layer? The **ozone layer** is a layer of the upper atmosphere about 15 to 30 kilometers above Earth's surface. The amount of ozone in this layer is very small. Yet even this small amount of ozone in the ozone layer protects people from the effects of too much ultraviolet radiation. These effects include sunburn, eye diseases, and skin cancer.

Because you read earlier that ozone is a pollutant, the fact that ozone can be helpful may sound confusing. The difference between ozone as a pollutant and ozone as a helpful gas is its location in the atmosphere. Ozone close to Earth's surface in the form of smog is harmful. Ozone higher in the atmosphere, where people cannot breathe it, protects us from too much ultraviolet radiation.

The Source of Ozone Ozone is constantly being made and destroyed. See **Figure 5**. When sunlight strikes an ozone molecule, the energy of the ultraviolet radiation is partly absorbed. This energy causes the ozone molecule to break apart into an oxygen molecule and an oxygen atom. The oxygen atom soon collides with another oxygen molecule. They react to form a new ozone molecule. Each time this cycle occurs, some energy is absorbed. That energy does not reach Earth's surface.

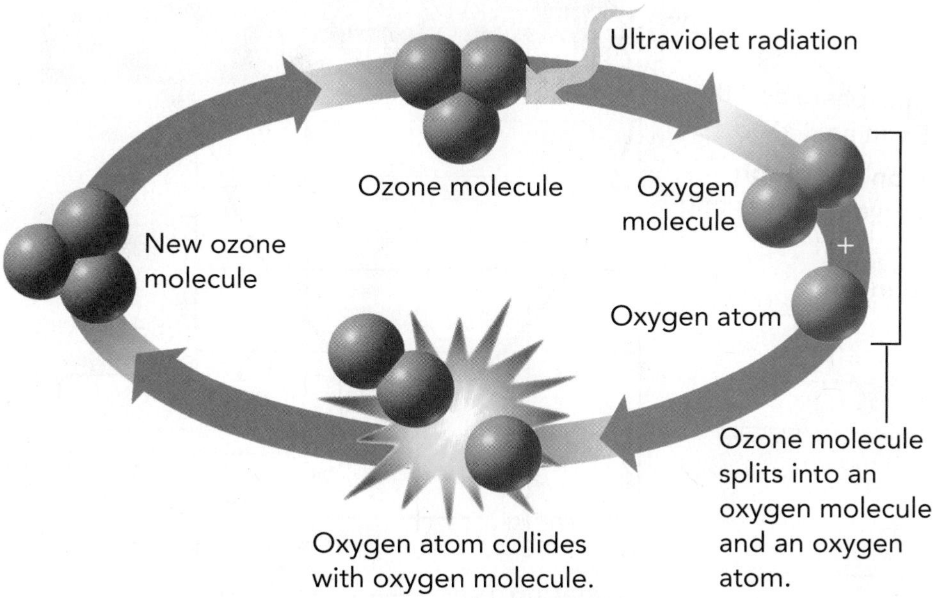

FIGURE 5 ·······································

Ozone Cycle

The ozone cycle prevents harmful ultraviolet radiation from reaching Earth's surface.

✎ **Sequence** Explain the ozone cycle in your own words.

_____

_____

_____

_____

_____

_____

_____

_____

_____

_____

_____

_____

_____

_____

Ultraviolet radiation

Ozone molecule

New ozone molecule

Oxygen molecule

Oxygen atom

+

Ozone molecule splits into an oxygen molecule and an oxygen atom.

Oxygen atom collides with oxygen molecule.

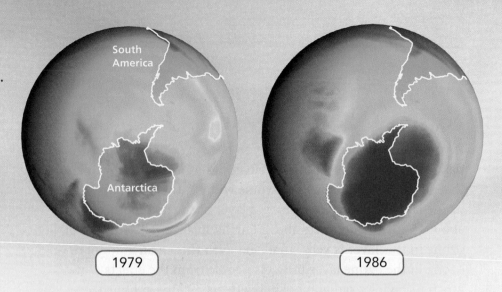

FIGURE 6 ·····
Ozone Hole
The ozone hole (shown in blue) is over Antarctica. The hole has grown over time, but it varies seasonally and from year to year.

South America

Antarctica

1979

1986

The Ozone Hole In the late 1970s, scientists observed from satellite images that the ozone layer over Antarctica was growing thinner each spring. The amount of ozone in the ozone layer was decreasing. This caused an area of severe ozone depletion, or an ozone hole. In **Figure 6,** you can see the size of the ozone hole in five selected years.

What is to blame for the ozone hole? 🔑 **Scientists determined that the major cause of the ozone hole is a group of gases called CFCs.** CFCs, or **chlorofluorocarbons,** are human-made gases that contain chlorine and fluorine. CFCs had been used in air conditioners, aerosol spray cans, and other household products. CFCs reach high into the atmosphere, and react with ozone molecules. The CFCs block the cycle in which ozone molecules absorb ultraviolet radiation. As a result, more ultraviolet light reaches Earth's surface.

FIGURE 7 ·····
Ozone and Ultraviolet Radiation
✏ The amount of ozone in the atmosphere and the amount of UV radiation reaching Earth are linked.

1. **Read Graphs** Label the curve on the graph representing ozone and the curve representing UV radiation.

2. **Summarize** Explain the graph in your own words.

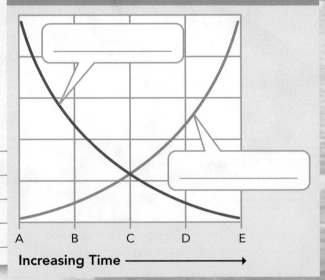

Ozone and UV Radiation Resulting From CFCs

A   B   C   D   E

Increasing Time ⟶

| 1993 | 2000 | 2004 |

What's Being Done
In 1990, many nations signed an agreement to eventually ban the use of ozone-depleting substances, including CFCs. Most uses of CFCs were banned in 2000. Some uses of CFCs are still allowed, but compared to the 1970s, few CFCs now enter the atmosphere. Unfortunately, CFC molecules remain in the atmosphere for a long time. Scientists predict that if the ban on ozone-depleting substances is maintained, the ozone layer will gradually recover.

When scientists discovered that CFCs were harming the atmosphere, they immediately began to search for substitutes. Refrigerators and air conditioners were redesigned to use less-harmful substances. Most spray cans were either replaced by pump sprays or redesigned to use other gases. Researchers developed new ways to make products such as plastic foam without using CFCs. As a result of this research and the development of CFC substitutes, far less CFCs now enter the atmosphere.

Relate Text and Visuals
Based on the photos, describe what happened to the hole in the ozone layer before CFCs were banned. What do you think could happen if the ban is maintained and enforced?

_____

_____

_____

_____

_____

_____

Do the Quick Lab
Analyzing Ozone.

Assess Your Understanding

2a. Explain How can ozone be both a pollutant and something beneficial to Earth?

_____

_____

_____

_____

b. Solve Problems What can countries do to help the ozone layer recover?

_____

_____

_____

_____

got it? ....

O **I get it!** Now I know the ozone layer was damaged by_____

_____

O **I need extra help with**_____

Go to **MY SCIENCE** COACH online for help with this subject.

How Can Air Pollution Be Reduced?

Air pollution can be reduced if we examine the sources. **The key to reducing air pollution is to control emissions.** In the United States, laws such as the Clean Air Act regulate the amount of certain pollutants that can be released into the air. Laws also encourage the development of new technology that reduces air pollution. Reducing emissions also requires your efforts.

Controlling Emissions From Factories At one time, industries dealt with emissions by building tall smokestacks. The stacks released wastes high into the air where they could blow away, but the pollutants still ended up somewhere. Now factories remove pollutants from their emissions with devices known as scrubbers that release water droplets. Pollutants dissolve in the water and fall into a container. The use of scrubbers explains why "smoke" from factories is white—it's not smoke, it's steam.

Controlling Emissions From Vehicles Cars and trucks now contain pollution-control devices. A catalytic converter is a part of the exhaust system that reduces emissions of carbon monoxide, hydrocarbons, and nitrogen oxides. This device causes the gases to react, forming less-harmful carbon dioxide and water. Laws can ensure that people use pollution-control devices. For example, in many states, cars must pass emissions tests to be allowed on the road.

What You Can Do You may not think there is much you can do to reduce air pollution. However, even small changes in your behavior can make a big difference.

You can help reduce air pollution by reducing certain types of energy use. Much air pollution is a result of burning fuels to provide electricity and transportation. Using less energy conserves fuel resources and reduces emissions. Turning off lights, computers, and televisions in empty rooms uses less energy and reduces emissions. When you take public transportation, carpool, walk, or ride a bicycle, there are fewer cars on the road. This means there are less emissions that contribute to air pollution.

FIGURE 8 ·······························

> INTERACTIVE ART

Your Solutions

✎ **Communicate** With a partner, list ways you can reduce air pollution in your everyday life.

_____

_____

_____

_____

_____

_____

_____

Apple Imports

Apples are grown in an orchard in Chile.

Trucks carry apples from the orchard to the airport.

Airplanes carry the apples from Chile to the United States.

More trucks bring the apples from the airport to shipping centers and grocery stores around the country.

FIGURE 9 ···

Where Does an Apple Really Come From?

Many things in our everyday lives, even where food comes from, can contribute to air pollution. ✎ **Analyze Costs and Benefits** Read the comic strip above. Then, fill in the boxes with pros and cons of buying apples that were grown locally instead of those grown in another country.

Pros

Cons

Lab zone® Do the Quick Lab *It's in the Air.*

🔑 Assess Your Understanding

got it? ···

○ **I get it!** Now I know the key to reducing air pollution is _____

_____

○ **I need extra help with** _____

_____

Go to MY SCIENCE ⬤ COACH *online for help with this subject.*

Water Pollution and Solutions

UNLOCK THE BIG ?

🗝 **Why Is Fresh Water a Limited Resource?**

🗝 **What Are the Major Sources of Water Pollution?**

🗝 **How Can Water Pollution Be Reduced?**

my planet diary

DISASTERS

A Flood of Sludge

In December 2008, over 4.5 billion liters of polluted water flooded the area around Kingston, Tennessee. A nearby coal-powered electric plant produced polluted water containing arsenic, lead, and other toxic chemicals. The toxic chemicals and coal ash mixed with water in a holding pond to form a thick sludge. When the dam holding back the pond broke, the water poured into rivers. The sludge water spilled over the land, damaging trees, homes, and other buildings. Local residents feared the flood would be dangerous to their health as well.

Communicate Discuss the question with a group of classmates. Then write your answer below.

Is water pollution a problem in your community? Why or why not?

_____

_____

_____

_____

_____

> PLANET DIARY Go to **Planet Diary** to learn more about water pollution and solutions.

 Lab zone® Do the Inquiry Warm-Up *How Does the Water Change?*

Why Is Fresh Water a Limited Resource?

Most of Earth's surface is covered by some form of water. Oceans cover nearly three fourths of Earth's surface. Around the poles are vast sheets of ice. From space you cannot even see many parts of Earth because they are hidden behind clouds of tiny water droplets. There seems to be so much water—it's hard to believe that it is a scarce resource in much of the world.

Vocabulary
- groundwater • pesticide • sewage • sediment

Skills
⟳ Reading: Outline
△ Inquiry: Design Experiments

How can water be scarce when there is so much of it on Earth's surface? 🔑 **Water is scarce on Earth because most of it—about 97 percent—is salt water.** Salt water cannot be used for drinking or watering crops. Also, about three quarters of the fresh water on Earth is ice. Most liquid fresh water is **groundwater,** water stored in soil and rock beneath Earth's surface. People use groundwater for drinking, but it is not always found near where people live. Cities in dry areas may draw their drinking water from hundreds of kilometers away.

Renewing the Supply
Fortunately, Earth's fresh water is renewable. Remember that water continually moves between the atmosphere and Earth's surface in the water cycle. Even though fresh water is renewable, there is not always enough of it in a given place at a given time.

Water Shortages
Water shortages occur when people use water faster than the water cycle can replace it. This is likely to happen during a drought when an area gets less rain. Many places never receive enough rain to meet their needs and use other methods to get water. Desert cities in Saudi Arabia get more than half of their fresh water by removing salt from ocean water, which is very expensive.

FIGURE 1 ·····································
Water
Most of Earth's surface is covered with water, but fresh water is still a limited resource.

✏ **Identify** Reread the text. Then, underline the reasons why fresh water is scarce.

Do the Quick Lab
Where's the Water?

🔑 Assess Your Understanding
got it? ··

○ **I get it!** Now I know that fresh water is limited on Earth because _____

_____

○ I need extra help with _____

Go to **my science** ⓢ **coach** online for help with this subject.

What Are the Major Sources of Water Pollution?

Since fresh water is scarce, water pollution can be devastating. Some pollutants, such as iron and copper, make water unpleasant to drink or wash in. Other pollutants, such as mercury or benzene, can cause sickness or even death.

🔑 **Most water pollution is the result of human activities. Wastes produced by agriculture, households, industry, mining, and other human activities can end up in water.** Water pollutants can be point or nonpoint pollution sources, classified by how they enter the water. A pipe gushing wastewater directly into a river or stream is an example of a point source. The pipe is a specific pollution source that can be easily identified. Nonpoint pollution sources include farm, street, and construction site runoff. The exact pollution source is hard to trace and identify.

Agricultural Wastes
Animal wastes, fertilizers, and pesticides are also sources of pollution. **Pesticides** are chemicals that kill crop-destroying organisms. Rain washes animal wastes, fertilizers, and pesticides into ponds, causing algae to grow. The algae block light and deplete the oxygen in the pond.

Household Sewage
The water and human wastes that are washed down sinks, showers, and toilets are called **sewage.** If sewage is not treated to kill disease-causing organisms, the organisms quickly multiply. People can become ill if they drink or swim in water containing these organisms.

FIGURE 2 ·····················

Farm Pollution
This scene may show common things found on a farm, but even common things can lead to water pollution.

✏️ **Relate Text and Visuals**
Circle the potential sources of water pollution in this scene.

Industry and Mining Wastes

Some plants, mills, factories, and mines produce wastes that can pollute water. Chemicals and metal wastes can harm organisms that live in bodies of water. Animals that drink from polluted bodies of water or eat the organisms that live in the water can also become ill.

Sediments

Water that causes erosion picks up **sediments,** or particles of rock and sand. Sediments can cover up the food sources, nests, and eggs of organisms in bodies of water. Sediments also block sunlight, preventing plants from growing.

Heat

Heat can also have a negative effect on a body of water. Some factories and power plants release water that has been used to cool machinery. This heated water can kill organisms living in the body of water into which it is released. This type of pollution is also known as thermal pollution.

Oil and Gasoline

An oil spill is a very dramatic form of water pollution. It can take many years for an area to recover from an oil spill because the oil floats on water and is difficult to collect. Another water pollution problem is caused by oil and gasoline that leak out of damaged underground storage tanks. The pollution can be carried far away from a leaking tank by groundwater.

⟳ Outline Look back in the text and fill in the graphic organizer below to outline causes of water pollution.

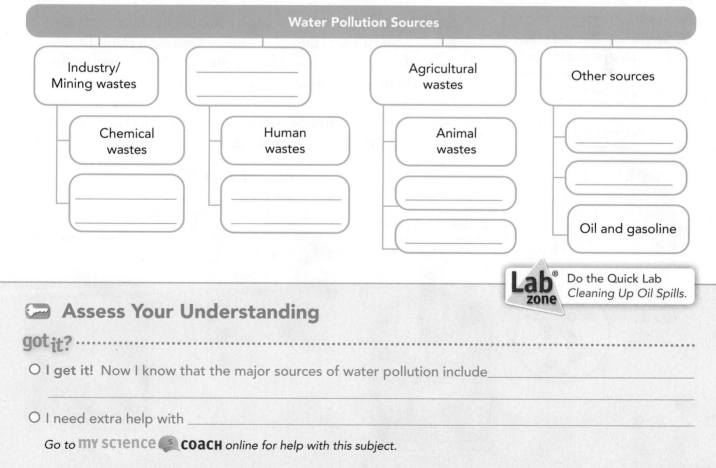

Water Pollution Sources

- Industry/Mining wastes
  - Chemical wastes
  - _____
- _____
  - Human wastes
  - _____
- Agricultural wastes
  - Animal wastes
  - _____
  - _____
- Other sources
  - _____
  - _____
  - Oil and gasoline

Lab zone Do the Quick Lab *Cleaning Up Oil Spills.*

🔑 Assess Your Understanding

got it? ....

○ **I get it!** Now I know that the major sources of water pollution include _____

_____

○ **I need extra help with** _____

Go to my science ⑤ COACH online for help with this subject.

How Can Water Pollution Be Reduced?

By working together, governments, industries, and individuals can improve water quality. Federal and state laws in the United States regulate the use of certain substances that can pollute water.

🔑 **The keys to keeping water clean are effective cleanup of oil and gasoline spills, proper sewage treatment, and reduction of pollutants.** There are also some important ways that people can reduce water pollution at home.

Cleaning Up Oil and Gasoline Spills

Nature can handle oil in small amounts. A natural cleaning process slowly takes place after oil spills. Certain bacteria living in the ocean feed on the oil. Of course, oil can cause much damage to an area in the time it takes the bacteria to work, so people often help clean up large spills. The hard work of many scientists and volunteers can minimize environmental damage from large spills.

Gasoline or oil that leaks from an underground tank is hard to clean up. If the pollution has not spread far, the soil around the tank can be removed. But pollution that reaches groundwater may be carried far away. Groundwater can be pumped to the surface, treated, and then returned underground. This can take many years.

Sewage Treatment

Most communities treat wastewater before returning it to the environment. Treatment plants handle the waste in several steps. During primary treatment, wastewater is filtered to remove solid materials. Then it is held in tanks where heavy particles settle out. During secondary treatment, bacteria break down the wastes. Sometimes the water is then treated with chlorine to kill disease-causing organisms. See **Figure 3.**

FIGURE 3 ·······························

Wastewater Treatment
There are several steps to proper sewage treatment.

✎ **Sequence** Put the steps of proper sewage treatment in order by writing the numbers one through four in the circles.

◯ Bacteria break down wastes.

◯ Water is filtered to remove solids.

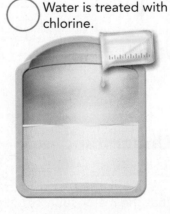
◯ Water is treated with chlorine.

◯ Heavy particles settle in tank.

Reducing Pollutants Instead of releasing wastes into the environment, industries can recycle their wastes. Once such programs are underway, companies often find they save money as well as reduce pollution. Other companies change their processes to produce less waste or less-harmful waste by using fruit acids as cleaning agents instead of toxic chemicals.

What You Can Do It is easy to prevent water pollution at home. Some common household water pollutants are paints and paint thinner, motor oil, and garden chemicals. You can avoid causing water pollution by never pouring these chemicals down the drain. Instead, save these materials for your community's next hazardous waste collection day.

know

The Exxon *Valdez* oil tanker spilled 40.9 million liters of oil into the Pacific Ocean on March 24, 1989. The oil eventually covered 28,000 square kilometers of ocean!

apply it!

Bacteria can be used to clean up oil spills. Some companies specialize in creating bacteria for cleaning up oil.

① Analyze Costs and Benefits Fill in the boxes with some pros and cons of using bacteria to clean oil spills.

Pros	Cons

② Design Experiments If you were creating bacteria for cleaning oil spills, what characteristics would you want to test the bacteria for? _____
_____

Pollution and Solutions

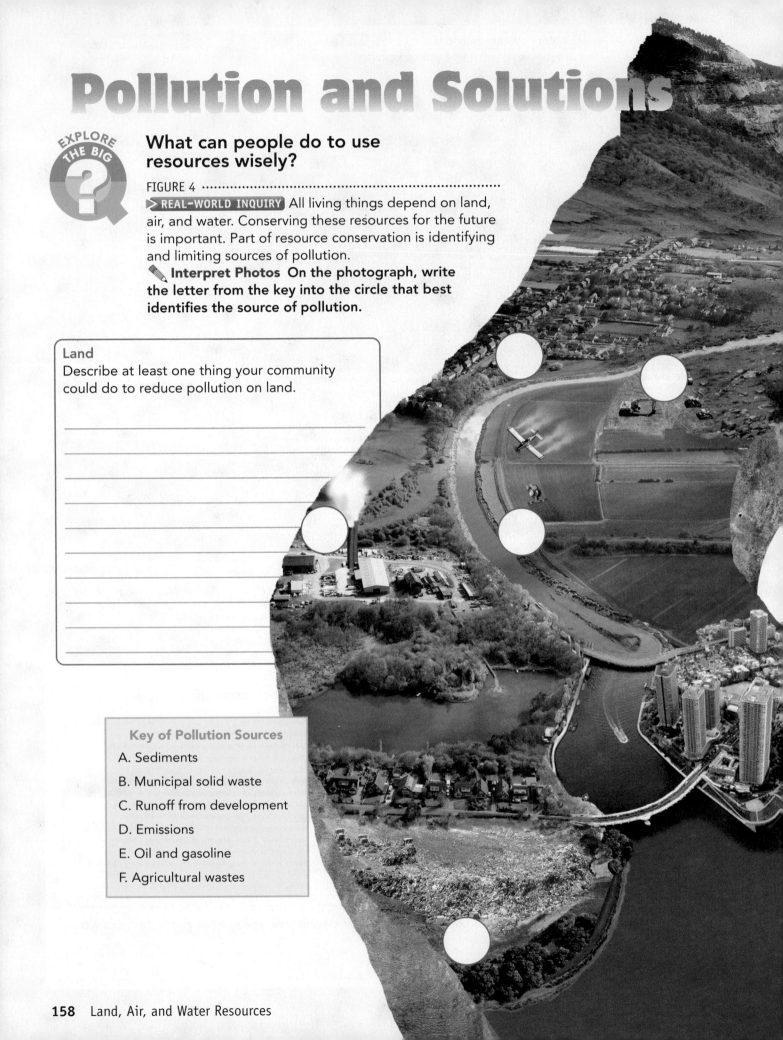

What can people do to use resources wisely?

FIGURE 4 ···

> **REAL-WORLD INQUIRY** All living things depend on land, air, and water. Conserving these resources for the future is important. Part of resource conservation is identifying and limiting sources of pollution.

✎ **Interpret Photos** On the photograph, write the letter from the key into the circle that best identifies the source of pollution.

Land
Describe at least one thing your community could do to reduce pollution on land.

_____

_____

_____

_____

_____

_____

_____

_____

_____

Key of Pollution Sources

A. Sediments

B. Municipal solid waste

C. Runoff from development

D. Emissions

E. Oil and gasoline

F. Agricultural wastes

Air
Describe at least one thing your community could do to reduce air pollution.

_____

_____

_____

_____

_____

_____

_____

Water
Describe at least one thing your community could do to reduce water pollution.

_____

_____

_____

_____

_____

_____

_____

Lab zone ® Do the Quick Lab
Getting Clean.

Assess Your Understanding

1a. Define What are sediments?

_____

_____

b. Explain How can bacteria help clean an oil spill in the ocean?

_____

_____

_____

c. ANSWER THE BIG ? What can people do to use resources wisely?

_____

_____

_____

_____

d. CHALLENGE Why might a company not want to recycle the waste they produce even if it would reduce water pollution?

_____

_____

_____

_____

_____

_____

got it? ·

○ **I get it!** Now I know that water pollution can be reduced by _____

_____

_____

○ **I need extra help with** _____

_____

_Go to_ MY SCIENCE ⓢ COACH _online for help with this subject._

Ocean Resources

UNLOCK THE BIG **Q?**

🔑 **What Are the Ocean's Living and Nonliving Resources?**

🔑 **What Are the Sources of Ocean Pollution?**

my PLANeT DiaRY

Are There Plenty of Fish in the Sea?

Huge schools of codfish used to swim off the eastern coast of North America. Sailors reported that sailing through crowded schools of cod slowed the boats down!

For more than 400 years, the seemingly endless cod supply supported a thriving fishing industry. But starting in the early 1900s, it became clear that the cod population was decreasing. Cod prices rose. There was more competition to catch fewer fish. In 1992, the Canadian government closed its cod fishery. Today, cod and many other fish species are struggling to return to healthy population sizes.

MISCONCEPTIONS

Communicate Discuss the question with a group of classmates. Write your answer below.

What do you think needs to happen for fish populations to reach healthy population sizes?

_____

_____

_____

_____

_____

_____

> PLANET DIARY   Go to **Planet Diary** to learn more about ocean resources.

Lab zone® Do the Inquiry Warm-Up *Is It From the Ocean?*

Vocabulary
• nodule
• upwelling

Skills
↻ Reading: Identify the Main Idea
△ Inquiry: Interpret Data

What Are the Ocean's Living and Nonliving Resources?

The ocean holds a variety of resources you often use, from edible fish and seaweeds to plants used in medicine to oil for vehicles.

Living Resources How many kinds of seafood have you eaten? 🔑 **People depend on ocean organisms for food. Ocean organisms also provide materials that are used in products such as detergents and paints.**

Harvesting Fish Many kinds of fishes are caught to be eaten. Anchovies, pollock, mackerel, herring, and tuna make up most of the worldwide catch. Nearly all fishes are harvested from coastal waters or areas with nutrients and plankton on which the fish feed.

If used wisely, fisheries naturally renew themselves each year. New fish hatch, replacing those that are caught, but only as long as the fishery is not overfished. Better technology has enabled people to quickly catch large numbers of fish. The fish can be caught faster than they can reproduce. When fish reproduction decreases, there are fewer fish each season. Eventually, the fish in the fishery may become very scarce.

apply it!

Imagine you are a fisheries scientist asked to evaluate a new harvesting strategy, pictured right. During each annual harvest, 40,000 fish are caught. Some people think the current population could support a larger harvest for 50 years into the future.

🐟 10,000 fish

❶ **Make Judgments** Should the harvest be increased? Why?

_____

_____

_____

❷ [CHALLENGE] Why is it important to carefully monitor fish populations before, during, and after setting harvest limits?

_____

Population before first harvest

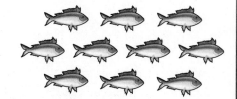

Population after first harvest

Population after second harvest

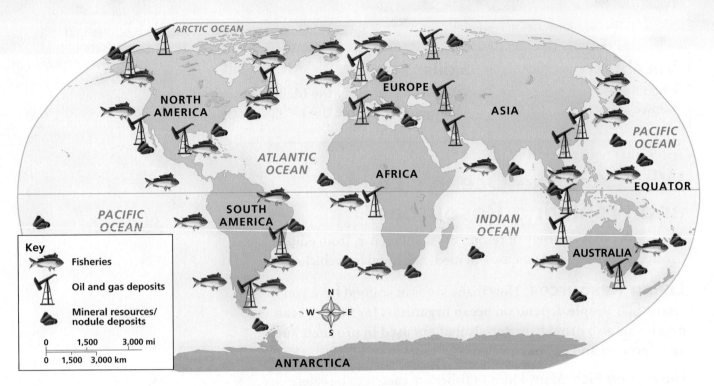

FIGURE 1 ···

> ART IN MOTION **Ocean Resources**

As you can see on the map, ocean resources are not evenly distributed among nations. ✎ **Interpret Maps** What problems do you think could arise from this distribution?

_____

_____

_____

_____

✎ **Identify the Main Idea** Why is aquaculture important in areas without ocean resources?

_____

_____

_____

_____

_____

Aquaculture As fish stocks decrease, aquaculture, or the farming of saltwater and freshwater organisms, is likely to become more common. Aquaculture has been practiced in some Asian countries for centuries.

Aquaculture involves creating an environment for the organisms. To help the organisms thrive, nutrient levels, water temperature, light, and other factors must be controlled. Oysters, abalone, and shrimp have successfully been farmed in artificial saltwater ponds and protected bays. Even landlocked regions can produce seafood using aquaculture. For example, salmon are now being raised in Nebraska fields that once were cattle ranches.

Other Ocean Products People harvest ocean organisms for many purposes besides food. Algae are an ingredient in many household products. Their gelatin-like texture make an ideal base for detergents, shampoos, cosmetics, paints, and even ice cream! Sediments containing the hard pieces of algae are used for abrasives and polishes. Many researchers think that other marine organisms may be important sources of chemicals for medicines in the future.

Nonliving Resources
The ocean also contains valuable nonliving resources. 🔑 **Some nonliving ocean resources include water, fuels, and minerals.**

Water Fresh water can be extracted from ocean water using a process called desalination. See **Figure 2.** Desalination provides fresh water for many dry areas, islands, ships, and submarines. However, the process also requires a large amount of energy to heat water for removing the salt.

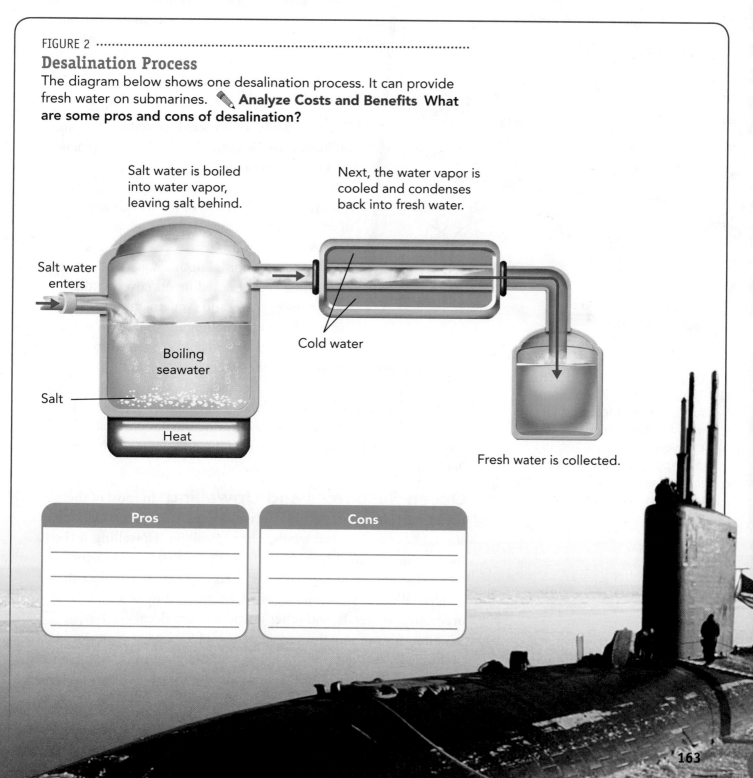

FIGURE 2 ···

Desalination Process
The diagram below shows one desalination process. It can provide fresh water on submarines. ✎ **Analyze Costs and Benefits** What are some pros and cons of desalination?

Salt water is boiled into water vapor, leaving salt behind.

Next, the water vapor is cooled and condenses back into fresh water.

Salt water enters

Cold water

Boiling seawater

Salt

Heat

Fresh water is collected.

Pros	Cons

Fuels The remains of dead marine organisms are the source of another nonliving resource. The remains sink to the bottom of the ocean, where they are buried by sediments. As more sediments accumulate, the buried remains decompose. Over hundreds of millions of years, the heat and pressure from the overlying layers gradually transform the organisms' remains into oil and natural gas. Scientists have also discovered methane hydrates, or methane trapped on ice, on the ocean bottom. Since methane is the main component of natural gas, methane hydrates could be an energy source in the future. However, techniques need to be developed to extract the methane from methane hydrates.

Minerals Minerals are solid substances that are obtained from the ground and the water. When fresh water is removed from ocean water, the salts that are left behind are a valuable mineral resource. More than half of the world's supply of magnesium, a strong, light metal, is obtained from seawater in this way.

The ocean floor is another source of mineral resources. From the sediments covering the ocean floor, gravel and sand are mined for use in building construction. In some areas of the world, diamonds and gold are mined from sand deposits. Manganese and other metals accumulate on the ocean floor. The metals concentrate around pieces of shell, forming black lumps called **nodules** (NAJH oolz). Nodules sometimes occur in waters as deep as 5,000 meters. Recovering the nodules is a difficult process. The technology for gathering the nodules is still being developed.

Ocean Resources and Upwelling

In most of the ocean, surface waters do not mix with deep ocean waters. Mixing sometimes occurs when winds cause upwelling. **Upwelling** is the movement of cold water upward from the deep ocean. As winds blow away the warm surface water, cold water rises to replace it.

Upwelling, as shown in **Figure 4,** brings up tiny ocean organisms, minerals, and other nutrients from deeper waters. Without this motion, the surface waters of the open ocean would be scarce in nutrients. Because nutrients are plentiful, areas of upwelling are usually home to huge schools of fish. These fish are an important resource to the people and animals that feed on them.

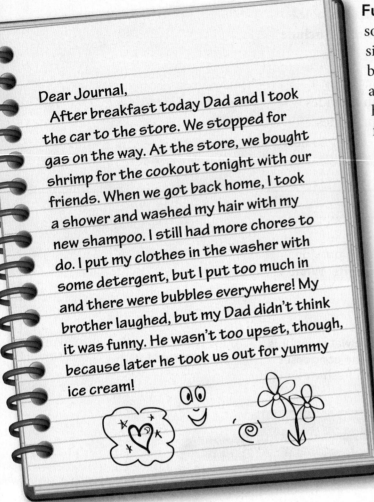

Dear Journal,
After breakfast today Dad and I took the car to the store. We stopped for gas on the way. At the store, we bought shrimp for the cookout tonight with our friends. When we got back home, I took a shower and washed my hair with my new shampoo. I still had more chores to do. I put my clothes in the washer with some detergent, but I put too much in and there were bubbles everywhere! My brother laughed, but my Dad didn't think it was funny. He wasn't too upset, though, because later he took us out for yummy ice cream!

FIGURE 3

Ocean Resource Journal
The ocean provides materials for many products that you might not realize are used in everyday life.

✏ **Apply Concepts** In this journal entry, underline every use of an ocean product.

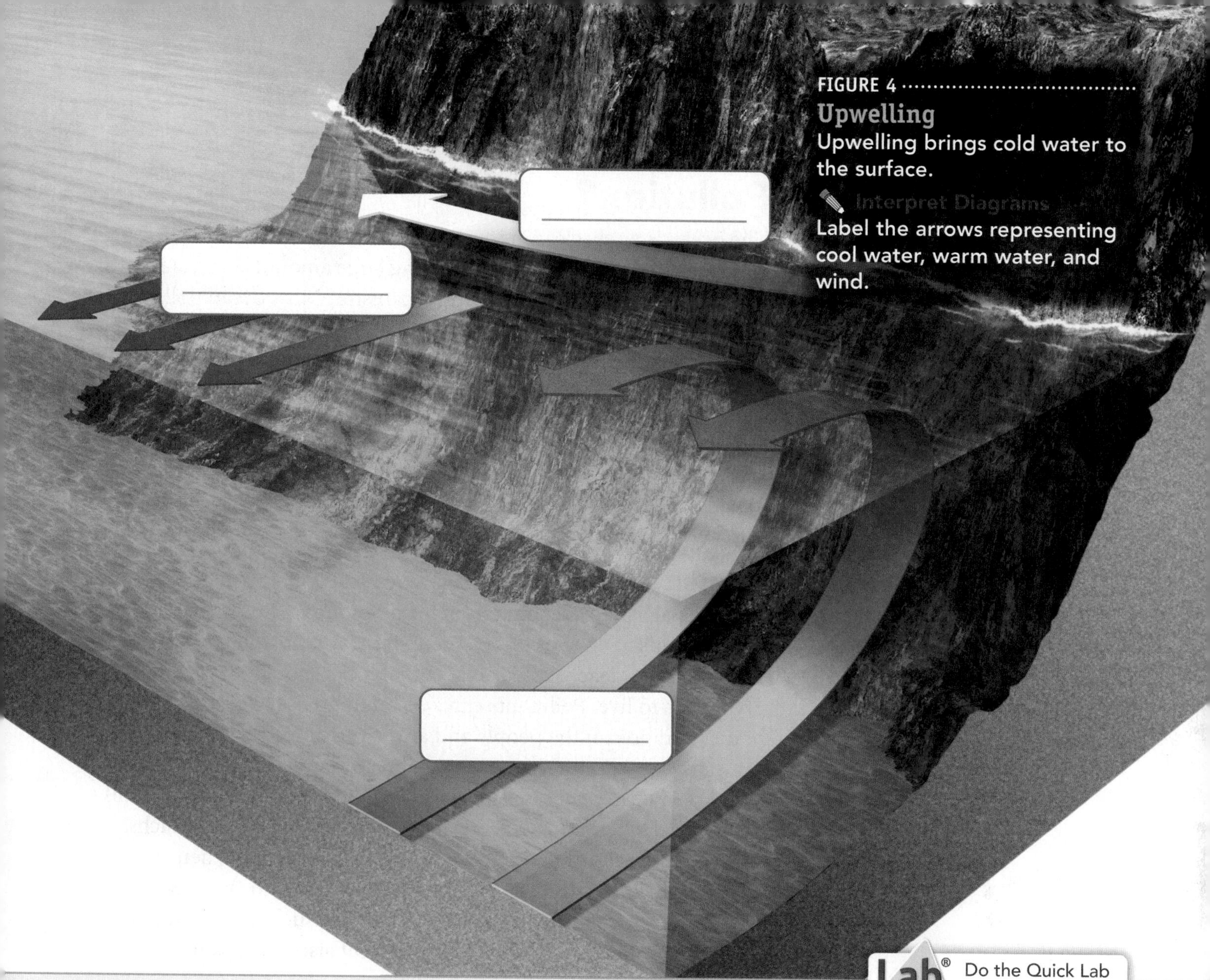

FIGURE 4 ·······························
Upwelling
Upwelling brings cold water to
the surface.

Interpret Diagrams
Label the arrows representing
cool water, warm water, and
wind.

_____

_____

_____

_____

Lab® Do the Quick Lab
zone *Seaweed Candy.*

🔑 **Assess Your Understanding**

1a. Review The practice of (aquaculture/upwelling)
can provide fish in areas not near an ocean.

b. Describe Where do the fuel deposits in the

ocean come from? _____

_____

_____

c. Relate Cause and Effect Explain how
upwelling supports organisms in open ocean.

_____

_____

_____

_____

_____

got it? ···

○ **I get it!** Now I know the living and nonliving resources in the ocean include_____

○ I need extra help with _____

Go to **MY SCIENCE** 🔵ˢ **COACH** online for help with this subject.

What Are the Sources of Ocean Pollution?

The ocean is a self-cleaning system. It can absorb some wastes without permanent damage. Dumping large amounts of wastes into the ocean threatens many marine organisms. Most ocean pollution, however, comes from the land. **Although some ocean pollution is the result of natural occurrences, most pollution is related to human activities.**

Natural Occurrences Some pollution is the result of weather. Heavy rains put fresh water into saltwater environments like marshes and swamps. This fresh water pollutes the ocean by lowering its salinity. It may kill organisms that cannot adjust.

Human Activities Sewage, chemicals, and trash dumped into coastal waters all come from human sources. Substances that run off fields and roads often end up in the ocean and can cause dead zones. A dead zone is an area that lacks enough oxygen for organisms to live. Pollutants can also build up in the organisms' bodies and poison the people and animals that feed on them. Trash can cause serious problems too. Air-breathing marine mammals can drown if they get tangled in fishing lines or nets. Other animals are harmed when they swallow plastic that blocks their stomachs.

Another major threat to ocean life is oil pollution. When an oil tanker or drilling platform is damaged, oil leaks into the ocean. Oil destroys the natural insulation of animals such as sea birds and otters. This affects their ability to float. Oil also harms animals when they swallow it.

do the math!

The graph shows some sources of oil pollution in the ocean. Give the graph a title and answer the questions.

1 **Interpret Data** Which source causes the most oil pollution?

_____

2 Of the five sources on the graph, how many are the result of human activity?

_____

3 **Solve Problems** What is one thing a coastal city could do to reduce oil pollution?

_____

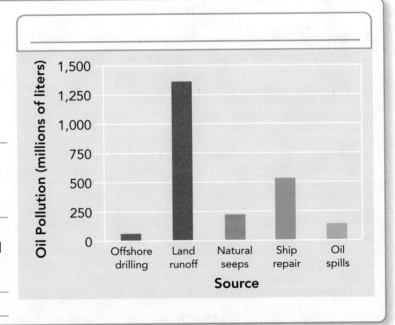

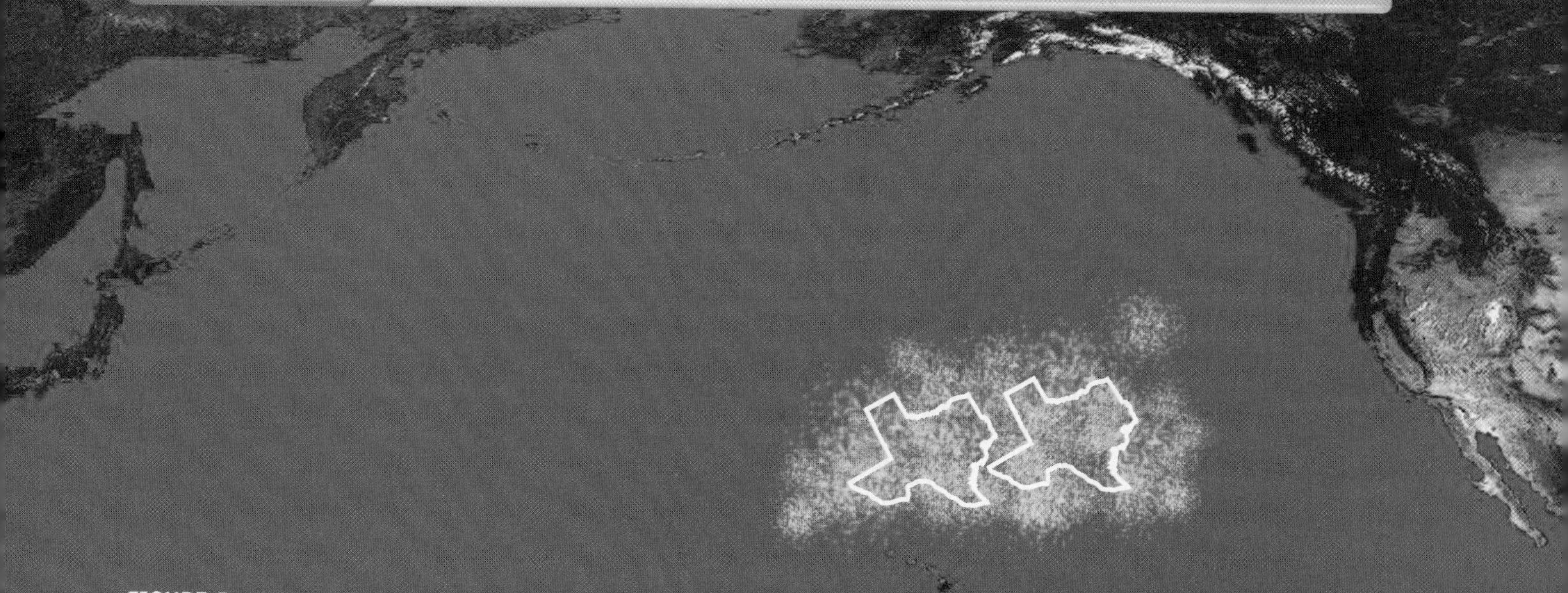

FIGURE 5 ···

Great Pacific Garbage Patch

There is an area of the Pacific Ocean with so much plastic trash in it that it could cover the state of Texas twice! Ocean currents bring trash from the continents to open water and keep it there. The surface water contains six times more plastic than living things!

✎ **List** How can you reduce ocean trash? Write your answers on the blank paper at the right.

Protecting Earth's Oceans

Who owns the ocean? Who is responsible for protecting it? Nations have struggled to answer these questions for hundreds of years. The world ocean is a continuous body of water with no boundaries. Because of this, it is difficult to determine who, if anyone, should control it. Nations must cooperate to protect the oceans.

The United Nations has established ocean boundaries. According to one treaty, a nation controls the first 22 kilometers off its coasts. The nation also controls the resources in the waters or on the ocean floor within 370 kilometers of its shore. This leaves approximately half of the ocean's surface waters as "high seas" owned by no nation. Ownership of the ocean floor beneath the high seas is still under debate.

Other international efforts have resulted in reducing ocean pollution. Examples include the creation of marine refuges and regulations for building safer oil tankers.

Lab zone Do the Quick Lab *Ocean Trash.*

🔑 **Assess Your Understanding**

got it? ···

○ **I get it!** Now I know most ocean pollution is caused by_____

_____

○ **I need extra help with** _____

_____

Go to my science ⓢ coach *online for help with this subject.*

4 Study Guide

To use resources wisely, people can reuse or _____ materials and they can properly dispose of hazardous wastes and other _____.

LESSON 1 Conserving Land and Soil

🗝 Three uses that change the land are agriculture, mining, and development.

🗝 Without soil, most life on land could not exist. Poor soil management results in three problems: erosion, nutrient depletion, and desertification.

Vocabulary
- litter • topsoil • subsoil • bedrock
- erosion • nutrient depletion • fertilizer
- desertification • drought • land reclamation

LESSON 2 Waste Disposal and Recycling

🗝 Solid waste is burned, buried, or recycled.

🗝 Recycling categories include metal, glass, paper, and plastic.

🗝 Hazardous wastes are stored depending on the type and potential danger.

Vocabulary
- municipal solid waste • incineration
- pollutant • leachate • sanitary landfill
- recycling • biodegradeable • hazardous waste

LESSON 3 Air Pollution and Solutions

🗝 A major source of outdoor air pollution is vehicle emissions. Indoor air pollution has a variety of causes.

🗝 The major cause of the ozone hole is CFCs.

🗝 Reducing air pollution requires reducing emissions.

Vocabulary
- emissions • photochemical smog • ozone
- temperature inversion • acid rain
- radon • ozone layer • chlorofluorocarbon

LESSON 4 Water Pollution and Solutions

🗝 Earth's water is about 97 percent salt water.

🗝 Most water pollution is caused by human activities.

🗝 The keys to keeping water clean include cleaning oil spills, proper sewage treatment, and the reduction of pollutants.

Vocabulary
- groundwater • pesticide • sewage • sediment

LESSON 5 Ocean Resources

🗝 Resources in the ocean include organisms such as fish and nonliving things such as oil.

🗝 Most ocean pollution is related to human activities.

Vocabulary
- nodule
- upwelling

Review and Assessment

LESSON 1 Conserving Land and Soil

1. What is an agricultural use of land?

a. growing crops on land

b. collecting water from land

c. building structures on land

d. removing minerals from land

2. Plant roots absorb nutrients and water from the layer of soil called _____.

3. Relate Cause and Effect What type of land use can result in nutrient depletion? Explain.

_____

_____

_____

_____

LESSON 2 Waste Disposal and Recycling

4. What is one benefit of recycling?

a. It increases the volume of solid waste.

b. If it is recycled, a material won't biodegrade.

c. It conserves resources and energy.

d. It uses more raw materials that need to be mined.

5. A _____
is a waste that can be harmful to human health or the environment.

6. 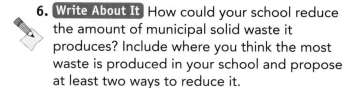 **Write About It** How could your school reduce the amount of municipal solid waste it produces? Include where you think the most waste is produced in your school and propose at least two ways to reduce it.

LESSON 3 Air Pollution and Solutions

7. Which of the following describes a pollutant that has been released into the air?

a. sewage   b. leachate

c. sediment   d. emissions

8. The _____ in the upper atmosphere prevents some of the sun's ultraviolet radiation from reaching Earth.

9. Predict Do you think the hole in the ozone layer will increase or decrease in size? Why?

_____

_____

_____

_____

10. Solve Problems Describe two ways a large city can reduce air pollution.

_____

_____

_____

_____

_____

_____

_____

LESSON 4 Water Pollution and Solutions

11. Why is fresh water a limited resource?

   a. because most water on Earth is in lakes

   b. because most water on Earth is in clouds

   c. because most water on Earth is in the ground

   d. because most water on Earth is salt water

12. A _____ is a chemical that kills crop-destroying organisms.

13. **Draw Conclusions** Rain may wash fertilizers into bodies of water, such as ponds. How might fertilizer affect a pond?

_____

_____

_____

_____

LESSON 5 Ocean Resources

14. The ocean contains living resources such as _____ and nonliving resources such as _____.

   a. fuel; water   **b.** fish; minerals

   c. seaweed; shrimp   **d.** organisms; pollution

15. _____ is the movement of cold water from the deep ocean to the surface.

16. **Relate Cause and Effect** How might oil used as fuel result in ocean pollution?

_____

_____

_____

_____

_____

APPLY THE BIG Q What can people do to use resources wisely?

17. Every individual, including young people, can make decisions to use resources wisely. **Use the terms *reduce, reuse,* and *recycle* to explain how the students in the picture below can help minimize solid waste.**

_____

_____

_____

_____

_____

_____

_____

_____

Standardized Test Prep

Multiple Choice

Circle the letter of the best answer.

1. According to the circle graph, what is the most common method of waste disposal in the United States?

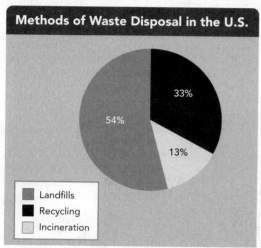

Methods of Waste Disposal in the U.S.

33%

54%

13%

- Landfills
- Recycling
- Incineration

   A composting   B recycling
   C incineration   D landfills

2. In which layer of soil would you expect to find rock fragments, nutrients, and decaying plant and animal matter?

   A litter   B topsoil
   C subsoil   D bedrock

3. What types of materials could be broken down in a compost pile?

   A all recyclable materials
   B biodegradable materials
   C all materials that can be incinerated
   D glass, metal, and other raw materials

4. How can sediments negatively affect an aquatic ecosystem?

   A by blocking sunlight
   B by causing algae to grow
   C by causing plants to grow
   D by changing the water temperature

5. What are the main sources of ocean pollution?

   A upwellings
   B natural causes
   C human activities
   D waves of sunlight reacting with water

Constructed Response

Use the diagram below and your knowledge of science to help you answer Question 6. Write your answer on a separate sheet of paper.

6. Compare and contrast the role of ozone in each of the images shown above.

Old MacDonald Had a Satellite

When listing the equipment needed for a farm, you might think of a tractor and irrigation equipment, but would you include a satellite on your list? Farming has come a long way since Old MacDonald's days! Precision farming uses high-tech tools, such as remote sensing and the Global Positioning System (GPS), to conserve resources and increase crop yields.

On large farms, soil fertility can vary in different areas. Before learning about precision farming, farmers usually averaged the amount of water and fertilizer that they needed for the whole farm. Then, they applied that amount evenly throughout their fields. Some areas might get too much fertilizer and water, while others might not get enough.

In precision farming, farmers can use data from GPS satellites to learn about what the soil on their farm needs. Satellite images of their farms can give farmers information about the fertility of specific fields, and whether these fields have enough nutrients and water. Because the farm machinery is equipped with a GPS receiver, the farmer can precisely adjust the amount of water, pesticides, or fertilizer applied to specific areas of a field, to make sure that each area gets exactly what it needs. This method reduces costs and increases crop yields. It also reduces the overuse of agricultural chemicals. Old MacDonald never had it this good!

Research It Find out more about how precision farming may protect water supplies from contamination or how these techniques can save farmers money. Create a poster display or multimedia presentation that explains your findings.

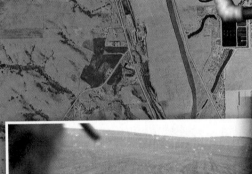

▲ Inside a crop-sprayer, a farmer uses a GPS receiver to read information from a GPS satellite about the soil in the field.

BEWARE of Greenwashing!

Many businesses claim to produce environmentally friendly products. But how can you know the truth? *Greenwashing* is a term that combines the words *green* and *whitewashing*. It refers to the practice of making a product, service, or company appear to be more environmentally friendly than it really is.

Sometimes, identifying greenwashing is difficult because advertisements can be very persuasive. Fortunately, thinking like a scientist can help. As you evaluate a company's environmental claims, consider the following questions.

✓ **Is there proof?** Is there a scientific basis for the claims made by the company?

✓ **Is there a trade-off?** Does creating or delivering the product or service have negative environmental effects that are greater than the benefits of the product or service?

✓ **Are the claims meaningless?** Some labels, such as "100% natural," have no scientific or regulatory meaning.

✓ **Who says so?** Has a reliable source tested the company's claims?

Apply It Find advertisements for products that claim to have environmental benefits. Use the questions above to evaluate the claims. Then, create a brochure to educate the public about greenwashing.

Now Safe for the Environment!

CFC free

With **Eco-sensitive** ingredients

HOW CAN WIND KEEP YOUR LIGHTS ON?

THE BIG ?

What are some of Earth's energy sources?

This man is repairing a wind turbine at a wind farm in Texas. Most wind turbines are at least 30 meters off the ground where the winds are fast. Wind speed and blade length help determine the best way to capture the wind and turn it into power. ▲Develop Hypotheses **Why do you think people are working to increase the amount of power we get from wind?**

_____

_____

_____

_____

_____

_____

▶ UNTAMED SCIENCE Watch the **Untamed Science** video to learn more about energy resources.

Energy Resources

5 Getting Started

Check Your Understanding

1. **Background** Read the paragraph below and then answer the question.

Aisha loves visiting her grandmother at work. Her grandmother says that the building she works in was designed to help conserve **natural resources.** Most of the building's electricity comes from **renewable resources,** such as sunlight and wind, instead of from **nonrenewable resources,** such as oil or coal.

> A **natural resource** is any material that occurs naturally in the environment and is used by people.
>
> A **renewable resource** is either always available or is naturally replaced in a short time.
>
> A **nonrenewable resource** is a resource that is not replaced within a useful time frame.

- What is one example of a natural resource?

_____

_____

> **MY READING WEB** If you had trouble completing the question above, visit **My Reading Web** and type in *Energy Resources.*

Vocabulary Skill

High-Use Academic Words High-use academic words are words that are used frequently in classrooms. Look for the words below as you read this chapter.

Word	Definition	Example
scarce	*adj.* rare; in limited supply	Tickets for the concert are becoming *scarce* because of the demand.
emit	*v.* to give off	When the oven is on, it *emits* heat, making the whole apartment warmer.

2. **Quick Check** Choose the word from the table above that best completes each sentence.

- Motor vehicles _____ chemicals that contribute to air pollution.

- As people continue to use oil faster than it can be replaced, it will become _____.

fossil fuel

solar energy

biomass fuel

energy conservation

Chapter Preview

LESSON 1
- fuel
- fossil fuel
- hydrocarbon
- petroleum
- refinery
- petrochemical

🔄 **Summarize**
△ **Communicate**

LESSON 2
- solar energy
- hydroelectric power
- biomass fuel
- gasohol
- geothermal energy
- nuclear fission
- reactor vessel
- fuel rod
- control rod

🔄 **Relate Cause and Effect**
△ **Infer**

LESSON 3
- efficiency
- insulation
- energy conservation

🔄 **Identify the Main Idea**
△ **Observe**

> VOCAB FLASH CARDS For extra help with vocabulary, visit **Vocab Flash Cards** and type in *Energy Resources.*

Fossil Fuels

🔑 **What Are the Three Major Fossil Fuels?**

🔑 **Why Are Fossil Fuels Nonrenewable Resources?**

DISASTERS

my pLaneT DiaRY

Hurricane Energy Crisis

On August 29, 2005, Hurricane Katrina struck the Gulf Coast. The storm flooded cities and towns. In New Orleans, tens of thousands of people were stranded on rooftops. Hundreds of thousands of evacuees fled to other parts of the country. Katrina also created another kind of crisis. The Gulf Coast has many factories that produce oil and gas for the entire country. These factories were shut down because of winds, power outages, and flooding. Gas stations ran out of gas. Prices soared. Many people couldn't afford to heat their homes. Some people burned wood instead. Others just got cold. The hurricane had created an energy crisis.

 Do the Inquiry Warm-Up *What's in a Piece of Coal?*

Communicate Discuss the questions with a group of classmates. Then write your answers below.

1. Due to global climate changes, more hurricanes are expected to hit the Gulf Coast. What might happen to gas and oil production?

_____

_____

2. How might alternative fuels provide a solution?

_____

_____

_____

_____

▶ PLANET DIARY Go to **Planet Diary** to learn more about fossil fuels.

Vocabulary
- fuel • fossil fuel • hydrocarbon
- petroleum • refinery
- petrochemical

Skills
- Reading: Summarize
- Inquiry: Communicate

What Are the Three Major Fossil Fuels?

Whether you travel in a car or a bus, walk, or ride your bike, you use some form of energy. The source of that energy is fuel. A **fuel** is a substance that provides energy, such as heat, light, motion, or electricity. This energy is the result of a chemical change.

Most of the energy used today comes from organisms that lived hundreds of millions of years ago. As these plants, animals, and other organisms died, their remains piled up. Layers of sand, rock, and mud buried the remains. Over time, heat and the pressure of the layers changed the remains into other substances. **Fossil fuels** are the energy-rich substances formed from the remains. 🔑 **The three major fossil fuels are coal, oil, and natural gas.**

Fossil fuels are made of hydrocarbons. **Hydrocarbons** are chemical compounds that contain carbon and hydrogen atoms. When the fossil fuels are burned, the atoms react. They combine with oxygen to form new molecules. These reactions release energy in the forms of heat and light.

Burning fossil fuels provides more energy per kilogram than burning other fuels. One kilogram of coal, for example, can provide twice as much energy as one kilogram of wood. Oil and natural gas can provide three times as much energy as an equal mass of wood.

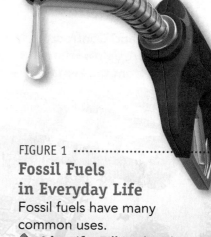

FIGURE 1

Fossil Fuels in Everyday Life
Fossil fuels have many common uses.

✏️ **Identify** Fill in the chart with ways that you or other people use the three fossil fuels in daily life.

Fossil Fuel	Common Uses	Uses in Your Life
Coal	• Used to generate half of all U.S. electricity • Used to make products like fertilizer and medicine • When heated, used to make steel	
Oil	• As gasoline and diesel fuels, used to power vehicles • Used to heat homes • Used to make plastics and other petroleum products	
Natural gas	• Used to generate electricity • Used to cook food • Used to heat homes	

Coal

People have burned coal to produce heat for thousands of years. For much of that time, wood was more convenient and cheaper than coal for most people. But during the 1800s, the huge energy needs of growing industries made it worthwhile to find, mine, and transport coal. Today, coal makes up about 22 percent of the fuel used in the United States. Most of that coal fuels electrical power plants.

Before coal can be used to produce energy, it has to be removed from the ground. Miners use machines to chop the coal into chunks and lift it to the surface. Coal mining can be a dangerous job. Thousands of miners have been killed or injured in mining accidents. Many more suffer from lung diseases. Fortunately, modern safety procedures and better equipment have made coal mining safer, although it is still very dangerous.

Coal is the most plentiful fossil fuel in the United States. It is fairly easy to transport and provides a lot of energy when burned. But coal also has some disadvantages. Coal mining can increase erosion. Runoff from coal mines can cause water pollution. Burning most types of coal results in more air pollution than using other fossil fuels. See **Figure 2.**

Figure 3 shows how plant remains build up over time and form coal.

FIGURE 2 ·····································

Pros and Cons of Coal Use
Coal mining, shown above, is a dangerous job.

✏ **Compare and Contrast**
Fill in the chart below using information from the text.

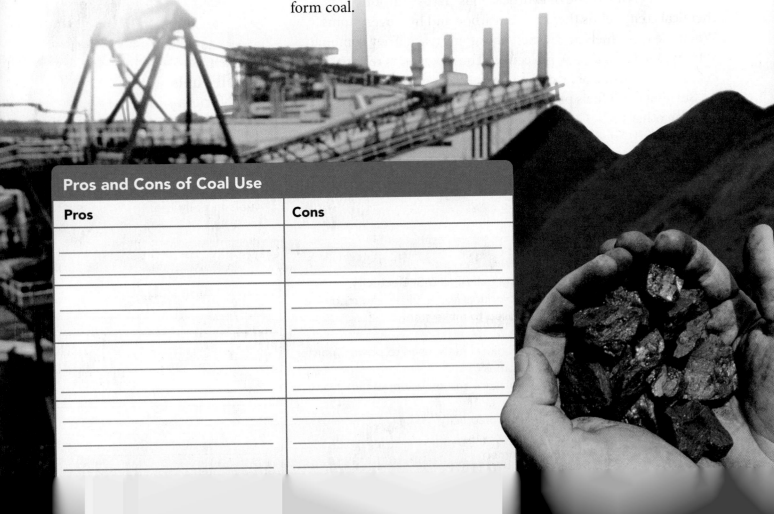

Pros and Cons of Coal Use	
Pros	**Cons**

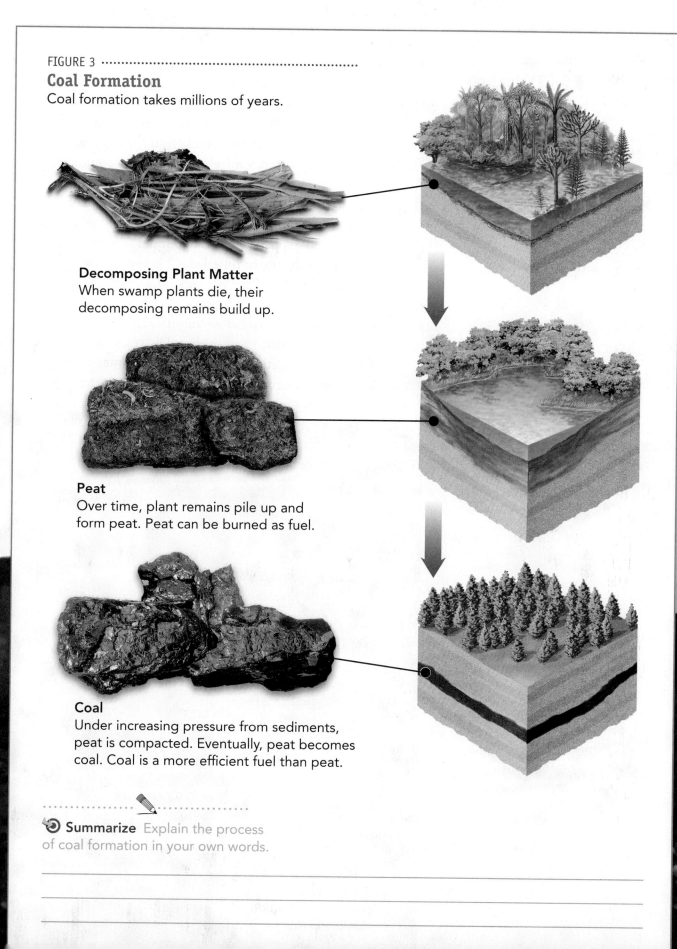

FIGURE 3 ···

Coal Formation

Coal formation takes millions of years.

Decomposing Plant Matter
When swamp plants die, their decomposing remains build up.

Peat
Over time, plant remains pile up and form peat. Peat can be burned as fuel.

Coal
Under increasing pressure from sediments, peat is compacted. Eventually, peat becomes coal. Coal is a more efficient fuel than peat.

Summarize Explain the process of coal formation in your own words.

_____

_____

_____

FIGURE 4 ··

▶ART IN MOTION Oil Formation

Oil is formed in a process similar to coal.

✎ **Interpret Diagrams** Use what you know to fill in the steps of oil formation in the diagrams below.

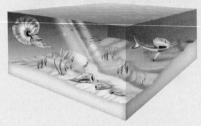

300–400 million years ago

_____
_____
_____

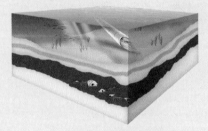

50–100 million years ago

_____
_____
_____

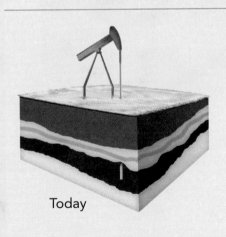

Today

_____
_____
_____
_____

Oil

Oil is a thick, black, liquid fossil fuel. It formed from the remains of small animals, algae, and other organisms that lived in oceans and shallow inland seas hundreds of millions of years ago. **Petroleum** is another name for oil. Petroleum comes from the Latin words *petra* (rock) and *oleum* (oil). Petroleum accounts for more than one third of the energy produced in the world. Fuel for most cars, airplanes, trains, and ships comes from petroleum. Many homes are heated by oil as well.

Most oil deposits are located underground in tiny holes in sandstone or limestone. **Figure 4** shows how oil is formed. The oil fills the holes somewhat like the way water fills the holes of a sponge. Because oil deposits are usually located deep below the surface, finding oil is difficult. Scientists can use sound waves to test an area for oil. Even using this technique, scientists may not always locate wells that will produce a usable amount of oil.

FIGURE 5 ························

Oil Pipeline
Workers build an oil pipeline in Russia.

When oil is first pumped out of the ground, it is called crude oil. To be made into useful products, crude oil must undergo a process called refining. A factory in which crude oil is heated and separated into fuels and other products is called a **refinery.** Many of the products that you use every day are made from crude oil. **Petrochemicals** are compounds that are made from oil. Petrochemicals are used to make plastics, paints, medicines, and cosmetics.

apply it!

Over 2,500 species of plants and animals live in Lake Baikal, in Russia. Eighty percent of these species live nowhere else on Earth. One of those species is the Baikal seal—one of only three freshwater seal species on Earth. The seal and other species were threatened when oil companies planned to build the world's longest oil pipeline within 800 meters of the lake's shore. The pipeline would bring oil from Russia's interior to China and ports along the Pacific Ocean. Citizens were concerned that oil leaks and spills would damage the lake. They worked together to convince the oil companies to move the pipeline 40 kilometers to the north. The design of the new pipeline protects the lake and also delivers oil to places that need it.

Communicate An oil pipeline is proposed in your area near a body of water you think is important. Using Lake Baikal as an example, write a letter to the editor of your local paper explaining what you think should be done about the pipeline and why. Give your letter a headline.

_____

_____

_____

_____

_____

_____

_____

_____

_____

_____

_____

_____

_____

_____

_____

Natural Gas Natural gas is a mixture of methane and other gases. Natural gas forms from some of the same organisms as oil. Because it is less dense than oil, natural gas often rises above an oil deposit, forming a pocket of gas in the rock.

Pipelines transport natural gas from its source to the places where it is used. If all the gas pipelines in the United States were connected, they would reach to the moon and back—three times! Natural gas can also be compressed into a liquid and stored in tanks as fuel for trucks and buses.

Natural gas has several benefits. It produces large amounts of energy, but has lower levels of many air pollutants compared to coal or oil. It is also easy to transport once pipelines are built. One cost of natural gas is that it is highly flammable. A gas leak can cause explosions and fires. If you use natural gas in your home, you probably are familiar with the "gas" smell alerting you when there is unburned gas in the air. You may be surprised to learn that natural gas actually has no odor. What causes the strong smell? Gas companies add a chemical with a distinct smell to the gas so that people can detect a gas leak.

FIGURE 6 ·······························

Natural Gas
A gas-top burner uses natural gas to cook food.

✎ **Analyze Costs and Benefits** Fill in the boxes with some costs and benefits of natural gas.

Costs of Natural Gas	Benefits of Natural Gas
_____	_____
_____	_____
_____	_____
_____	_____
_____	_____
_____	_____

Lab ® Do the Quick Lab *Observing Oil's Consistency.*
zone

🗝 Assess Your Understanding

1a. Define What are petrochemicals?

_____

_____

_____

b. Make Judgments Should the federal government decide where to build oil or natural gas pipelines? Explain.

_____

_____

_____

got it? ···

○ **I get it!** Now I know that the three major fossil fuels are_____

○ **I need extra help with** _____

Go to **MY SCIENCE** ⓢ **COACH** *online for help with this subject.*

Why Are Fossil Fuels Nonrenewable Resources?

The many advantages of using fossil fuels as an energy source have made them essential to modern life.  **Since fossil fuels take hundreds of millions of years to form, they are considered nonrenewable resources.** Earth's known oil reserves, or the amount of oil that can currently be used, took 500 million years to form. Fossil fuels will run out if they are used faster than they are formed.

Many nations that consume large amounts of fossil fuels have very small reserves or supplies. They have to buy oil, natural gas, and coal from nations with large supplies to make up the difference. The United States, for example, uses about one quarter of all the oil produced in the world. But only two percent of the world's oil supply is located in this country. The uneven distribution of fossil fuel reserves has often been a cause of political problems in the world.

do the math!

Use the graph to answer the questions below.

1 Read Graphs Which energy source generates the most electricity in the United States? _____

2 Calculate What percentage of the fuels in the graph are fossil fuels? _____

3 CHALLENGE How might this graph look in 50 years? Give reasons to support your answer. _____
_____
_____

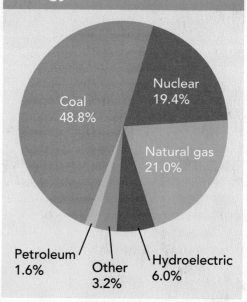

Recent Electricity Production in the United States by Energy Source

Coal 48.8%
Nuclear 19.4%
Natural gas 21.0%
Petroleum 1.6%
Other 3.2%
Hydroelectric 6.0%

Lab zone — Do the Quick Lab *Fossil Fuels.*

Assess Your Understanding

got it?

○ I get it! Now I know that fossil fuels are nonrenewable because_____
_____

○ I need extra help with _____

Go to my science COACH online for help with this subject.

Alternative Sources of Energy

UNLOCK THE BIG ?

🗝 **What Are Some Renewable Sources of Energy?**

🗝 **How Does a Nuclear Power Plant Produce Electricity?**

my pLaneT DiaRY

BIOGRAPHY

An Unlikely Decision

T. Boone Pickens's family taught him the value of hard work during the Great Depression of the 1930s. At 11, he delivered newspapers. By 26, he founded his own oil and gas company and became rich. In 2007, T. Boone Pickens surprised everyone by announcing plans to build the world's largest wind farm. He insisted the country must replace oil with wind and solar power. Even though he still promotes oil, he was one of the first oil businessmen to admit a change was needed. "I've been an oil man all my life," Pickens said, "but this is one emergency we can't drill our way out of."

Communicate Discuss these questions with a group of classmates. Write your answers below.

1. Why do you think Pickens's decision was so surprising?

_____

_____

2. Do you think more focus should be put on finding sources of energy other than oil? Why or why not?

_____

_____

▶ PLANET DIARY Go to **Planet Diary** to learn more about renewable energy.

Lab zone® Do the Inquiry Warm-Up *Can You Capture Solar Energy?*

What Are Some Renewable Sources of Energy?

Coal, oil, and natural gas are not the only energy options available on Earth. 🗝 **Renewable sources of energy include sunlight, water, wind, biomass fuels, and geothermal energy.** Other energy options include nuclear power and hydrogen. Scientists are trying to put these energy sources to work.

Vocabulary

- solar energy • hydroelectric power • biomass fuel
- gasohol • geothermal energy • nuclear fission
- reactor vessel • fuel rod • control rod

Skills

↻ Reading: Relate Cause and Effect

△ Inquiry: Infer

Solar Energy

The warmth you feel on a sunny day is **solar energy,** or energy from the sun. The sun constantly gives off energy in the forms of light and heat. Solar energy is the source, directly or indirectly, of most other renewable energy resources. In one hour, Earth receives enough solar energy to meet the energy needs of the world for an entire year. Solar energy does not cause pollution. It will not run out for billions of years.

So why hasn't solar energy replaced energy from fossil fuels? One reason is that solar energy is only available when the sun is shining. Another problem is that the energy Earth receives from the sun is very spread out. To obtain a useful amount of power, it is necessary to collect solar energy from a large area.

Solar Power Plants One way to capture the sun's energy involves using giant mirrors. In a solar power plant, rows of mirrors focus the sun's rays to heat a tank of water. The water boils. This creates steam. The steam can then be used to generate electricity.

Solar Cells Solar energy can be converted directly into electricity in a solar cell. When light hits the cell, an electric current is produced. Solar cells power some calculators, lights, and other small devices.

↻ **Relate Cause and Effect**
Underline one way solar energy is collected and circle the way it is used.

did you know?

Photovoltaic cells, or solar cells, are named for the Greek word for light, *photo*, and electricity pioneer Alessandro Volta.

FIGURE 1

Everyday Solar Power

Many objects, including calculators, street lights, and even backpacks that charge electronic devices, can be powered by the sun.

✎ **Describe** What object in your everyday life would you like to run on solar power? Would you want the sun to be its only power source? Why?

_____

_____

_____

_____

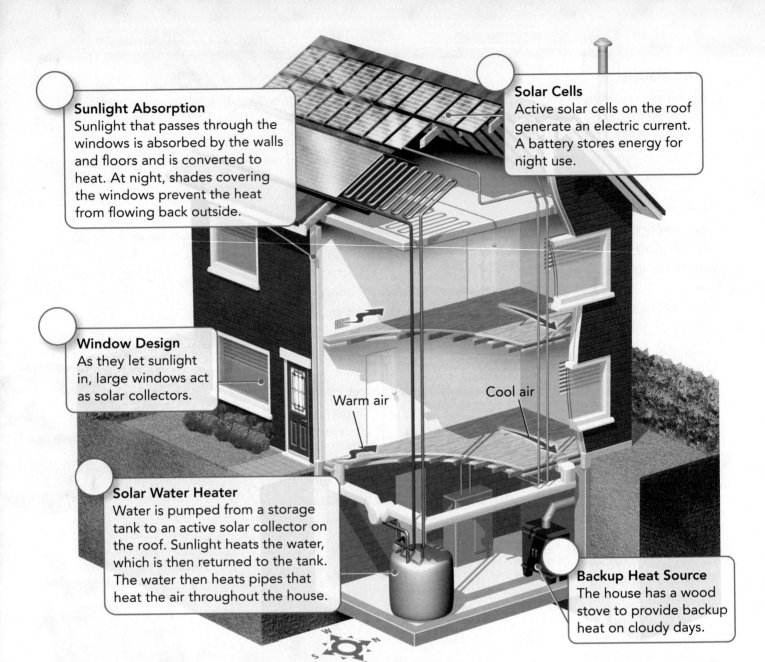

Sunlight Absorption
Sunlight that passes through the windows is absorbed by the walls and floors and is converted to heat. At night, shades covering the windows prevent the heat from flowing back outside.

Solar Cells
Active solar cells on the roof generate an electric current. A battery stores energy for night use.

Window Design
As they let sunlight in, large windows act as solar collectors.

Warm air

Cool air

Solar Water Heater
Water is pumped from a storage tank to an active solar collector on the roof. Sunlight heats the water, which is then returned to the tank. The water then heats pipes that heat the air throughout the house.

Backup Heat Source
The house has a wood stove to provide backup heat on cloudy days.

FIGURE 2 ·······························
Solar-Powered House
This house takes advantage of active and passive solar heating.

△**Infer** Draw a checkmark in the blank circles on the passive sources of solar energy. Draw a star in the blank circles on the active sources.

Passive Solar Heating Solar energy can be used to heat buildings with passive solar systems. A passive solar system converts sunlight into heat, or thermal energy. The heat is then distributed without using pumps or fans. Passive solar heating is what occurs in a parked car on a sunny day. Solar energy passes through the car's windows and heats the seats and other car parts. These parts transfer heat to the air, warming the inside of the car. The same principle can be used to heat a home.

Active Solar Heating An active solar system captures the sun's energy, and then uses pumps and fans to distribute the heat. First, light strikes the dark metal surface of a solar collector. There, it is converted to thermal energy. Water is pumped through pipes in the solar collector to absorb the thermal energy. The heated water then flows to a storage tank. Finally, pumps and fans distribute the heat throughout the building. Refer to **Figure 2.**

Hydroelectric Power
Solar energy is the indirect source of water power. In the water cycle, energy from the sun heats water on Earth's surface. The heat turns the water into water vapor. The vapor condenses and falls back to Earth as rain, sleet, hail, or snow. As the water flows over land, it provides another source of energy.

Hydroelectric power is electricity produced by flowing water. A dam across a river blocks the flow of water, creating a body of water called a reservoir. When a dam's gates are opened, water flows through tunnels at the bottom of the dam. As the water moves through the tunnels, it turns turbines (like a fan's blades). The turbines are connected to a generator. Once a dam is built, generating electricity is inexpensive. But dams can prevent some fish species from breeding. They can also damage aquatic habitats.

Capturing the Wind
Like water power, wind energy is also an indirect form of solar energy. The sun heats Earth's surface unevenly. As a result, different areas of the atmosphere have different temperatures and air pressures. The differences in pressure cause winds to form as air moves from one area to another.

Wind can be used to turn a turbine and generate electricity. Wind farms consist of many wind turbines. Together, the wind turbines generate large amounts of power. Wind is the fastest-growing energy source in the world. Wind energy does not cause pollution. In places where fuels are difficult to transport, wind energy is the major source of power if it is available.

Nuclear Power
Like water and wind power, nuclear power does not produce air pollution since no fuel is burned. Instead, the energy released from the splitting of atoms is used to create steam that turns turbines. This process can be dangerous and even cause explosions if too much energy is released. Wastes generated by nuclear plants can be dangerous if disposed of improperly.

FIGURE 3 ·······················

Hydroelectric and Wind Power

Hydroelectric and wind power do not rely on fossil fuels.

✎ **Compare and Contrast** List similarities and differences between water and wind power in the Venn diagram.

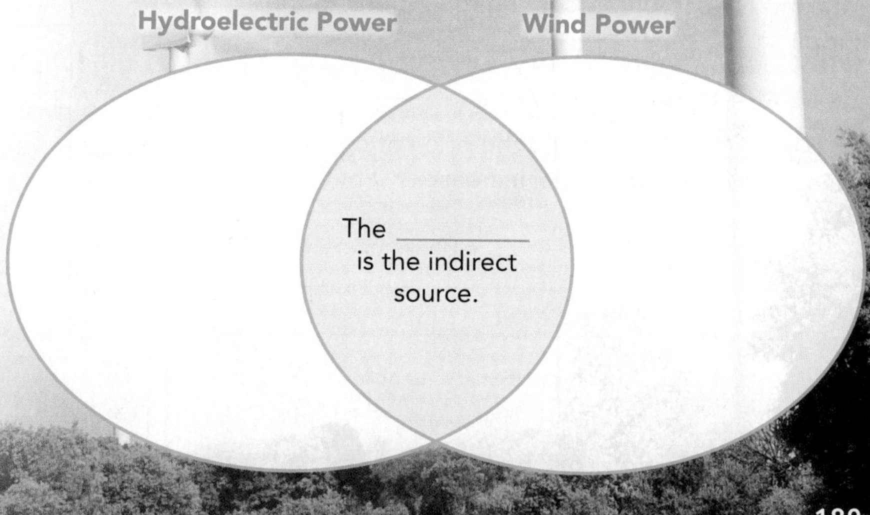

Hydroelectric Power   Wind Power

The _____ is the indirect source.

Biomass Fuels Wood was probably the first fuel ever used for heat and light. Wood belongs to a group of fuels called **biomass fuels.** Biomass fuels are made from living things. Other biomass fuels include leaves, food wastes, and even manure. As fossil fuel supplies shrink, people are taking a closer look at biomass fuels. For example, when oil prices rose in the early 1970s, Hawaiian farmers began burning sugar cane wastes to generate electricity.

In addition to being burned as fuel, biomass materials can be converted into other fuels. For example, corn, sugar cane, and other crops can be used to make alcohol. Adding alcohol to gasoline forms **gasohol.** Gasohol can be used as fuel for cars. Bacteria can produce methane gas by decomposing biomass materials in landfills. That methane can be used to heat buildings. And some crops, such as soybeans, can produce oil. The oil can be used as fuel, which is called biodiesel fuel.

Biomass fuels are renewable resources. But it takes time for new trees to replace those that have been cut down. And it is expensive to produce alcohol and methane in large quantities. As a result, biomass fuels are not widely used today in the United States. But as fossil fuels become scarcer, biomass fuels may provide another source for meeting energy needs.

FIGURE 4 ·····················

Corn Power
Biomass fuels come from living things, such as corn. It takes about 11.84 kilograms of corn to make one gallon of fuel!

apply it!

What can happen when a food crop is used for fuel? The relationship is plotted with two curves on the graph.

❶ Interpret Graphs According to the graph, as demand for corn increases, what happens to the supply?

_____

❷ CHALLENGE How would the price of corn change as demand for fuel increases? Why?

_____
_____
_____
_____

Supply and Demand for Food and Fuel Crops

— Demand
— Supply

Amount of Corn

Increasing Time ⟶

Tapping Earth's Energy Below Earth's surface are pockets of very hot liquid rock called magma. In some places, magma is very close to the surface. The intense heat from Earth's interior that warms the magma is called **geothermal energy.**

In certain regions, such as Iceland and New Zealand, magma heats underground water to the boiling point. In these places, the hot water and steam can be valuable sources of energy. For example, in Reykjavík, Iceland, 90 percent of the homes are heated by water warmed underground in this way. Geothermal energy can also be used to generate electricity, as shown in **Figure 5.**

Geothermal energy does have disadvantages. There are only a few places where Earth's crust is thin enough for magma to come close to the surface. Elsewhere, very deep wells would be needed to tap this energy. Drilling deep wells is very expensive. Even so, geothermal energy is likely to become a good method for meeting energy needs for some locations in the future.

FIGURE 5 ·····································

Geothermal Power in Iceland

Geothermal power plants like the one shown here use heat from Earth's interior to generate electricity.

✎ **Infer** On the diagram below, draw Earth's crust and show where magma might be located in relation to Iceland's surface.

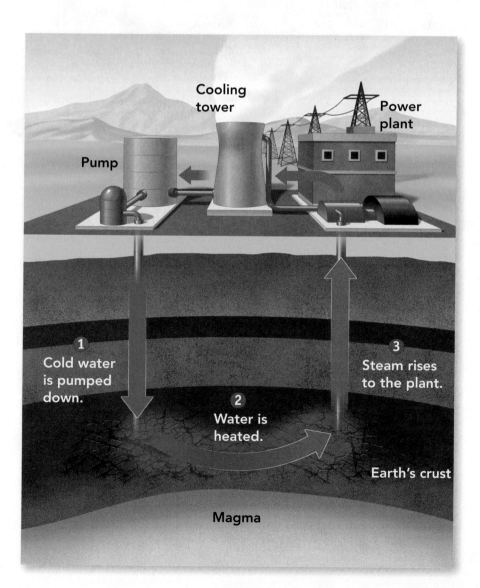

Pump

Cooling tower

Power plant

1 Cold water is pumped down.

2 Water is heated.

3 Steam rises to the plant.

Earth's crust

Magma

Earth's crust

Magma

The Energy Around Us

What are some of Earth's energy sources?

FIGURE 6 ....

> **INTERACTIVE ART** People use many energy sources in their daily lives. Each source has its pros and cons.

✎ **Analyze Costs and Benefits** In the boxes, write one pro and one con about each energy source pictured.

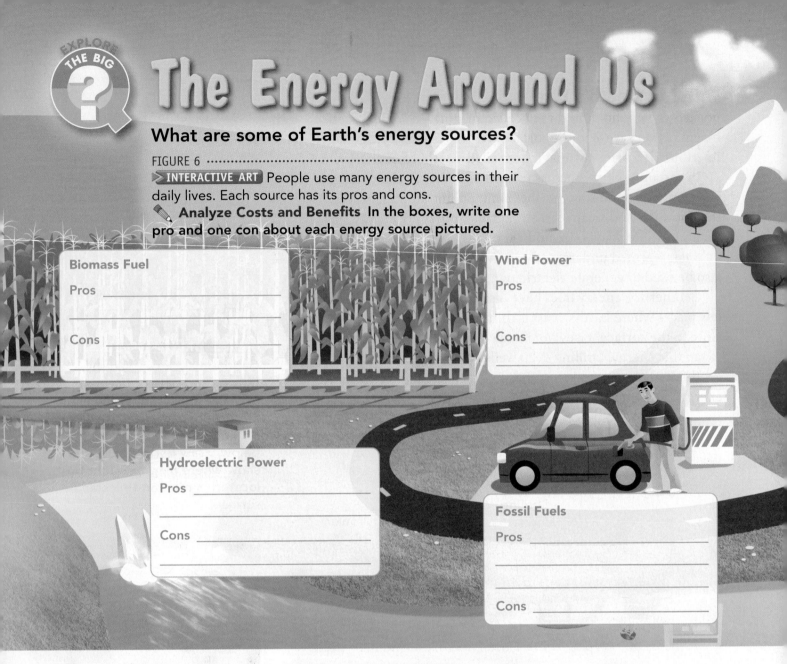

Biomass Fuel

Pros _____

_____

Cons _____

_____

Wind Power

Pros _____

_____

Cons _____

_____

Hydroelectric Power

Pros _____

_____

Cons _____

_____

Fossil Fuels

Pros _____

_____

_____

Cons _____

Vocabulary High-Use Academic Words The word *emit* means "to give off." What do vehicles that run on hydrogen fuel cells emit?

_____

_____

_____

Electric Cars and Hydrogen Fuel Cells You may have heard about or even seen battery-powered electric cars. But what about cars that use hydrogen fuel cells? Both technologies, battery-powered electric cars and hydrogen fuel cells, have been developed to use renewable energy. See **Figure 6**.

Electric cars run entirely on batteries, and you plug them into an outlet to recharge them. The electricity used can be generated by power plants that use hydroelectric or solar energy. Some electric cars have adaptors that let you recharge them in minutes.

Some cars can run on hydrogen. They have tanks called hydrogen fuel cells that hold hydrogen instead of gasoline. Many power plants can use excess energy to break water molecules apart to make hydrogen. This hydrogen can then be pumped into cars. Cars that run on hydrogen fuel cells emit water vapor, not exhaust.

Solar Power

Pros _____

_____

Cons _____

_____

Geothermal Energy

Pros _____

_____

Cons _____

_____

Hydrogen

Hydrogen Power

Pros _____

_____

Cons _____

_____

_____

Nuclear Power

Pros _____

_____

Cons _____

_____

Lab zone® Do the Lab Investigation *Design and Build a Solar Cooker.*

🔑 Assess Your Understanding

1a. Review What forms of energy are provided by the sun? _____

b. Explain Are biomass fuels renewable? Why? _____

_____

c. ANSWER THE BIG ? What are some of Earth's energy sources?

_____

_____

_____

_____

_____

_____

got it? ....

○ **I get it!** Now I know that alternative energy sources include _____

_____

○ **I need extra help with** _____

Go to **MY SCIENCE** ⬤ S **COACH** online for help with this subject.

How Does a Nuclear Power Plant Produce Electricity?

Nuclear power plants generate much of the world's electricity. They generate about 20 percent of the electricity in the United States and more than 70 percent in France. Controlled nuclear fission reactions take place inside nuclear power plants. **Nuclear fission** is the splitting of an atom's nucleus into two nuclei. The splitting releases a lot of energy. 🔑 **In a nuclear power plant, the heat released from fission reactions is used to turn water into steam. The steam then turns the blades of a turbine to generate electricity.** Look at the diagram of a nuclear power plant in **Figure 7**. In addition to the generator, it has two main parts: the reactor vessel and the heat exchanger.

Reactor Vessel The **reactor vessel** is the part of the nuclear reactor in which nuclear fission occurs. The reactor contains rods of radioactive uranium called **fuel rods.** When several fuel rods are placed close together, a series of fission reactions occurs.

If the reactor vessel gets too hot, control rods are used to slow down the chain reactions. **Control rods,** made of the elements cadmium, boron or hafnium, are inserted near the fuel rods. The elements absorb particles released during fission and slow the speed of the chain reactions. The control rods can then be removed to speed up the chain reactions again.

FIGURE 7 ··

> INTERACTIVE ART **Nuclear Power Plants**

Nuclear power plants are designed to turn the energy from nuclear fission reactions into electricity.

✎ **Interpret Diagrams Where does nuclear fission occur in the plant?**

_____

_____

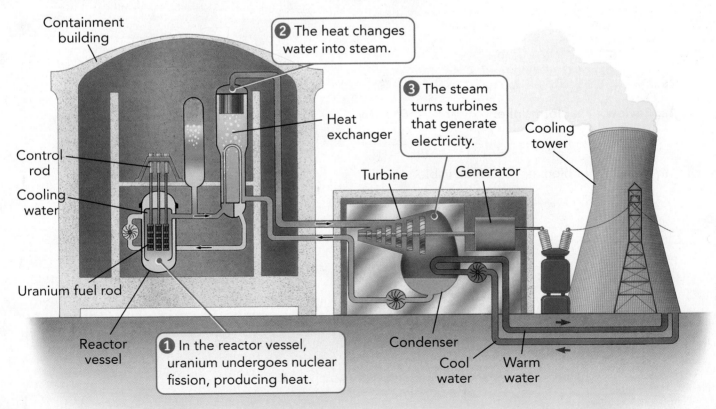

Containment building

❷ The heat changes water into steam.

❸ The steam turns turbines that generate electricity.

Heat exchanger

Cooling tower

Control rod

Cooling water

Turbine

Generator

Uranium fuel rod

Reactor vessel

❶ In the reactor vessel, uranium undergoes nuclear fission, producing heat.

Condenser

Cool water

Warm water

Heat Exchanger   Heat is removed from the reactor vessel by water or another fluid that is pumped through the reactor. This fluid passes through a heat exchanger. There, the fluid boils water to produce steam. The steam runs the electrical generator. The steam is condensed again and pumped back to the heat exchanger.

The Risks of Nuclear Power   At first, people thought that nuclear fission would provide an almost unlimited source of clean, safe energy. But accidents at nuclear power plants have led to safety concerns. In 1986, the reactor vessel in a nuclear power plant in Chernobyl, Ukraine, overheated. The fuel rods generated so much heat that they started to melt. This condition is called a meltdown. The excess heat caused a series of explosions, which injured or killed dozens of people immediately. In addition, radioactive materials escaped into the environment and killed many more people.

Plant operators can avoid accidents at nuclear facilities through careful planning and by improving safety features. A more difficult problem is the disposal of radioactive wastes. Radioactive wastes remain dangerous for many thousands of years. Scientists must find ways to store these wastes safely for very long periods of time.

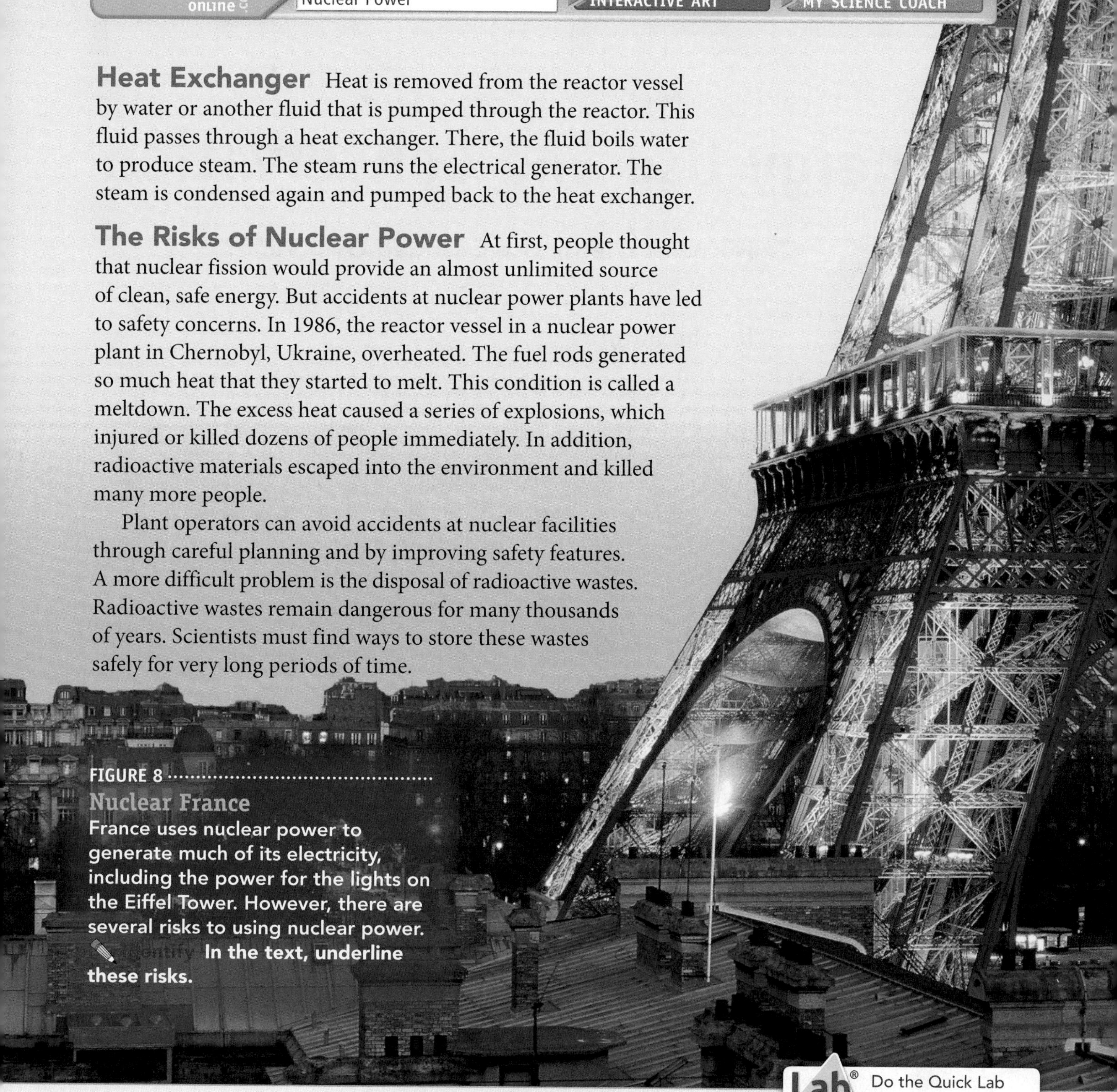

FIGURE 8 ·······························

Nuclear France
France uses nuclear power to generate much of its electricity, including the power for the lights on the Eiffel Tower. However, there are several risks to using nuclear power. ✎ Identify **In the text, underline these risks.**

Lab zone ® Do the Quick Lab *Producing Electricity.*

🔑 Assess Your Understanding

got_it? ··

○ **I get it!** Now I know that nuclear power plants produce energy by _____

_____

○ **I need extra help with** _____

   Go to **my science** ⑤ **coach** *online for help with this subject.*

3 Energy Use and Conservation

UNLOCK THE BIG

🔑 **How Has Energy Use Changed Over Time?**

🔑 **How Can We Ensure There Will Be Enough Energy for the Future?**

my planet Diary

House of Straw

What was that first little pig thinking? Was he just lazy—building a house of straw as quickly as he could without much thought? Or was he helping the environment? It turns out that straw is one of the best materials for keeping warm air inside in cold weather and keeping hot air outside in hot weather. Builders place stacks of straw along the exterior walls of a building and then seal the straw with mud. Bales of straw are natural and cheap, since straw is left over after grain is harvested. It's no wonder that more and more people are using straw to insulate their homes!

TECHNOLOGY

Communicate Write your answers below.

1. How does using straw for insulation save energy?

_____

_____

_____

2. Why is using straw for insulation good for the environment?

_____

_____

_____

▸ PLANET DIARY Go to **Planet Diary** to learn more about energy use and conservation.

Lab zone® Do the Inquiry Warm-Up *Which Bulb Is More Efficient?*

Vocabulary
- efficiency
- insulation
- energy conservation

Skills
- Reading: Identify the Main Idea
- Inquiry: Observe

How Has Energy Use Changed Over Time?

Energy, beyond using your own muscle power, is essential to the way most people live. The methods people use to obtain energy have changed, especially in the last 200 years. **For most of human history, people burned wood for energy. Only recently have fossil fuels become the main energy source.**

Eventually, people harnessed the power of other renewable resources. Ships used tall sails to capture wind energy. Flowing water turned wheels connected to stones that ground grain into flour.

Wood, wind, and water were also the main sources of energy in the United States until the nineteenth century. Coal gained in popularity as a fuel during the westward expansion of the railroads. Coal remained the dominant fuel until 1951, when it was replaced by oil and natural gas.

Today, scientists are continually looking for new and better fuels to meet the world's energy needs. As fossil fuel supplies continue to decrease, the interest in renewable energy sources has increased. With more focus on protecting the environment, scientists are working to meet our energy needs while reducing and eliminating many sources of pollution.

Identify the Main Idea
Energy use has changed over time. On the timeline, label and shade the periods in which coal and oil were the dominant fuel sources in the United States.

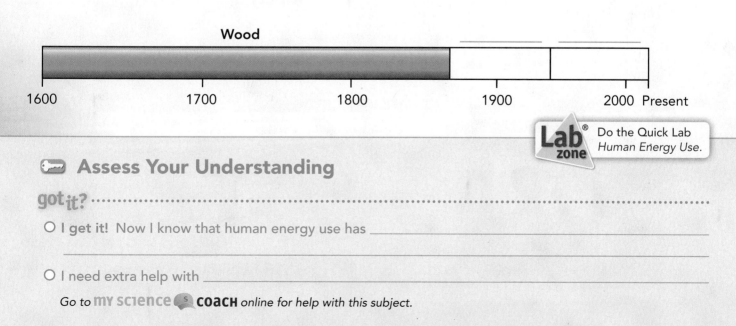

Wood

1600   1700   1800   1900   2000 Present

Lab zone Do the Quick Lab Human Energy Use.

Assess Your Understanding

got it?

- ○ I get it! Now I know that human energy use has _____

_____

- ○ I need extra help with _____
  Go to my science COACH online for help with this subject.

197

How Can We Ensure There Will Be Enough Energy for the Future?

What would happen if the world ran out of fossil fuels today? The heating and cooling systems in most buildings would stop functioning. Forests would disappear as people began to burn wood for heating and cooking. Cars, buses, and trains would be stranded wherever they ran out of fuel. About 70 percent of the world's electric power would disappear. Since televisions, computers, and telephones depend on electricity, communication would be greatly reduced. Lights and most home appliances would no longer work.

Although fossil fuels won't run out immediately, they also won't last forever. Most people think that it makes sense to use fuels more wisely now to avoid fuel shortages in the future. 🔑 **One way to preserve our current energy resources is to increase the efficiency of our energy use. Another way is to conserve energy whenever possible.** Refer to **Figure 1.**

FIGURE 1 ·······························

▶ REAL-WORLD INQUIRY **Wasting Energy**
Many things, such as lights and appliances, use energy. If people do not use these things properly, energy can be wasted.
⚠ **Observe Circle everything in this scene that is wasting energy.**

Energy Efficiency One way to make energy resources last longer is to use fuels more efficiently. **Efficiency** is the percentage of energy that is actually used to perform work. The rest of the energy is "lost" to the surroundings, usually as heat. People have developed many ways to increase energy efficiency.

Heating and Cooling One method of increasing the efficiency of heating and cooling systems is insulation. **Insulation** is a layer of material that traps air. This helps block the transfer of heat between the air inside and outside a building. You have probably seen insulation made of fiberglass. It looks like pink cotton candy. A layer of fiberglass 15 centimeters thick insulates a room as well as a brick wall 2 meters thick!

Trapped air can act as insulation in windows too. Many windows consist of two panes of glass with space in between them. The air between the panes of glass acts as insulation.

Lighting Much of the electricity used for home lighting is wasted. For example, less than 10 percent of the electricity that an incandescent light bulb uses is converted into light. The rest is given off as heat. In contrast, compact fluorescent bulbs use about one fourth as much energy to provide the same amount of light.

FIGURE 2 ·······························

Solutions to Wasting Energy
There are many ways to save energy in a home.
✎ **Explain** Pick at least three of the things you circled in the scene and explain what people could do to stop wasting energy.

Ways to Conserve Energy

Transportation Engineers have improved the energy efficiency of cars by designing better engines and batteries. For instance, many new cars use high-efficiency hybrid engines that go twice as far on a tank of fuel than other cars. Buses in some cities are now entirely electric, running on high-power rechargeable batteries. New kinds of batteries allow some electric cars to drive hundreds of kilometers before recharging.

Another way to save energy is to reduce the number of cars on the road. In many communities, public transit systems provide an alternative to driving. Other cities encourage carpooling and bicycling. Many cities now set aside lanes for cars containing two or more people.

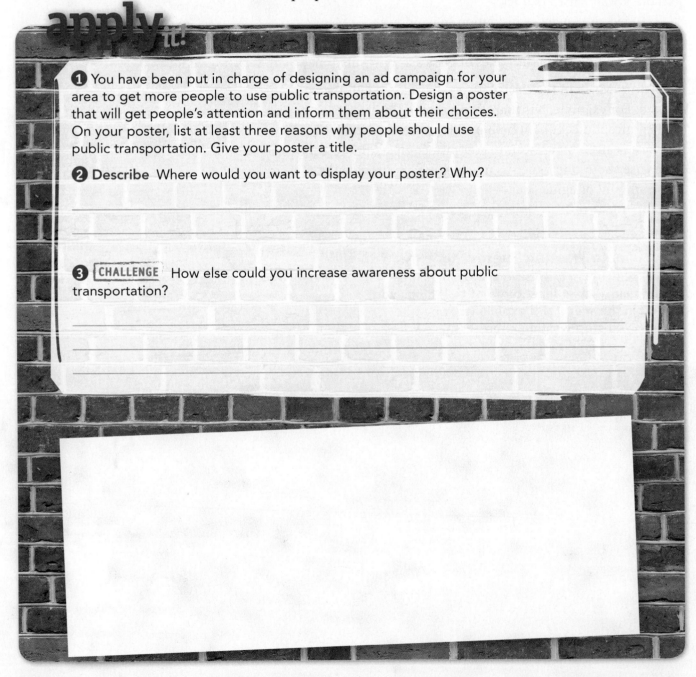

apply it!

1 You have been put in charge of designing an ad campaign for your area to get more people to use public transportation. Design a poster that will get people's attention and inform them about their choices. On your poster, list at least three reasons why people should use public transportation. Give your poster a title.

2 Describe Where would you want to display your poster? Why?

_____

_____

3 [CHALLENGE] How else could you increase awareness about public transportation?

_____

_____

_____

Energy Conservation

Energy Conservation Another approach to making energy resources last longer is conservation. **Energy conservation** means reducing energy use.

You can reduce your personal energy use by changing your behavior in some simple ways. For example, if you walk to the store instead of getting a ride, you are conserving the gasoline it would take to drive to the store.

While these suggestions seem like small things, multiplied by millions of people they add up to a lot of energy saved for the future.

FIGURE 3 ·····························

Energy Conservation in Your Everyday Life
Even students like you can conserve energy.
✎ **Communicate** With a partner, think of ways you can conserve energy in your daily life. Write your answers in the notebook.

Lab zone® Do the Quick Lab *Future Energy Use.*

🔑 Assess Your Understanding

1a. Define What does it mean to say that something is "energy efficient"?

_____

_____

_____

_____

b. Solve Problems What are some strategies a city could use to increase energy conservation?

_____

_____

_____

_____

got it? ···

○ **I get it!** Now I know that ensuring that the future has enough energy requires _____

_____

○ I need extra help with _____

Go to MY SCIENCE ⓢ COACH online for help with this subject.

5 Study Guide

Earth has many energy sources, including _____ such as coal; the sun, which can be used for _____; and flowing water, which can be used for hydroelectric power.

LESSON 1 Fossil Fuels

🔑 The three major fossil fuels are coal, oil, and natural gas.

🔑 Since fossil fuels take hundreds of millions of years to form, they are considered nonrenewable resources.

Vocabulary
- fuel • fossil fuel
- hydrocarbon
- petroleum • refinery
- petrochemical

LESSON 2 Alternative Sources of Energy

🔑 Renewable sources of energy include sunlight, water, wind, biomass fuels, and geothermal energy.

🔑 In a nuclear power plant, the heat released from fission reactions is used to change water into steam. The steam then turns the blades of a turbine to generate electricity.

Vocabulary
- solar energy • hydroelectric power • biomass fuel • gasohol
- geothermal energy • nuclear fission
- reactor vessel • fuel rod • control rod

LESSON 3 Energy Use and Conservation

🔑 For most of human history, the main fuel source was wood. Only recently have fossil fuels become the main energy source.

🔑 One way to preserve our current energy resources is to increase the efficiency of our energy use. Another way is to conserve energy whenever possible.

Vocabulary
- efficiency • insulation • energy conservation

Review and Assessment

LESSON 1 Fossil Fuels

1. What is one similarity among oil, coal, and natural gas?

   a. They are all petrochemicals.

   b. They all must be processed in a refinery.

   c. They are all gases at room temperature.

   d. They are all formed from the remains of dead organisms.

2. Fossil fuels take hundreds of millions of years to form, and therefore are considered _____ energy sources.

3. Compare and Contrast Describe one main use for each fuel: coal, oil, and natural gas.

_____

_____

_____

_____

_____

4. Sequence How does coal form?

_____

_____

_____

_____

_____

_____

_____

5. **Write About It** Imagine a day without fossil fuels. Describe your day, from when you wake up until when you eat lunch. Identify each time you would have used energy from fossil fuels.

LESSON 2 Alternative Sources of Energy

6. Which of the following is not a biomass fuel?

   a. gasohol   **b.** methane from landfills

   c. hydrogen   **d.** sugar cane wastes

7. Running water can be used as an energy source to produce _____ power.

8. Apply Concepts Fill in the boxes with two benefits and two costs of hydrogen power.

Benefits	Costs
_____	_____
_____	_____
_____	_____
_____	_____

9. Interpret Photos Explain how a nuclear power plant, like the one pictured below, produces energy.

_____

_____

_____

_____

LESSON 3 Energy Use and Conservation

10. What is efficiency?

   a. the percentage of energy that is lost to the environment as heat

   b. the percentage of energy that is used to perform work

   c. the percentage of energy that is conserved when work is done

   d. the percentage of energy that is wasted when electronics are left on

11. _____

involves using less energy, helping energy

resources last longer.

12. Draw Conclusions How is energy use today different from energy use 200 years ago?

_____

_____

_____

_____

_____

_____

_____

13. Solve Problems Describe three actions a person can take to conserve energy.

_____

_____

_____

_____

_____

_____

_____

_____

APPLY THE BIG ? What are some of Earth's energy sources?

14. Earth's energy sources include both renewable and nonrenewable resources. Name at least three sources of energy that could be used in a classroom like the one below. Then describe the ideal energy source for generating most of your school's electricity and explain why you chose this source.

_____

_____

_____

_____

_____

_____

_____

_____

_____

_____

_____

_____

_____

Standardized Test Prep

Multiple Choice

Circle the letter of the best answer.

1. Which statement is best supported by the table below?

2007 Global Oil Production and Use		
Country	Oil production global rank	Oil use global rank
United States	3	1
Russia	1	6
China	5	3
Brazil	15	8

   A   Brazil produces more oil than China.
   B   Russia produces the most oil.
   C   China consumes the most oil.
   D   The United States consumes and produces the most oil in the world.

2. Which of the following is not a fossil fuel?

   A   oil
   B   coal
   C   natural gas
   D   wood

3. The interior of a car heats up on a sunny day because of

   A   solar cells.
   B   active solar heating.
   C   passive solar heating.
   D   direct solar heating.

4. How does increasing the efficiency of energy use help preserve energy resources?

   A   by increasing the energy resources available
   B   by doing less work while giving off more heat
   C   by using less energy to do the same amount of work
   D   by increasing the amount of energy needed to generate electricity

5. How does a nuclear power plant produce energy?

   A   with solar panels
   B   through nuclear fission reactions
   C   with geothermal heat
   D   through nuclear meltdown reactions

Constructed Response

Use the diagram below and your knowledge of science to help you answer Question 6. Write your answer on a separate sheet of paper.

6. Describe how energy is produced in the diagram above. Then, describe one advantage and one disadvantage of this source.

How Low Is Low Impact?

▲ This electric car is charged by attaching an electric cord to an outlet. However, the source of the electricity may be a fossil fuel-based power plant.

Hybrid engines, windmills, low-impact this, alternative-energy that—everywhere you look, people are trying to find ways to create energy by using renewable resources. Sometimes, a technology seems to conserve energy, but in reality it has hidden costs. For example, electric cars do not release air pollutants during use, but the method that is used to generate the electricity for the car may cause pollution. Is the electricity really "clean"?

Evaluating the costs and benefits of different technologies is an important scientific skill. Use the following questions to sharpen your decision-making skills.

What is the source? What materials are used to create or power the technology? How are they obtained?

What are the products? What is produced when the technology is created or used? How do these products affect the environment? How are these products stored, recycled, or disposed of?

How does it affect our lives? Does using a technology encourage people to use more energy? If it does, do the benefits of the technology outweigh the environmental costs?

Every technology has costs and benefits. However, it is important to be able to evaluate new technologies to find out if the benefits outweigh the costs!

Write About It In a group, discuss the questions listed above. Can you think of ways to add to them or to change them? Then, create an Environmental Decision-Making Guide and use it to evaluate two of the energy technologies described in this chapter.

Life on an Oil Rig

This professional's office is on a huge steel platform that is half the area of a football field, surrounded by water. With much of Earth's oil located under the ocean floor, petroleum engineers must go where the oil is. Many of them work on offshore oil rigs—large drilling platforms that extract oil from under the ocean floor.

Conditions far out in the the ocean can be harsh or dangerous. Large equipment, fires, and even hurricanes threaten workers' safety. However, far out in the ocean, workers on oil rigs can see sharks, manta rays, and other marine life.

Petroleum engineers study geology, physics, and chemistry to understand the properties of rock formations that contain oil. They use high-tech remote sensing equipment to find oil and computer modeling software to figure out how to get the oil out of the ocean's floor.

Write About It Find out more about life on an offshore oil rig. Then, write a diary or blog entry that describes a week in the life of an offshore petroleum engineer.

OFFSHORE PETROLEUM ENGINEER

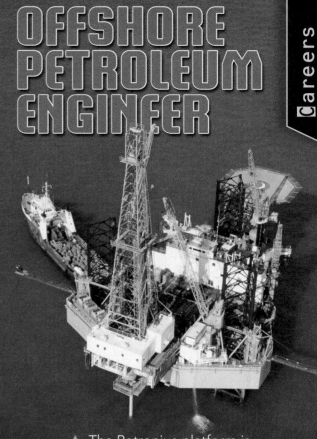

▲ The Petronius platform is located in the Gulf of Mexico.

Hydrokinetic Energy

Whirlpool! Maelstrom! Vortex! Do these words make you think of a rushing spiral of water, sucking fish and boats into its center? Not all vortexes sink ships. Fish and whales cause little vortexes when they swim. As the animals move, they create turbulence in the water. Turbulent water moves away from the animal and gives it a little push.

An engineer named Michael Bernitsas has developed a device that uses this effect to generate electricity. As currents push water around a cylindrical device, a vortex forms. As the vortex moves away from the device, the cylinder moves up and down. The device then converts that mechanical energy into electrical energy. Bernitsas has even improved the device by adding mechanical "fish tails" to the generators! Bernitsas is still testing his system, but he hopes that it can someday be used to help meet society's needs for a renewable source of energy.

Design It Find out more about how fish swim. Then, design a model that shows how the body of a fish moves in the water. In your model, show where a vortex would form as the fish swims.

207

GLOSSARY

abiotic factor A nonliving part of an organism's habitat. (6)
factor abiótico La parte sin vida del hábitat de un organismo.

acid rain Rain or another form of precipitation that is more acidic than normal, caused by the release of molecules of sulfur dioxide and nitrogen oxide into the air. (145)
lluvia ácida Lluvia u otra forma de precipitación que es más ácida de lo normal, debido a la contaminación del aire con moléculas de dióxido de azufre y óxido de nitrógeno.

adaptation An inherited behavior or physical characteristic that helps an organism survive and reproduce in its environment. (19)
adaptación Comportamiento o característica física hereditaria que le permite a un organismo sobrevivir y reproducirse en su ambiente.

aquaculture The practice of raising fish and other water-dwelling organisms for food. (107)
acuicultura Técnica del cultivo de peces y otros organismos acuáticos para consumo humano.

bedrock Rock that makes up Earth's crust; also the solid rock layer beneath the soil. (130)
lecho rocoso Roca que compone la corteza terrestre; también, la capa sólida de roca debajo del suelo.

biodegradable Capable of being broken down by bacteria and other decomposers. (138)
biodegradable Sustancia que las bacterias y otros descomponedores pueden descomponer.

biodiversity The total number of different species on Earth, including those on land, in the water, and in the air. (108)
biodiversidad Número total de especies diferentes que habitan la Tierra, incluyendo especies terrestres, marinas y del aire.

biogeography The study of where organisms live and how they got there. (73)
biogeografía Estudio del hábitat de los organismos y de cómo han llegado a ese hábitat.

biomass fuel Fuel made from living things. (190)
combustible de biomasa Combustible creado a partir de seres vivos.

biome A group of ecosystems with similar climates and organisms. (58)
bioma Grupo de ecosistemas con organismos y climas parecidos.

biotic factor A living or once living part of an organism's habitat. (6)
factor biótico Parte viva, o que alguna vez tuvo vida, del hábitat de un organismo.

birth rate The number of births per 1,000 individuals for a certain time period. (11)
tasa de natalidad Número de nacimientos por 1.000 individuos durante un período de tiempo determinado.

boreal forest Dense forest of evergreens located in the upper regions of the Northern Hemisphere. (64)
bosque boreal Bosque denso donde abundan las plantas coníferas y que se encuentra en las regiones más al norte del Hemisferio Norte.

canopy A leafy roof formed by tall trees in a rain forest. (61)
dosel Techo de hojas que forman los árboles en la selva tropical.

captive breeding The mating of animals in zoos or wildlife preserves. (115)
reproducción en cautiverio Apareamiento de animales en zoológicos y reservas naturales.

carnivore A consumer that obtains energy by eating only animals. (44)
carnívoro Consumidor que adquiere su energía al alimentarse de animales solamente.

carrying capacity The largest population that a particular environment can support. (16)
capacidad de carga Población mayor que un ambiente en particular puede mantener.

chlorofluorocarbons Human-made gases containing chlorine and fluorine (also called CFCs) that are the main cause of ozone depletion. (148)
clorofluorocarbonos Gases generados por el hombre, que contienen cloro y flúor (también llamados CFC) y que son la causa principal del deterioro de la capa de ozono.

clear-cutting The process of cutting down all the trees in an area at once. (104)
tala total Proceso de cortar simultáneamente todos los árboles de un área.

climate The average annual conditions of temperature, precipitation, winds, and clouds in an area. (58)
clima Condiciones promedio anuales de temperatura, precipitación, viento y nubosidad de un área.

commensalism A type of symbiosis between two species in which one species benefits and the other species is neither helped nor harmed. (26)
comensalismo Tipo de relación simbiótica entre dos especies en la cual una especie se beneficia y la otra especie ni se beneficia ni sufre daño.

community All the different populations that live together in a particular area. (8)
comunidad Todas las poblaciones distintas que habitan en un área específica.

competition The struggle between organisms to survive as they attempt to use the same limited resources in the same place at the same time. (21)
competencia Lucha por la supervivencia entre organismos que se alimentan de los mismos recursos limitados en el mismo lugar y al mismo tiempo.

condensation The change in state from a gas to a liquid. (51)
condensación Cambio del estado gaseoso al estado líquido.

coniferous tree A tree that produces its seeds in cones and that has needle-shaped leaves coated in a waxy substance to reduce water loss. (64)
árbol conífero Árbol que produce sus semillas en piñones y que tiene hojas en forma de aguja y cubiertas por una sustancia cerosa que reduce la pérdida de agua.

conservation The practice of using less of a resource so that it can last longer. (97)
conservación Práctica que consiste en reducir el uso de un recurso para prolongar su duración.

consumer An organism that obtains energy by feeding on other organisms. (44)
consumidor Organismo que obtiene energía al alimentarse de otros organismos.

continental drift The hypothesis that the continents slowly move across Earth's surface. (73)
deriva continental Hipótesis según la cual los continentes se desplazan lentamente en la superficie de la Tierra.

control rod A cadmium rod used in a nuclear reactor to absorb neutrons from fission reactions. (194)
varilla de control Varilla de cadmio que se usa en un reactor nuclear para absorber los neutrones emitidos por reacciones de fisión.

D

death rate The number of deaths per 1,000 individuals for a certain time period. (11)
tasa de mortalidad Número de muertes per 1.000 individuos durante un período de tiempo determinado.

deciduous tree A tree that sheds its leaves during a particular season and grows new ones each year. (63)
árbol caducifolio Árbol que pierde las hojas durante una estación específica y al que le salen hojas nuevas cada año.

decomposer An organism that gets energy by breaking down biotic wastes and dead organisms, and returns raw materials to the soil and water. (45)
descomponedor Organismo que obtiene energía al descomponer desechos bióticos y organismos muertos, y que devuelve materia prima al suelo y al agua.

desert A dry region that on average receives less than 25 centimeters of precipitation per year. (59)
desierto Región seca en la que se registra un promedio menor de 25 centímetros de precipitación anual.

desertification The advance of desert-like conditions into areas that previously were fertile; caused by overfarming, overgrazing, drought, and climate change. (132)
desertificación Paso de condiciones desérticas a áreas que eran fértiles; resulta de la agricultura descontrolada, el uso exagerado de los pastos, las sequías y los cambios climáticos.

dispersal The movement of organisms from one place to another. (74)
dispersión Traslado de los organismos de un lugar a otro.

drought A long period of low precipitation. (132)
sequía Período prolongado de baja precipitación.

E

ecological footprint The amount of land and water that individuals use to meet their resource needs and to absorb the wastes that they produce. (96)
espacio ecológico Cantidad de tierra y agua que los individuos usan para cubrir sus necesidades y absorber sus desechos.

GLOSSARY

ecology The study of how organisms interact with each other and their environment. (9)
ecología Estudio de la forma en que los organismos interactúan entre sí y con su medio ambiente.

ecosystem The community of organisms that live in a particular area, along with their nonliving environment. (9)
ecosistema Comunidad de organismos que viven en un área específica, y el medio ambiente que los rodea.

efficiency The percentage of input work that is converted to output work. (199)
eficacia Porcentaje de trabajo aportado que se convierte en trabajo producido.

emergent layer The tallest layer of the rain forest that receives the most sunlight. (61)
capa emergente Capa superior de la selva tropical, que recibe la mayor cantidad de luz solar.

emigration Movement of individuals out of a population's area. (12)
emigración Traslado de individuos fuera del área de una población.

emissions Pollutants that are released into the air. (143)
gases contaminantes Contaminantes liberados al aire.

endangered species A species in danger of becoming extinct in the near future. (113)
especie en peligro de extinción Especie que corre el riesgo de desaparecer en el futuro próximo.

energy conservation The practice of reducing energy use. (201)
conservación de energía Práctica de reducción del uso de energía.

energy pyramid A diagram that shows the amount of energy that moves from one feeding level to another in a food web. (48)
pirámide de energía Diagrama que muestra la cantidad de energía que fluye de un nivel de alimentación a otro en una red alimentaria.

environmental science The study of the natural processes that occur in the environment and how humans can affect them. (90)
ciencias del medio ambiente Estudio de los procesos naturales que ocurren en el medio ambiente y de cómo los seres humanos pueden afectarlos.

erosion The process by which water, ice, wind, or gravity moves weathered particles of rock and soil. (131)
erosión Proceso mediante el cual el agua, el hielo, el viento o la gravedad mueven partículas de roca y suelo expuestas al ambiente.

estuary A kind of wetland formed where fresh water from rivers mixes with salty ocean water. (70)
estuario Tipo de pantanal que se forma donde el agua dulce de los ríos se junta con el agua salada del océano.

evaporation The process by which molecules at the surface of a liquid absorb enough energy to change to a gas. (51)
evaporación Proceso mediante el cual las moléculas en la superficie de un líquido absorben suficiente energía para pasar al estado gaseoso.

exotic species Species that are carried to a new location by people. (74)
especies exóticas Especies que las personas trasladan a un nuevo lugar.

exponential growth Growth pattern in which individuals in a population reproduce at a constant rate, so that the larger a population gets, the faster it grows. (99)
crecimiento exponencial Patrón de crecimiento en el cual los individuos de una población se reproducen a una tasa constante, de modo que mientras más aumenta la población, más rápido crece ésta.

extinction The disappearance of all members of a species from Earth. (113)
extinción Desaparición de la Tierra de todos los miembros de una especie.

F

fertilizer A substance that provides nutrients to help crops grow better. (131)
fertilizante Sustancia que proporciona nutrientes para ayudar a que crezcan mejor los cultivos.

fishery An area with a large population of valuable ocean organisms. (106)
pesquería Área con una gran población de organismos marinos aprovechables.

food chain A series of events in an ecosystem in which organisms transfer energy by eating and by being eaten. (46)
cadena alimentaria Serie de sucesos en un ecosistema por medio de los cuales los organismos transmiten energía al comer o al ser comidos por otros.

food web The pattern of overlapping feeding relationships or food chains among the various organisms in an ecosystem. (46)
red alimentaria Patrón de las relaciones de alimentación intercruzadas o de cadenas alimentarias entre los diferentes organismos de un ecosistema.

fossil fuel Coal, oil, or natural gas that forms over millions of years from the remains of ancient organisms; burned to release energy. (179)
combustible fósil Carbón, petróleo o gas natural que se forma a lo largo de millones de años a partir de los restos de organismos antiguos; se queman para liberar energía.

fuel A substance that provides energy as the result of a chemical change. (179)
combustible Sustancia que libera energía como resultado de un cambio químico.

fuel rod A uranium rod that undergoes fission in a nuclear reactor. (194)
varilla de combustible Varilla de uranio que se somete a la fisión en un reactor nuclear.

G

gasohol A mixture of gasoline and alcohol. (190)
gasohol Mezcla de gasolina y alcohol.

gene A sequence of DNA that determines a trait and is passed from parent to offspring. (112)
gen Secuencia de ADN que determina un rasgo y que se pasa de los progenitores a los hijos.

geothermal energy The intense heat energy that comes from Earth's interior. (191)
energía geotérmica Energía intensa que proviene del interior de la Tierra.

grassland An area populated mostly by grasses and other nonwoody plants that gets 25 to 75 centimeters of rain each year. (62)
pradera Área poblada principalmente por hierbas y otras plantas no leñosas, y donde caen entre 25 y 75 centímetros de lluvia cada año.

groundwater Water that fills the cracks and spaces in underground soil and rock layers. (153)
aguas freáticas Agua que llena las grietas y huecos de las capas subterráneas de tierra y roca.

H

habitat An environment that provides the things a specific organism needs to live, grow, and reproduce. (5)
hábitat Medio que provee lo que un organismo específico necesita para vivir, crecer y reproducirse.

habitat destruction The loss of a natural habitat. (114)
destrucción del habitat Pérdida de un hábitat natural.

habitat fragmentation The breaking of a habitat into smaller, isolated pieces. (114)
fragmentación del hábitat Desintegración de un hábitat en porciones aisladas más pequeñas.

hazardous waste A material that can be harmful if it is not properly disposed of. (140)
desecho peligroso Material que puede ser dañino si no se elimina adecuadamente.

herbivore A consumer that obtains energy by eating only plants. (44)
herbívoro Consumidor que obtiene su energía al alimentarse de plantas solamente.

host An organism that a parasite lives with, in, or on, and provides a source of energy or a suitable environment for the parasite to live. (26)
huésped Organismo en el cual vive un parásito y que le sirve de fuente de energía o de medio ambiente.

hydrocarbon An organic compound that contains only carbon and hydrogen atoms. (179)
hidrocarburo Compuesto orgánico que contiene átomos de carbón e hidrógeno solamente.

hydroelectric power Electricity produced by the kinetic energy of water moving over a waterfall or dam. (189)
energía hidroeléctrica Electricidad producida a partir de la energía cinética del agua que baja por una catarata o presa.

I

immigration Movement of individuals into a population's area. (12)
inmigración Movimiento de individuos al área de una población.

incineration The burning of solid waste. (135)
incineración Quema de desechos sólidos.

insulation Material that traps air to help block heat transfer between the air inside and outside of a building. (199)
aislante Material que atrapa el aire para ayudar a bloquear el paso del calor del aire adentro y afuera de un edificio.

intertidal zone An area between the highest high-tide line on land to the point on the continental shelf exposed by the lowest low-tide line. (70)
zona intermareal Área entre el punto más alto de la marea alta y el punto más bajo de la marea baja.

K

keystone species A species that influences the survival of many other species in an ecosystem. (109)
especie clave Especie que tiene un impacto en la supervivencia de muchas otras especies de un ecosistema.

L

land reclamation The process of restoring land to a more natural, productive state. (133)
recuperación de la tierra Proceso que consiste en restaurar la tierra y llevarla a un estado productivo más natural.

leachate Polluted liquid produced by water passing through and dissolving chemicals from buried wastes in a landfill. (136)
lixiviado Líquido contaminado producido por el agua que pasa por y disuelve químicos provenientes de desechos bajo la tierra y en rellenos sanitarios.

limiting factor An environmental factor that causes a population to decrease in size. (15)
factor limitante Factor ambiental que causa la disminución del tamaño de una población.

litter The very top layer of fertile soil made of dead leaves and grass. (130)
mantillo Capa superior del suelo fértil, que está formada por hojas y pasto muertos.

M

municipal solid waste Waste produced in homes, businesses, schools and in a community. (135)
desechos sólidos urbanos Desechos generados en los hogares, los negocios, las escuelas y las comunidades.

mutualism A type of symbiosis in which both species benefit from living together. (25)
mutualismo Tipo de relación simbiótica entre dos especies en la cual ambas especies se benefician de su convivencia.

N

natural resource Anything naturally occuring in the environment that humans use. (88)
recurso natural Cualquier elemento natural ambiental que el ser humano usa.

natural selection The process by which organisms that are best adapted to their environment are most likely to survive and reproduce. (19)
selección natural Proceso mediante el cual los organismos que se adaptan mejor a su ambiente tienen mayor probabilidad de sobrevivir y reproducirse.

neritic zone The area of the ocean that extends from the low-tide line out to the edge of the continental shelf. (70)
zona nerítica Área del océano que se extiende desde la línea de bajamar hasta el borde de la plataforma continental.

niche How an organism makes its living and interacts with the biotic and abiotic factors in its habitat. (20)
nicho Forma en que un organismo vive e interactúa con los factores bióticos y abióticos de su hábitat.

nitrogen fixation The process of changing free nitrogen gas into nitrogen compounds that plants can absorb and use. (54)
fijación del nitrógeno Proceso que consiste en transformar el gas de nitrógeno libre en compuestos de nitrógeno que las plantas pueden absorber y usar.

nodule A lump on the ocean floor that forms when metals such as manganese build up around pieces of shell. (164)
nódulo Protuberancia formada en el suelo oceánico cuando metales, como el manganeso, se depositan sobre pedazos de concha.

nonpoint source A widely spread source of pollution that is difficult to link to a specific point of origin. (89)
fuente dispersa Fuente muy extendida de contaminación que es difícil vincular a un punto de origen específico.

nonrenewable resource A natural resource that is not replaced in a useful time frame. (94)
recurso no renovable Recurso natural que no se restaura, en un período relativamente corto, una vez se utiliza.

nuclear fission The splitting of an atom's nucleus into two smaller nuclei and neutrons, releasing a large quantity of energy. (194)
fisión nuclear Separación del núcleo de un átomo en núcleos y neutrones más pequeños, en la cual se libera una gran cantidad de energía.

nutrient depletion The situation that arises when more soil nutrients are used than the decomposers can supply. (131)
agotamiento de nutrientes Situación que se produce cuando se usan más nutrientes del suelo de lo que los descomponedores pueden proporcionar.

O

omnivore A consumer that obtains energy by eating both plants and animals. (44)
omnívoro Consumidor que adquiere su energía al alimentarse de plantas y animales.

organism A living thing. (5)
organismo Ser vivo.

ozone A form of oxygen that has three oxygen atoms in each molecule instead of the usual two; toxic to organisms where it forms near Earth's surface. (144)
ozono Forma de oxígeno que tiene tres átomos de oxígeno en cada molécula, en vez de dos; donde se forma en la superficie terrestre, es tóxico para los organismos.

ozone layer The layer of the upper atmosphere that contains a higher concentration of ozone than the rest of the atmosphere. (147)
capa de ozono Capa superior de la atmósfera que contiene una concentración mayor de ozono que el resto de la atmósfera.

P

parasite The organism that benefits by living with, on, or in a host in a parasitism interaction. (26)
parásito Organismo que se beneficia al vivir con o en un huésped, en una relación parasítica.

parasitism A type of symbiosis in which one organism lives with, on, or in a host and harms it. (26)
parasitismo Tipo de relación simbiótica en la cual un organismo vive con o en un huésped y le hace daño.

permafrost Permanently frozen soil found in the tundra biome climate region. (65)
permagélido Suelo que está permanentemente congelado y que se encuentra en el bioma climático de la tundra.

pesticide A chemical that kills insects and other crop-destroying organisms. (154)
pesticida Químico usado para matar insectos y otros organismos que destruyen los cultivos.

petrochemical A compound made from oil. (183)
petroquímico Compuesto que se obtiene del petróleo.

petroleum Liquid fossil fuel; oil. (182)
petróleo Combustible fósil líquido.

photochemical smog A brownish thick haze that is a mixture of ozone and other chemicals formed when pollutants react with sunlight. (144)
neblina tóxica fotoquímica Nubosidad gruesa de color marrón, resultado de la mezcla del ozono y otras sustancias químicas que se forman cuando los contaminantes reaccionan a la luz del sol.

pioneer species The first species to populate an area during succession. (29)
especies pioneras La primera especie que puebla un área durante la sucesión.

poaching Illegal killing or removal of wildlife from their habitats. (114)
caza ilegal Matanza o eliminación de la fauna silvestre de su hábitat.

point source A specific source of pollution that can be identified. (89)
fuente localizada Fuente específica de contaminación que puede identificarse.

pollutant A substance that causes pollution. (136)
contaminante Sustancia que provoca contaminación.

GLOSSARY

pollution Contamination of Earth's land, water, or air. (89)
polución Contaminación del suelo, el agua o el aire de la Tierra.

population All the members of one species living in the same area. (8)
población Todos los miembros de una especie que viven en el mismo lugar.

population density The number of individuals in an area of a specific size. (14)
densidad de población Número de individuos en un área de un tamaño específico.

precipitation Any form of water that falls from clouds and reaches Earth's surface as rain, snow, sleet, or hail. (51)
precipitación Cualquier forma del agua que cae de las nubes y llega a la superficie de la tierra como lluvia, nieve, aguanieve o granizo.

predation An interaction in which one organism kills another for food or nutrients. (22)
depredación Interacción en la cual un organismo mata a otro para alimentarse u obtener nutrientes de él.

predator The organism that does the killing in a predation interaction. (22)
depredador Organismo que mata durante la depredación.

prey An organism that is killed and eaten by another organism in a predation interaction. (22)
presa Organismo que es consumido por otro organismo en el proceso de depredación.

primary succession The series of changes that occur in an area where no soil or organisms exist. (29)
sucesión primaria Serie de cambios que ocurren en un área donde no existe suelo ni organismos.

producer An organism that can make its own food. (43)
productor Organismo que puede generar su propio alimento.

R

radon A colorless, odorless, radioactive gas. (146)
radón Gas radioactivo que no tiene color ni olor.

rain forest A forest that receives at least 2 meters of rain per year, mostly occurring in the tropical wet climate zone. (60)
selva tropical Bosque donde caen al menos 2 metros de lluvia al año, principalmente en la zona climática tropical húmeda.

reactor vessel The part of a nuclear reactor in which nuclear fission occurs. (194)
cuba de reactor Parte de un reactor nuclear donde ocurre la fisión.

recycling The process of reclaiming and reusing raw materials. (137)
reciclaje Proceso de recuperar y volver a usar materias primas.

refinery A factory in which crude oil is heated and separated into fuels and other products. (183)
refinería Planta en la que el petróleo crudo se calienta y fracciona en combustibles y otros productos.

renewable resource A resource that is either always available or is naturally replaced in a relatively short time. (93)
recurso renovable Recurso que está siempre disponible o que es restituido de manera natural en un período relativamente corto.

S

sanitary landfill A landfill that holds nonhazardous waste such as municipal solid waste, construction debris, and some agricultural and industrial wastes. (136)
relleno sanitario Vertedero que contiene desechos que no son peligrosos, como desechos sólidos municipales, de construcción y algunos tipos de desechos industriales y resultantes de la agricultura.

savanna A grassland located close to the equator that may include shrubs and small trees and receives as much as 120 centimeters of rain per year. (62)
sabana Pradera que puede tener arbustos y árboles pequeños, ubicada cerca del ecuador y donde pueden caer hasta 120 centímetros de lluvia al año.

scavenger A carnivore that feeds on the bodies of dead or decaying organisms. (44)
carroñero Carnívoro que se alimenta de los restos de organismos muertos o en descomposición.

secondary succession The series of changes that occur in an area where the ecosystem has been disturbed, but where soil and organisms still exist. (30)
sucesión secundaria Serie de cambios que ocurren en un área después de la perturbación de un ecosistema, pero donde todavía hay suelo y organismos.

sediment Small, solid pieces of material that come from rocks or the remains of organisms; earth materials deposited by erosion. (155)
sedimento Trozos pequeños y sólidos de materiales que provienen de las rocas o de los restos de organismos; materiales terrestres depositados por la erosión.

selective cutting The process of cutting down only some tree species in an area. (104)
tala selectiva Proceso que consiste en cortar solo algunas especies de árboles de un área.

sewage The water and human wastes that are washed down sinks, toilets, and showers. (154)
aguas residuales Agua y desechos humanos que son desechados por lavamanos, servicios sanitarios y duchas.

solar energy Energy from the sun. (187)
energía solar Energía del Sol.

species A group of similar organisms that can mate with each other and produce offspring that can also mate and reproduce. (8)
especie Grupo de organismos semejantes que pueden aparearse y producir descendencia fértil.

subsoil The layer of soil below topsoil that has less plant and animal matter than topsoil and contains mostly clay and other minerals. (130)
subsuelo Capa de suelo debajo del suelo superior que tiene menos materia de plantas y animales que el suelo superior, y que principalmente contiene arcilla y otros minerales.

succession The series of predictable changes that occur in a community over time. (28)
sucesión Serie de cambios predecibles que ocurren en una comunidad a través del tiempo.

sustainable use The use of a resource in ways that maintain the resource at a certain quality for a certain period of time. (96)
uso sostenible Uso de un recurso que permite que ese recurso mantenga cierta calidad por un período de tiempo determinado.

sustainable yield An amount of a renewable resource that can be harvested regularly without reducing the future supply. (105)
rendimiento sostenible Cantidad de un recurso renovable que puede ser recolectado constantemente sin reducir el abastecimiento futuro.

symbiosis Any relationship in which two species live closely together and that benefits at least one of the species. (25)
simbiosis Cualquier relación en la cual dos especies viven muy cerca y al menos una de ellas se beneficia.

─────────── **T** ───────────

temperature inversion A condition in which a layer of warm air traps polluted air close to Earth's surface. (144)
inversión térmica Condición en la que una capa de aire caliente atrapa aire contaminado cerca de la superficie de la Tierra.

threatened species A species that could become endangered in the near future. (113)
especie amenazada Especie que puede llegar a estar en peligro de extinción en el futuro próximo.

topsoil The crumbly, topmost layer of soil made up of clay and other minerals and humus (nutrients and decaying plant and animal matter). (130)
suelo superior Capa superior arenosa del suelo formada por arcilla, otros minerales y humus (nutrientes y materia orgánica de origen vegetal y animal).

tundra An extremely cold, dry biome climate region characterized by short, cool summers and bitterly cold winters. (65)
tundra Bioma de la región climática extremadamente fría y seca, que se caracteriza por veranos cortos y frescos e inviernos sumamente fríos.

─────────── **U** ───────────

understory A layer of shorter trees and vines that grows in the shade of a forest canopy. (61)
sotobosque Capa de árboles de poca altura y plantas trepadoras que crecen bajo la sombra del dosel de un bosque.

upwelling The movement of cold water upward from the deep ocean that is caused by wind. (164)
corriente de ascenso Movimiento ascendente de aguas frías desde las profundidades del mar, causado por los vientos.

INDEX

Page numbers for key terms are printed in **boldface** type.

ACKNOWLEDGMENTS

Staff Credits

The people who made up the *Interactive Science* team—representing composition services, core design digital and multimedia production services, digital product development, editorial, editorial services, manufacturing, and production—are listed below.

Jan Van Aarsen, Samah Abadir, Ernie Albanese, Zareh MacPherson Artinian, Bridget Binstock, Suzanne Biron, MJ Black, Nancy Bolsover, Stacy Boyd, Jim Brady, Katherine Bryant, Michael Burstein, Pradeep Byram, Jessica Chase, Jonathan Cheney, Arthur Ciccone, Allison Cook-Bellistri, Rebecca Cottingham, AnnMarie Coyne, Bob Craton, Chris Deliee, Paul Delsignore, Michael Di Maria, Diane Dougherty, Kristen Ellis, Theresa Eugenio, Amanda Ferguson, Jorgensen Fernandez, Kathryn Fobert, Julia Gecha, Mark Geyer, Steve Gobbell, Paula Gogan-Porter, Jeffrey Gong, Sandra Graff, Adam Groffman, Lynette Haggard, Christian Henry, Karen Holtzman, Susan Hutchinson, Sharon Inglis, Marian Jones, Sumy Joy, Sheila Kanitsch, Courtenay Kelley, Chris Kennedy, Toby Klang, Greg Lam, Russ Lappa, Margaret LaRaia, Ben Leveillee, Thea Limpus, Dotti Marshall, Kathy Martin, Robyn Matzke, John McClure, Mary Beth McDaniel, Krista McDonald, Tim McDonald, Rich McMahon, Cara McNally, Melinda Medina, Angelina Mendez, Maria Milczarek, Claudi Mimo, Mike Napieralski, Deborah Nicholls, Dave Nichols, William Oppenheimer, Jodi O'Rourke, Ameer Padshah, Lorie Park, Celio Pedrosa, Jonathan Penyack, Linda Zust Reddy, Jennifer Reichlin, Stephen Rider, Charlene Rimsa, Stephanie Rogers, Marcy Rose, Rashid Ross, Anne Rowsey, Logan Schmidt, Amanda Seldera, Laurel Smith, Nancy Smith, Ted Smykal, Emily Soltanoff, Cindy Strowman, Dee Sunday, Barry Tomack, Patricia Valencia, Ana Sofia Villaveces, Stephanie Wallace, Christine Whitney, Brad Wiatr, Heidi Wilson, Heather Wright, Rachel Youdelman

Photography

All uncredited photos copyright © 2011 Pearson Education.

Cover, Front and Back
tr Raymond Kasprzak/Shutterstock; **m** David Aubrey/Photolibrary New York; **b** Tamara Kulikova/Shutterstock.

Front Matter
Page vi, Gary Bell/Zefa/Corbis; **vii,** Marko König/imagebroker/Corbis; **viii,** DEA/W. BUSS/De Agostini/Getty Images; **ix,** Benedict Luxmoore/Arcaid/Corbis; **x,** Greg Smith/Corbis; **xi laptop, TV screens, touch-screen phone,** iStockphoto.com; **xiii tr,** iStockphoto.com; **xv br,** JupiterImages/Getty Images; **xviii t,** iStockphoto.com; **xx–xxi,** Robert Postma/Design Pics/Corbis.

Chapter 1
Pages xxii–1, Gary Bell/Zefa/Corbis; **3 t,** Photodisc/Getty Images; **3 m,** age Fotostock/SuperStock; **3 b,** Imagebroker/Alamy; **4 bkgrnd,** Ruth Hofshi/PhotoStock-Israel/Alamy; **4 tr,** David Haring/DUPC/Getty Images; **4 bl,** Jörn Köhler; **4 br,** Wildlife/A.Visage/Peter Arnold Inc.; **5 bkgrnd,** Bruno Morandi/Robert Harding World; **5 inset,** Tom Brakefield/Getty Images; **8–9,** Jason O. Watson / Alamy; **10,** Thomas Ash/Shutterstock; **11,** Chris Johns/National Geographic Stock; **12,** Photodisc/Getty Images; **13,** Kim Taylor/Nature Picture Library; **15,** Wichita Eagle/MCT/Getty Images; **16–17,** catolla/

Fotolia; **16 inset,** Tim Mannakee/Grand Tour/Corbis; **17 tr,** Taylor S. Kennedy/National Geographic Society; **18,** Alex Wild; **21 tr,** Glenn Bartley/All Canada Photos/Corbis; **21 mr and mb,** Jim Zipp/Photo Researchers, Inc.; **21 bl,** Michael P. Gadomski/Photo Researchers, Inc.; **22 tr,** Bill Curtsinger/National Geographic Stock; **22 r,** Sándor F. Szabó/iStockphoto.com; **22 bl,** Klaas Lingbeek-van Kranen/GettyImages; **22 bc,** Imagebroker/Alamy; **23 tl,** Jeff Hunter/Getty Images; **23 tr,** Michael D. Kern/Nature Picture Library; **23 cl,** Ethan Daniels/Alamy; **23 cr,** age Fotostock/SuperStock; **23 bl,** Fabrice Bettex/Alamy; **23 br,** Nature's Images/Photo Researchers, Inc.; **25 l,** Mogens Trolle/Shutterstock; **25 r,** Steve Byland/Fotolia; **26 l,** Jeff Foott/Getty Images; **26 tr,** WaterFrame/Alamy; **26 br,** USGA; **27 t,** Steve Jones/Stocktrek Images/Corbis; **27 c,** Bruce Dale/National Geographic/Getty Images; **27 b,** Dietmar Nill/Nature Picture Library; **28,** Ilene MacDonald/Alamy; **32,** WaterFrame/Alamy.

Interchapter Feature
Page 36, Photo courtesy of Roger del Moral; **37 t,** Dave & Les Jacobs/Blend Images/Getty Images; **37 b,** Chris Gomersall/Alamy.

Chapter 2
Pages 38–39, Marko König/imagebroker/Corbis; **41 t,** Dorling Kindersley; **41 b,** Karen Huntt/Getty Images; **42,** Ian McAllister/Photolibrary New York; **43 inset,** Edward Kinsman/Photo Researchers, Inc.; **43 b,** Jerome Wexler/Photo Researchers, Inc.; **46 t,** Dorling Kindersley; **46 m,** Jerry Young/Dorling Kindersley; **46 b,** Peter Blottman/iStockphoto.com; **47 snail,** Nicholas Homrich/iStockphoto.com; **47 heron,** Judy Foldetta/iStockphoto.com; **47 frog,** Geoff Brightling/Dorling Kindersley; **47 shrew,** Rollin Verlinde/Dorling Kindersley; **47 garter snake,** Jerry Young/Dorling Kindersley; **47 mushrooms,** Neil Fletcher/Dorling Kindersley; **47 crayfish,** Frank Greenaway/Dorling Kindersley/Courtesy of the Natural History Museum, London; **47 fox,** Dorling Kindersley; **47 grasshopper,** Jerry Young/Dorling Kindersley; **47 plants,** Peter Blottman/iStockphoto.com; **48 t,** Eric Isselée/iStockphoto.com; **48 tm,** Dave King/Dorling Kindersley; **48 bm,** Frank Greenaway/Dorling Kindersley; **48 b,** Kim Taylor and Jane Burton/Dorling Kindersley; **50,** Juniors Bildarchiv/Alamy; **52,** Emma Firth/Dorling Kindersley; **54,** Dr. Paul A. Zahl/Photo Researchers, Inc.; **58,** Imagebroker/Alamy; **59 bkgrnd,** Karen Huntt/Getty Images; **59 inset,** Floridapfe from S.Korea Kim in cherl/Getty Images; **60–61,** Peter Chadwick/Dorling Kindersley; **61 c,** Theo Allofs/Corbis; **62 l,** Stefan Huwiler/Rolf Nussbaumer Photography/Alamy; **62 c,** Arco Images GmbH/Alamy; **62 r,** David_Steele/Fotolia; **63 tr,** mlorenz/Shutterstock; **63 br,** Tim Shepard, Oxford Scientific Films/Dorling Kindersley; **64 t,** Randy Green/Getty Images; **64 b,** Tom Brakefield/Corbis; **65,** deberarr/Fotolia; **66,** blickwinkel/Alamy; **68–69,** PIER/Getty Images; **68 m,** Sandy Felsenthal/Corbis; **72,** Ken Findlay/Dorling Kindersley; **74 l,** Martin M. Bruce/SuperStock; **74 r,** Geoff du Feu/Getty Images; **75,** Inge Johnsson/Alamy; **76,** Peter Blottman/iStockphoto.com; **77,** Cheerz/Dreamstime.com.

Interchapter Feature
Page 80, Westend 61 GmbH/Alamy; **81 bkgrnd,** Brent Waltermire/Alamy; **81 inset,** Jupiterimages/Creatas/Alamy.

Chapter 3

Pages 82–83, Kent Gilbert/AP Images; **85 t,** Mark Bolton/Photolibrary New York; **85 m,** C Squared Studios/Photodisc/Getty Images; **85 m inset,** C Squared Studios/Photodisc/Getty Images; **85 b,** Digital Vision/Photolibrary New York; **86,** Michael Patrick O'Neill/Alamy; **87,** Frank Krahmer/Masterfile; **88–89,** Gavin Hellier/Jon Arnold Images Ltd/Alamy; **90 bkgrnd,** photowings/Shutterstock; **90 inset,** Mark Bolton/Photolibrary New York; **92 bkgrnd,** AP Images; **92 inset,** Derek Dammann/iStockphoto.com; **94 tl,** C Squared Studios/Photodisc/Getty Images; **94 tl inset,** C Squared Studios/Photodisc/Getty Images; **95 tl,** Liba Taylor/Corbis; **95 tr,** Alfred Cheng Jin/Reuters/Landov; **95 bl,** Gary Braasch/Corbis; **98 bkgrnd,** endless image/F1online digitale Bildagentur GmbH/Alamy; **98 inset,** London Scientific Films/Oxford Scientific/Photolibrary New York; **100–101,** Digital Vision/Photolibrary New York; **102,** Yann Arthus–Bertrand/Corbis; **103 shoes,** Matthew Gonzalez/iStockphoto.com; **103 basketball,** Nick Schlax/iStockphoto.com; **103 can,** javier fontanella/iStockphoto.com; **103 crayons,** Anna Yu/iStockphoto.com; **103 polish,** Plainview/iStockphoto.com; **103 comb,** iStockphoto.com; **103 scissors,** Long Ha/iStockphoto.com; **106,** Michael Melford/National Geographic/Getty Images; **107,** Edward J.Westmacott/Alamy; **108 r,** Jerome Whittingham/iStockphoto.com; **109 l,** PhotographerOlympus/iStockphoto.com; **109 c,** Burke/Triolo Productions/Brand X/Corbis; **109 tr,** iStockphoto.com; **109 r,** iStockphoto.com; **109 b,** kikkerdirk/Fotolia; **111,** kiamsoon/iStockphoto.com; **112,** mbongo/Fotolia; **113 tr,** ©2007 James D. Watt/Image Quest Marine; **113 l,** Hawaii Dept. of Land and Natural Resources, Betsy Gange/AP Images; **113 br,** David Cobb/Alamy; **115 tl,** Markus Botzek/zefa/Corbis; **115 tr,** Kevin Schafer/Alamy; **115 tm,** James Caldwell/Alamy; **115 bl,** Kim Mitchell/ Whooping Crane Eastern Partnership; **115 bm,** www.operationmigration.org; **115 br,** Mike Briner/Alamy; **116,** Nevio Doz/Marka/age Fotostock; **117,** DEA/W. BUSS/De Agostini/Getty Images.

Interchapter Feature

Page 122, VStock/Alamy; **123 t,** MPI/Getty Images; **123 b and inset,** Photo courtesy of Melissa Scanlan.

Chapter 4

Pages 124–125, Benedict Luxmoore/Arcaid/Corbis; **127 t,** Dorling Kindersley; **127 b,** NASA/Goddard Space Flight Center Scientific Visualization Studio; **128,** Creatas/SuperStock; **129 t,** Dorling Kindersley; **129 m,** fotoshoot /Alamy; **129 b,** Ron Chapple/Corbis; **130,** Dorling Kindersley; **131 l,** Dana Edmunds/Design Pics/Corbis; **131 r,** Rest/iStockphoto.com; **132,** Robert Harding Picture Library/Alamy; **134–135,** Andrew Brookes/Corbis; **136–137,** Rami Ba/iStockphoto.com; **137 tr,** cosma/Fotolia; **138,** Angela Hampton Picture Library/Alamy; **139 tl,** Imagebroker/Alamy; **139 tr,** ©2004 The Christian Science Monitor/Getty Images; **139 ml,** Martin Williams/Alamy; **139 mr,** Stan Gilliland/AP Images; **139 bl,** Adam Borkowski/iStockphoto.com; **139 br,** Mark Boulton/Photo Researchers, Inc.; **140 bottle,** Feng Yu/iStockphoto.com; **140 soda can,** Feng Yu/iStockphoto.com; **140 cup,** Eric Mulherin/iStockphoto.com; **140 battery,** Dorling Kindersley; **140 pizza box,** Fenykepez/iStockphoto.com; **140 apple core,** Dorling Kindersley; **140 newspaper,** Andy Crawford/Dorling Kindersley; **140 mobile phone,** Paul Wilkinson/Dorling Kindersley; **140 tin can,** Dorling Kindersley; **140 bl,** gabyjalbert/iStockphoto.com; **140 bm,** James Steidl/iStockphoto.com; **140 br,** Don Wilkie/iStockphoto.com; **140 waste sign,** Richard Goerg/iStockphoto.com; **141,** Thinkstock/Jupiter Images; **142 b,** David Parsons/Getty Images; **143,** Guillermo Arias/AP Images; **144,** P. Baeza/Publiphoto/Photo Researchers, Inc.; **145 bkgrnd,** Will McIntyre/Photo Researchers, Inc; **145 tl,** Fletcher & Baylis/Photo Researchers, Inc.; **148–149,** Dorling Kindersley; **148 tl and tr,** NASA/Goddard Space Flight Center Scientific Visualization Studio; **149 all,** NASA/Goddard Space Flight Center Scientific Visualization Studio; **150,** Charles Orrico/SuperStock; **152–153,** Dorling Kindersley; **152 m,** Wade Payne/AP Images; **157,** John Gaps III/AP Images; **160 t,** Dorling Kindersley; **160 b,** Jeffrey L. Rotman/Corbis; **163,** The Stocktrek Corp/Brand X/Corbis; **167,** NASA/Goddard Space Flight Center Scientific Visualization Studio; **168,** fotoshoot/Alamy; **169,** Zima/iStockphoto.com; **170,** Spencer Grant/PhotoEdit Inc.

Interchapter Feature

Page 172 bkgrnd, Corbis; **172 bl,** Angela Waite/Alamy.

Chapter 5

Pages 174–175, Greg Smith/Corbis; **177 t,** Kiyoshi Takahase Segundo/iStockphoto.com; **177 tm,** Rosenfeld Images Ltd./Photo Researchers, Inc.; **177 bm,** Ed Bock/Corbis; **177 b,** Larry Dale Gordon/Getty Images; **178–179,** Phil Coale/AP Images; **178 bl,** Doug Loehr/Bellefontaine Examiner/AP Images; **179 rm,** Kiyoshi Takahase Segundo/iStockphoto.com; **180 bkgrnd and br,** Tim Wright/Corbis; **180 tl,** Craig Aurness/Corbis; **181 t,** Colin Keates/Dorling Kindersley, Courtesy of the Natural History Museum, London; **181 m and b,** Andreas Einsiedel/Dorling Kindersley; **182–183,** ITAR–TASS/Grigory Sysoyev/Newscom; **183 bl,** MISHA JAPARIDZE/ASSOCIATED PRESS; **183 inset,** vusovich/Fotolia; **184,** Caro/Alamy; **186,** Ethan Miller/Getty Images; **187 tr,** Rosenfeld Images Ltd./Photo Researchers, Inc; **187 mr,** Krys Bailey/Alamy; **187 bl,** Voltaic Systems; **187 br,** Patrick Lynch/Alamy; **189,** José Luis Gutiérrez/iStockphoto.com; **190 t,** casadaphoto/Shutterstock; **190 b,** Jonah Manning/iStockphoto.com; **195,** Simeone Huber/Getty Images; **196,** Courtesy of Skip Baumhower/AP Images; **200 bkgrnd,** michael1959/iStockphoto.com; **200 t,** Justin Sullivan/Getty Images; **201,** Larry Dale Gordon/Getty Images; **202 t,** Andreas Einsiedel/Dorling Kindersley; **202 b,** Rosenfeld Images Ltd./Photo Researchers, Inc.; **203,** fototrm12/Fotolia; **204,** Photolibrary New York.

Interchapter Feature

Page 206 bkgrnd, DBURKE/Alamy; **206 inset,** David Pearson/Alamy; **207 t,** GlowImages/Alamy; **207 b,** Amana Images Inc./Alamy.

this is your book

you can write in it

this is your book

you can write in it

this is your book

you can write in it

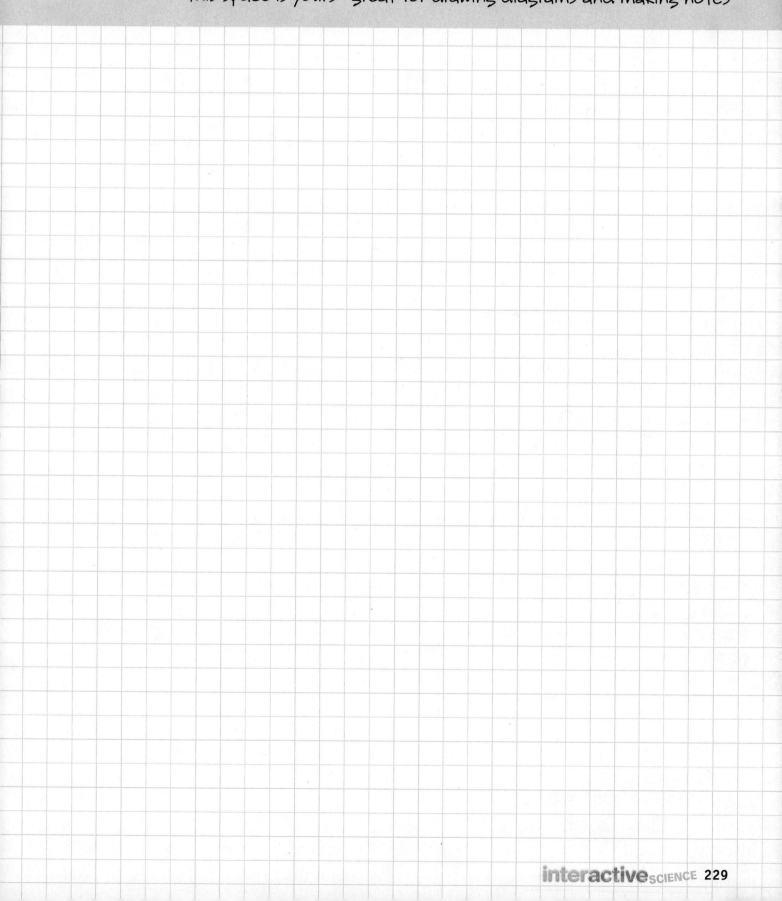

this is your book

you can write in it

this is your book

you can write in it

take note

this space is yours—great for drawing diagrams and making notes

this is your book

you can write in it